The Imaginative Landscape
of
Christopher Columbus

The Imaginative Landscape
of
Christopher Columbus

VALERIE I. J. FLINT

PRINCETON UNIVERSITY PRESS

PRINCETON, NEW JERSEY

Copyright © 1992 by Princeton University Press
Published by Princeton University Press,
Princeton, New Jersey
In the United Kingdom: Princeton University Press, Oxford

Library of Congress Cataloging-in-Publication Data

Flint, Valerie I. J. (Valerie Irene Jane), 1936–
    The imaginative landscape of Christopher. Columbus/Valerie I. J.
Flint.
      p. cm.
    Includes bibliographical references and index.
    ISBN 0-691-05681-1 (alk. paper)
    1. Columbus, Christopher.   Knowledge and learning.   2. Cosmology,
Medieval.   3. Geography — 15th–16th centuries.   I. Title.
E112.F57   1992
970.01′5 — dc20   92-230

This book has been composed in Baskerville

Production services by Fisher Duncan,
10 Barley Mow Passage, Chiswick, London W4 4PH, UK
Printed in the United King

Contents

v

List of Illustrations

Acknowledgments

This book is deeply dependent upon the generosity of others. To the Leave Committee of my own university I owe grants of sabbatical leave and long-vacation leave, to the Research Committee, a grant towards interlibrary borrowing and a long-vacation airfare. Two fellowships, a Visiting Fellowship at Clare Hall, Cambridge, and a Fellowship at the Hermon Dunlap Smith Center of the Newberry Library, Chicago, gave access to collections and working conditions very hard to equal. I am especially grateful to Mr. Fairclough of the Map Room of the Cambridge University Library, and his staff, for their unstinting help, and to Drs. David Buisseret and James Akerman of the Hermon Dunlap Smith Center at the Newberry for timely direction to recent materials. The Auckland University Library (especially the interloans section), and my own department, displayed yet again their capacity to triumph over distance and difficult demands. Invitations to lecture at Oxford and Princeton Universities and to give a conference paper at the University of Gröningen in Holland gave me the opportunity to set at least some of my ideas in order. It was once more a pleasure to work with the Princeton University Press.

Among the many other individuals to whom I am indebted, both professionally and personally, I should like especially to mention Drs. Martin and Teresa Brett, Dr. Marjorie Chibnall, Professor Raewyn Dalziel, Professor Peter Dronke, Professor Tony Grafton, Professor Michael Reeve. None can, of course, be held responsible for my views or my mistakes.

Finally, my aunt and uncle, Vera and Jim Pullen, and my sister Toni Brisby, and her family, provided limitless hospitality during my own adventures overseas. The book is dedicated to them.

Valerie I. J. Flint
Auckland, New Zealand, 1991

—————— *Introduction* ——————

Our knowledge about the real achievements of Christopher Columbus is now abundant. We are well informed about the four voyages and the discoveries the great admiral made in each of them, about certain of the navigational methods he used, about the peoples, animals, plants, and possible products he found, about the settlements in the New World he attempted to make, and succeeded in making. Not all of this knowledge, of course, is free from controversy, but much is agreed. I cannot attempt to add to it here.[1] This book will be preoccupied instead with information of another kind. Whilst drawing deeply and gratefully upon those facts about Columbus's real achievements which are for the most part established, it will be concerned in the first place rather with "fantasy," than with "fact." I shall attempt in it to reconstruct, and understand, not the New World Columbus found, but the Old World which he carried with him in his head.

This Old World held great power. It gave energy to, and directed, many of Columbus's endeavors in the first place, and much of it remained obdurately in place in his head to the last.

---

1. For convenience, I have set out in outline in an appendix that which I take to be, in general, agreed about the four voyages of Columbus, and about the main events of his life. A most inspiriting survey of previous work on Columbus is to be found in J. Larner, "The Certainty of Columbus: Some Recent Studies," *History* 73 (1988), 3–23. My attention was drawn to this article by Dr. Peter Linehan.

Thus, though some of it could later, with justice, be described as fanciful, it was so real at the time to so many of the most important actors upon this particular stage, that it had a decisive impact upon the eventual establishment of "objective reality." Here fact and fantasy become so hard to distinguish that the word *fantasy* loses its usual meaning, and fantasy of a certain sort becomes proper, indeed vital, to the complete understanding of fact itself. This is my main reason for exploring this now almost forgotten world.

I describe this inner world, this "cosmology," as "medieval" in the first section of the book. This adjective is in some ways unnecessary, in others, inaccurate. In that Columbus was born and educated in the second half of the fifteenth century, obviously his mental world was medieval, or late medieval at least. Yet some of his ideas break across such arbitrary frontiers. Columbus's fierce belief in the providence of God, for instance, and his insistence upon looking only at the positive side of apparent disasters, have many modern echoes, political, religious, psychiatric—and economic. So does his desire (a desire made manifest in the *Book of Prophecies* he compiled) to have the Bible underwrite his most treasured schemes. Thus, though such views and impulses were certainly to be found in abundance in the Middle Ages, we cannot confine them all to this period, and some are valued today. The term *medieval* is a hard one to use, for time barriers rarely confine thought. Much of the thought-world of Columbus *was*, however, rooted firmly in, and sustained by, a past which has now largely vanished, but which had, nonetheless, many strengths. This book will try to recapture some of this past.

The great discoverer's medieval mental world had many dimensions to it. It was built in part, of course, of practical experience, as are all mental worlds; but personal devotion fired by private reflection, reading, and, above all perhaps, dramatic storytelling, sacred and secular, contributed more to its makeup than has always been recognized. In his earlier life in Italy, Portugal or Spain, Columbus acquired a reverence for the medieval church's liturgy and devotional practices which was profoundly important to him, and which helped to stimulate an imagination which was in any case excitable. He clearly respected the Bible, especially, it seems, the more adventurous and mysterious parts of it. He accumulated favorite books along the way, which he annotated avidly. He found inspiration in the examples of persons who had performed signal services for, and with the help of, Christianity in the past, especially in stories about Christian seafarers and pilgrims. His ideas were patterned with geographical pictures and descriptions as strange as they were elaborate, some drawn from the Bible, some from these very stories. He drew energy from the parts faraway Eastern countries had previously played (or were thought to have played) in the encouragement of Christians, and from the past and present threats posed by Christianity's enemies. He came to express strong views upon the supreme importance of a certain form of medieval Christianity in the history of man as a whole, and appeared to suffer anxieties about how this form could best be both defended and extended. The gold Columbus required of his westward voyage was, he declared, sought primarily for Christian purposes, especially for the recapture and subsequent security of Christian lands from the infidel, and for the extension of the Christian message to those who had not yet received it.

I shall contend here that a surprising number of Columbus's descriptions of what he found were influenced by, and reflect, particular expectations; and that many of these expectations were, to us, extraordinary ones. Fervent reading, listening and observation — and there is much to suggest that Columbus was an exceptionally fervent person — both led to the creation of a vivid inner vision, and allowed, even impelled, this inner vision to color almost all he saw. Scenes preenacted, as it were, behind his eyes, were reenacted before them, and were then reported to the admiral's sovereigns with all the imaginative and emotional intensity which drives the visionary. That Columbus's descriptions were colored in this way does not, of course, render them any the less valuable; but, in that they may be a little less straightforward, and possibly more manipulative than they seem at first sight, it does add an extra and important dimension to our own understanding of them. We need urgently to incorporate this dimension into our assessment of the admiral's achievement as a whole. It may well be, further, that this achievement is a speaking illustration of a deep truth; namely, that beautifully painted mental pictures[2] and powerfully held beliefs, even when they lose touch with that form of fact we incline to call scientific, may help those open to them towards remarkable and life-enhancing deeds. "Optimistic blunders"[3] might bring, for some, great blessings with them. It is arguable, indeed, that certain of the most apparently fantastic of Columbus's ideas were *precisely* the ones which allowed him to make the most important of his real discoveries.

I shall focus, therefore, directly upon the admiral, and call primarily upon his own sayings and writings about his discoveries, and upon the books he treasured. This policy poses problems in itself. Not all of the words Columbus uttered or wrote are, of course, accessible, and some of those which are may have undergone very extensive editing (perhaps by the admiral himself, perhaps by his admirers or detractors). As I write now, we still await a definitive study of the admiral's library, and the recent discovery of the *Libro Copiador*, with its seven *cartas-relaciones* (narrative letters) by Columbus, five previously unknown, shows that we may yet hope that more might be found.[4] Of those of Columbus's writings and readings

---

2. Some of them were literally pictures, for instance that of the Santa Maria la Antigua, the great painting of the Virgin in Seville after which Columbus named the present Antigua.

3. I take this phrase from C. R. Beazely, *The Dawn of Modern Geography* iii (Oxford, 1906), 502. Beazley applied it to Columbus but, since he carried his own magnificent study only to 1420, he gave himself no chance to explore it.

4. A. Rumeu de Armas, *Libro Copiador de Cristóbal Colón. Correspondencia Inedita con*

which have now reached us, some are inaccessible to readers only of English. I have tried to meet a few of these difficulties by proceeding in two main ways; firstly by making a close examination of all that *is* known and available, secondly by citing English translations where I can, and by translating and paraphrasing where I cannot. Here, as a prefatory guide, I set out all the accessible material we have upon Columbus's own words. Interestingly, it seems that the more disappointments with which he met, the more articulate and the more obstinately rooted in his inner imaginative landscape his ideas seem to have become. For us, therefore, the later writings might be the more important.

In 1493, Columbus wrote a journal of his first voyage for presentation to the monarchs Ferdinand and Isabella of Aragon. They kept the original, sending him back only a copy. Both have since disappeared. The admiral's son Ferdinand, however, used the journal in his life of his father,[5] and the Dominican

---

los Reyes Católicos Sobre los Viajes a America (Madrid, 1989). The *Libro Copador* is a sixteenth century copy-book of letters by Columbus, probably Italian in origin and found in a private collection from the island of Mallorca. It has in it nine letters in all; the five *cartas-relationes* just mentioned, two short personal letters written by the admiral to his sovereigns, also previously unknown, and additional texts of two well-known accounts, one of the third voyage and one of the fourth, see below. The copy-book seems to have been put together with an especial eye to the exploration and colonization of Hispaniola. It is of surpassing interest not merely because of the new materials it contains, but because it may draw directly upon the admiral's own archives. The copy appears in some instances, however, to be a careless one. Professor John Elliott both drew my attention to this discovery in the first place and, in the face of my failure to find it in England at the time of writing, generously lent me his personal copy. I am greatly in his debt.

5. He presumably had his father's own copy, and he quotes from it, on occasion, directly. Ferdinand Columbus's *Life of the Admiral* was written originally in Spanish. The Spanish version does not survive, and the *Life* did not appear until 1571, when it was published in Venice in an Italian translation. It may be read in English in B. Keen, *Ferdinand Columbus, Life of Columbus* (London, 1960), but there are difficulties both about the authenticity of the original manuscript of the *Life*, and about its translation from the Spanish to the Italian; see Larner, "The Certainty," 8.

historian, Bartolomé de Las Casas, had access to it also, either to Columbus's own first copy, or to a transcript of it. In the course of preparing material for his *Historia de las Indias* (written for the greater part between the years ca. 1550–1563), Las Casas made an abstract of this journal. His abstract contains both direct quotations and abridgments, and has survived. There remains some concern, unhappily impossible wholly to allay, about the extent of Las Casas's modification of the original, but in that Ferdinand Columbus's *Life*, in its present state, reiterates certain passages almost word for word, the balance of probability lies in favor of the faithfulness of Las Casas's abstract to Columbus's first text. We still have no idea, of course, quite when the admiral wrote up the entries in his journal, or, indeed, whether he edited it after his return.[6] This rendering of the journal, a letter dated 15 February 1493 and addressed to Luis de Santangel (*escribano de racion*, or financial secretary, to King Ferdinand) in which Columbus gives a shortened account of his discoveries to his sovereigns, and the very similar first letter of the *Libro Copiador*, dated 4 March 1493 and this time addressed directly to the sovereigns themselves, are our only available primary sources for the admiral's own views upon this first voyage.[7]

6. Jane is particularly gloomy about the journal of the first voyage; "since the extent to which the original was edited cannot be even approximately determined, the evidence of the Journal for the ideas of Columbus before he reached the Indies can only be accepted with reserve"; C. Jane, *Select Documents Illustrating the Four Voyages of Columbus* i (London, 1930), xxvii. This compilation provides the original texts of all Jane translates into English.

7. An English translation of Columbus's well-known February 1493 letter to Santangel and Las Casas's rendering of the journal may conveniently be found in C. Jane, *The Journal of Christopher Columbus* (London, 1960). My references will be to this translation of the journal. Formerly a relatively rare book, it was reprinted (lacking some of the finer illustrations) in 1989 by Bonanza Books, New York. The Spanish version of the letter is printed in C. Jane, *Select Documents*, i, 2–19, but the English translation there is not the best. The letter of 4 March is printed in Spanish in Rumeu de Armas, *Libro*, ii, 435–443. The 1493 letter was extraordinarily popular. The Spanish version was rushed into print in April

The journal of the second voyage is lost. We do have, however, Columbus's prefatory letter to Ferdinand and Isabella (written April 1493), in which he sets out for them his ideas and ambitions,[8] letters two to five of the *Libro Copiador*,[9] and Columbus's official report about the colonization of Hispaniola, dated 30 January 1494, and usually known as the *Torres Memorandum*.[10] We can supplement these by turning to Andres Bernaldez, to whom Columbus gave details to help with the former's *Historia de los Reyes Catolicos* (written before 1500). We can also turn to Ferdinand Columbus, who claims again, on occasion, to report his father's very own words, in part from the lost journal.[11] The letters in the *Libro Copiador* add substance to the belief that Ferdinand and Bernaldez did indeed have direct access to the admiral's own writings.[12]

1493 and was re-published seventeen times before 1500. It was then translated into Latin and nine editions of this translation were published in Italy between 1493 and 1494, some illustrated very fancifully indeed. Some of Columbus's imaginative reconstructions were thus at first published extremely energetically, but the interest of printers and translators seems later to have borne an inverse relationship to Columbus's own heightening of his accounts. At the time of writing a new collection of sources is announced; D. P. Henige, *In Search of Columbus: the Sources for the First Voyage* (Tucson, 1991). The best and fullest collection of Columbus material in the original languages (excepting, of course, the *Libro Copiador*) is to be found in the official Italian publication which followed the 1892 celebrations; *Raccolta di Documenti e Studi Pubblicati dalla R. Commissione Columbiana* (Rome, 1892–1894), 14 vols. and supplement.

8. *Transl.* S. E. Morison, *Journals and Other Documents on the Life and Voyages of Christopher Columbus* (New York, 1963), 199–202. This also contains English versions of the first journal and letter and much other important material. I shall cite it frequently, especially for its excellent annotations.

9. Rumeu de Armas, *Libro*, ii, 447–541.

10. Jane, *Select Documents*, i, 74–113.

11. For Bernaldez, see Jane, *Select Documents*, i, 114–167, and for Ferdinand, most conveniently, Morison, *Journals*, 246–251.

12. Rumeu de Armas, *Libro*, i, 107–113.

We are somewhat better off for the third voyage, for the admiral wrote three very forceful reports about it, and we have early versions of them. Firstly, he compiled another journal along the way (as he says), which he sent to his sovereigns. Las Casas made an abstract of the journal once again, and this abstract, like that of the first journal, has survived. Secondly, Columbus wrote a full account to the sovereigns in a separate letter (dated 18 October 1498), and, thirdly, he sent, in October 1500, a further informative letter to Dona Juana de Torres, friend of Queen Isabella and governess to the latter's son.[13] For the fourth voyage Ferdinand himself becomes a primary source for his father's views, for he accompanied the admiral on it. We have also one more letter from Columbus to his sovereigns about this fourth voyage, the so-called "Lettera Rarissima," dated 7 July 1503.[14]

Columbus's annotations to his books will be discussed fully in Chapter 2; I shall not therefore review the editions and translations of them here. A word should perhaps be said,

13. Las Casas's abstract of the journal, an extract from the letter to the sovereigns, and the letter to Dona Juana are translated into English in Morison, *Journals*, 253–298. Difficulties similar to those which attach to the abstract of the journal of the first voyage attach also to that of the third. The *Libro Copiador* provides, as its sixth letter, an independent copy of the letter to the sovereigns, perhaps made from the admiral's own archive. This copy has, however, been in some parts carelessly made. Rumeu de Armas, *Libro*, i, 358–372 (text ii, 545–564).

14. Translations of the relevant passages from Ferdinand's *Life* and of the "Letter Rarissima" may be found in Morison, *Journals*, 321–385. The "Lettera Rarissima" features also as the last letter (9) of the *Libro Copiador*; Rumeu de Armas, *Libro*, ii, 575–594. This copy, like the *Libro Copiador's* version of the letter to the sovereigns on the third voyage, may have been made directly from Columbus's own archive. It is of great importance, for the only other known Spanish text of the "Lettera Rarissima" survives solely in a copy of the seventeenth century. This and the text in the *Libro Copiador* are remarkably close. Some of Columbus's cartas-relaciones (including the letters about the third and fourth voyages), some extracts from the journals and Ferdinand's *Life*, and a few other sources may be found in English in *transl.* J. M. Cohen, *The Four Voyages of Christopher Columbus* (Harmondsworth, 1969). Because this is a convenient and available collection I shall cite it in addition to Morison, *Journals*, on occasion.

however, about his *Book of Prophecies*. This consists primarily
of a *catena* of extracts from the Bible and from well-known ancient
and medieval authors, together with a few verse fragments in
Spanish, and a part of a letter to Ferdinand and Isabella written
ca. 1501–1502.[15] The *Book of Prophecies* was put together over
a period of years, chiefly perhaps between the years 1501 and
1505, and Columbus's work upon it may have become all the
more intense after the unhappy experiences of the third voyage.
He was helped in its compiling by a friend, the Carthusian
Gaspar Gorricio of Novara, from the monastery of Santa Maria
de las Cuevas. Unhappily, the *Book of Prophecies* was never
completed. Even so, it may be regarded as a high point in,
perhaps even the apotheosis of, the most markedly medieval
aspects of the great admiral's inspiration.[16]

Each of the chapters which follow has been prompted by a
passage or passages Columbus seems actually to have written
himself. These passages show, and with an especial clarity, that
the admiral's chosen habitation, the support for many of the
most inventive of his energies, was a world very different from
the one in which he lived from day to day. This world may,
in addition, have been the source of some of the shrewder of
his schemes. I touched earlier upon the word *manipulative*.
A word such as this carries certain implications with it. It might

15. It is printed by C. de Lollis, *Scritti di Cristoforo Colombo*. *Raccolta*, I(ii),
75–160. Morison chooses, appropriately, passages from the *Book of Prophecies*
as chapter headings in his fundamental book on Columbus; S. E. Morison,
Admiral of the Ocean Sea, 2 vols., (Boston, 1942). At the time of writing a new
edition of the *Book of Prophecies* is announced, together with a translation into
English; D. C. West, *The Libro de las Profecias of Christopher Columbus* (Gainesville,
1991).

16. The *Book of Prophecies* is discussed in an excellent article by P. M. Watts,
"Prophecy and discovery: on the spiritual origins of Christopher Columbus's
'Enterprise of the Indies'," *American Historical Review* 90 (1–2) (1985), esp. 85.
I am grateful for this reference too to Professor John Elliott. Dr. Watts and
I might not in the end quite agree about the ultimate place and purpose
of the *Book of Prophecies*, nor about the true aims of Columbus's medieval reading
as a whole, but I am much indebted to her learning.

suggest, for example, that Columbus used his inner world, his imaginative landscape, deliberately; perhaps to draw others into it with him, perhaps to make, with its help, an impression upon these others which would serve his ends. Such a suggestion takes us to the edge of dangerous and uncharted waters. The definitive resolution of the problems of how original at the time was the admiral's vivid cosmology or how well related to the views of his contemporaries, how personal it was to Columbus or how widely it was shared, how innocently he moved within it or with what cunning he employed it — all of these await a larger study, if, indeed, they are capable of resolution at all. It may never be possible accurately to draw a line between that which Columbus himself truly believed, and that which he exploited for effect. But, in addition to this attempted re-creation of the admiral's medieval inner universe, a few suggestions about how he used the imaginative fuel it gave him will be made along the way. I hope that this enquiry, limited as it is, might at least help to show how great a debt was owed to the middle ages by so-called "renaissance man."

Author's Note

The terms *edit.* and *transl.* are used throughout especially in footnotes and Bibliography, to show that the given work contains both a full edition (as opposed to a transcription) and a translation.

PART I

The Medieval Background

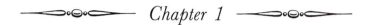

Chapter 1

"*Mappemondes*"

Columbus speaks directly of ""mappemondes,"" (*mappae mundi*, or maps of the world) twice in his journal of the first voyage. In the entry for 24 October 1492 he writes (of Cuba);

> the Indians of these islands and those whom I carry with me in the ships give me to understand by signs, for I do not know their language, it is the island of Cipangu, of which marvellous things are recounted; and in the spheres which I have seen and in the drawing of mappemondes, it is this region.

Though the word *mappemonde* could, at this period, denote a geographical treatise, it is clear from this passage that Columbus meant actual maps. Under the entry for 14 November Las Casas tells us further that as Columbus sailed among the islands off the northeastern coast of Cuba;

> he says that he believes that these islands are those without number which in the mappemondes are placed at the end of the east. And he said that he believed that in them there were very great riches and precious stones and spices, and that they extend very far to the south, and spread out in every direction.[1]

1. C. Jane, *The Journal of Christopher Columbus* (London, 1960), 43 and 62.

It is easy to understand how it was that Columbus set store by mappae mundi and carried pictures of them in his mind, for throughout the Middle Ages they had been both a popular and an effective way of conveying geographical knowledge. Unfortunately, we cannot be quite sure which of these maps he had seen. In 1474 the Florentine physician Paolo Toscanelli wrote a letter to Fernão Martins in Portugal, urging upon King Alfonso V the western route to the Indies. Columbus acquired this letter, perhaps in the early 1480s, and derived great encouragement from it. He may, at the same time, have acquired the "graphic sketch" which accompanied the original letter. Toscanelli wrote also independently to Columbus, enclosing a map which he described as a "chart . . . which would have better been shewn in the form of a round sphere." Both may have contained elements of mappae mundi of the kind we shall shortly examine. Neither of Toscanelli's enclosures has survived.[2] Copies of treatises *Imago Mundi* were, however, frequently accompanied by world maps, and Columbus had, we know, his own treasured copy of the *Imago Mundi* of Pierre d'Ailly. Perhaps, then, this was the source of at least one of his world maps, of some of his ideas about the islands of the Indies—and of a good deal more. I have therefore included an exceptionally fine copy of an early *Imago Mundi* world map as an illustration of how such "mappemondes" could be set out, and in order to give some indication of the type of geographical knowledge they sought to purvey (Plate 1).[3]

---

2. The Toscanelli correspondence may be read in translation in S. E. Morison, *Journals and Other Documents on the Life and Voyages of Christopher Columbus* (New York, 1963), 13–14. Morison plausibly suggests that the sphere-like representation may be related to Behaim's globe of 1492, which echoes Toscanelli's famous, hopeful, and flawed reckoning of the distance the western voyage must cover; see below. There is an attempted reconstruction of Toscanelli's chart in A. E. Nordenskiöld, *Periplus* (Stockholm, 1897), 166, Fig. 78 (this is reproduced below as Plate 12).

3. Ms. Corpus Christi College Cambridge, 66, f. 2 (Plate 1). The treatise called *Imago Mundi* which this map illustrates, that of Honorius Augustodunensis, was one of Pierre d'Ailly's chief sources.

As Columbus set out upon his first voyage in 1492, Martin Behaim, at Nuremberg, was engaged in the construction of his famous globe. The impossibility of establishing any direct link between Columbus and Behaim is one of the great frustrations of this crucial period in the history of discovery. Try as we may, it cannot be proved that Columbus either met Behaim or knew of his globe,[4] but it is, I think, virtually certain that Columbus was informed and inspired by sources and maps of the kind upon which Martin Behaim drew.[5] Columbus may, indeed, have had a globe similar to that of Martin Behaim with him on this first voyage,[6] and some of its information may even have imprinted itself upon the reports made of the admiral's discoveries.[7]

The *Imago Mundi* map, just mentioned, is especially closely associated with, and may even have been a model for, the famous late thirteenth century Hereford Map. The Hereford Map, a circular display map or "wheel," is now one of the most

---

4. Ravenstein suggests that they might have met in Portugal in the late 1480s, but agrees that there is no proof. E. G. Ravenstein, *Martin Behaim, His Life and His Globe* (London, 1908), 32–33. Ravenstein's study is still the best we have on Behaim's globe, and contains magnificent facsimiles. There is also a fine reconstruction of it to be seen in the English National Maritime Museum, at Greenwich.

5. S. E. Morison, *Journals*, 81. The similarity between Toscanelli's, Columbus's and Behaim's estimates of the distance across the Atlantic is especially striking; Ravenstein, *Martin Behaim*, 64. Ravenstein suggests that Toscanelli may have communicated with Behaim through their mutual friend Regiomontanus (Johan Müller), who published his *Ephemerides* in Nuremberg, and who had been in touch with Toscanelli as early as 1463. On the use in contemporary Nuremberg of sources upon which Columbus certainly drew see E. P. Goldschmidt, *Hieronymus Münzer und seiner Bibliothek* (London, 1938), 43–50. I owe this reference to Professor Tony Grafton.

6. So Ravenstein, *Martin Behaim*, 32–34, 57–58.

7. This material will be discussed more fully in Chapter 4, Marvels of the East.

treasured possessions of the cathedral chapter of Hereford.[8] This especially magnificent mappa mundi measures fully fifty-two inches in diameter and, in the late Middle Ages, possibly did duty as an altar piece in the cathedral. Columbus may also have been familiar, then, with display maps of this kind.[9] Their particular placing in great centers of worship might, indeed, have made an especially deep impression upon so fervent a Christian.[10] The Hereford Map, too, is an excellent general example of the stimuli, ideas and even justifications which might be gained from world maps by an enthusiastic explorer, and I shall therefore draw upon it greatly here.[11]

Mappae mundi, large and small, came into the European Middle Ages with Christianity, and were one of the agents in the spread of this religion. The model for some of the earliest

---

8. The association is made clear in an admirable, though now rare, book upon the Hereford Map and related maps; W. L. Bevan and H. W. Phillott, *Medieval Geography, an Essay in Illustration of the Hereford Mappa Mundi* (London, 1873), xxxvi–xxix. They place CCCC 66 in the twelfth century, but an early thirteenth century date is more likely. The eastern section is reproduced here in Plate 6.

9. The thirteenth century Ebstorf Map, a slightly earlier world map, related to the Hereford Map, measured almost twelve feet across, and was also used as an altarpiece by the monks of the abbey. This map was destroyed in the Second World War, but a good reproduction may be found in R. V. Tooley et al., *A History of Cartography* (London, 1969), 23.

10. The Hereford Map is crowned by a representation of the Day of Judgment, in which the Virgin Mary is given a prominent position as intercessor; ibid., 15–16. Such symbolism was, again, dear to Columbus.

11. Display maps were also valued by great secular houses, to the glories of which Columbus was very susceptible. Countess Adela of Blois, in the early twelfth century, had one on her bedroom floor (covered with glass to preserve it from dust); O. A. W. Dilke, *Greek and Roman Maps* (London, 1985), 153. There was one on the wall in the "Sala dello Scudo" of the Doge's palace in Venice in the mid-fifteenth century; H. Yule, *The Book of Ser Marco Polo* i (London, 1903), 110. One of the most famous and spectacular of all world maps, the Catalan Atlas of ca. 1375, was given as a present to a reigning monarch. Columbus may have seen a world map closely related to this, see below. The map which acted as model for Behaim's globe was subsequently mounted and hung on the wall of the Nuremberg chancellery; Ravenstein, *Martin Behaim*, 58–59.

of the known ones seems to have accompanied the commentary
on the Apocalypse (or Book of Revelations) composed in the
last quarter of the eighth century by the Spanish monk Beatus
of Liébana.[12] A note to the commentary tells us that this
accompanying map depicted the missions of the twelve apostles,
possibly in illustration both of Matthew 13 (the parable of the
sower), and of Matthew 28:19, in which the apostles were
commanded to preach to all nations. The model Beatus Map,
it should be noted, was also forged in the fire of fierce
contemporary controversy, for Beatus, when he wrote his
commentary, was engaged in a battle against a Christian
heresy.[13] The need to defend the true faith imparted to it, then,
an even greater urgency. Urgency of such a kind is a general
characteristic of medieval maps of the world. They were, for
the greater part, less geographical descriptions than religious
polemics; less maps than a species of morality. Mappae mundi
are also to be found in company with copies of the Psalter (Plate
2),[14] and, especially, with some of the works of a Spanish
Christian pastor and prosyletizer even more distinguished than
Beatus; Archbishop Isidore of Seville (d. 636).[15] We can see,

---

12. Beatus of Liébana (d. 798) was teacher and adviser to Queen Adosinda of
Leon, for whom he wrote this commentary. It was extraordinarily popular in
the Middle Ages, and the illustrations that often accompanied it were widely
known and copied, even into stone, as at Vézelay and Moissac. The original
map that went with the commentary has not survived, but we have many
derivatives in manuscripts from the tenth to the thirteenth century.

13. That of "adoptionism" — the notion that Christ was, as divine, the natural
son of God but, as human, merely an adopted son.

14. For example, the so-called "Psalter Map" of the British Library, found
in the mid-thirteenth century manuscript Ms. London, B.L.Add.28681, f. 9
(Plate 2).

15. Mappae mundi accompanying works by Isidore are illustrated in Visconde
de Santarem, *Atlas Composé de Mappemondes et de Cartes Hydrographiques et Historiques*
i (Paris, 1845), 1. They usually accompanied copies of Isidore's *De Natura Rerum*,
but were sometimes with his *Etymologies*. Many are mentioned in C. R. Beazely,

even from these few examples, that such maps were, from the beginning, associated with books of the Bible especially important to the Christian liturgy and to preaching—with books, that is, expected to be particularly helpful in the extension of the Christian message—with energetic pastors, and with the early Christian heritage of Spain.

Mappae mundi took passages from the Apocalypse, the Gospels, the Psalter and other books of the Bible as their principal guides through the uncharted territories of the habitable world. Ezechiel provided two emphatic statements about the physical placing of Jerusalem:

> Thus says the Lord God: This is Jerusalem; I have set her in the centre of the nations, with countries round about her. (5:5)

and (of the inhabitants of Jerusalem):

> the people who were gathered from the nations . . . who dwell at the centre of the earth. (38:12)

The Book of Ezechiel was yet one more book of the Bible especially well attuned to prosyletism and was, together with the Apocalypse and Psalter, again heavily so employed. The Psalms spoke too of God's "working salvation in the midst of the earth" (74[73]:12). Jerusalem, then, could perhaps be taken as the center-point of the earth's surface and, once this was established, the remaining parts of the world be distributed in accordance with their supposed relationship to Jerusalem. The information provided in Genesis, perhaps the most important

The Dawn of Modern Geography ii (London, 1897), 628–629. The latter work is still fundamental to all understanding of medieval geography, but Beazely's views upon medieval mappae mundi need now to be replaced by the magnificent chapter by D. Woodward in eds. J. B. Harley and D. Woodward, *The History of Cartography* i (Chicago and London, 1987), 286–370.

preaching book of all, could then also be brought usefully to bear upon the problem. Thus, instead of the north being at the top of the map, as now, such biblically inspired geographers placed the east there, for Paradise, said Genesis, was in the east (Genesis 2:8), and that was man's first home and his final interest. The Terrestrial Paradise also demanded a somewhat uphill journey of those who would attain it, and this too could be nicely indicated by putting it at the top. The second book of Genesis taught that the Terrestrial Paradise was every bit as much a part of creation as was Adam, and it seemed, therefore, that it must have its place on the globe.

The habitable world was divided then into three continents, in accordance with God's delivery of the dry land to be peopled by the three sons of Noah after the flood (Genesis 9:18-19).[16] The continent of Asia occupied, as a general rule, half the space allotted to the lands God created, and, being the largest portion, was assumed to be the domain of Shem, the firstborn. Europe (Japhet) and Africa (Ham) divided the remaining half of the lands between them. Jerusalem stood on the western edge of Asia, with the Mediterranean, appropriately central too (but to the lower part of the map), lapping up to Jerusalem and dividing Europe from Africa.

To the north (that is, to the left of the onlooker) an arm of the Mediterranean representing the River Don or Black Sea would often divide Europe from Asia. To the south, or right, the Mediterranean might extend into another gulf, dividing Asia from Africa and sometimes meeting the River Nile, as Pliny said it did. The lands were usually (though not invariably)

---

16. This division had the additional support of Pliny, *Natural History* III, i, 3; "The whole circuit of the earth is divided into three parts, Europe, Asia and Africa. The starting point is in the West, at the Straits of Gibraltar, where the Atlantic Ocean bursts in and spreads out into the inland seas. On the right as you enter from the ocean is Africa and on the left Europe, with Asia between them; the boundaries are the river Don and the river Nile." *Edit.* H. Rackham, *Pliny Natural History* ii (Loeb, London, and Harvard, 1961), 4–5.

Plate 2. *The so-called "Psalter Map," from the mid-thirteenth century Ms. London, B.L.Add.28681, f. 9. Reproduced by permission of the British Library.*

Plate 3. *The so-called "Cotton Map," from the tenth century Ms. London, B.L. Cotton Tiberius B.V., f. 56v. Reproduced by permission of the British Library.*

Plate 4. The "Columbus" Map and Chart. Ms. Paris, Bibliothèque Nationale, Res. Ge.AA 562. Reproduced by permission of the Bibliothèque Nationale, Paris.

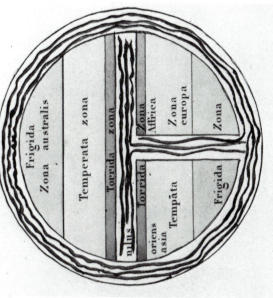

Planisphère du XIIᵉ Siècle qui se trouve dans un M.s.s. de l'Imago Mundi de Honoré d'Autun.

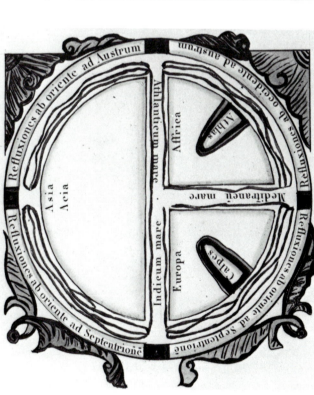

Planisphère du Traité intitulé Imago Mundi d'Honoré d'Autun XIIᵉ Siècle.

Plate 5. (A). TO map from a twelfth century copy of the Imago Mundi of Honorius Augustodunensis. (B). Macrobian zone and climate map. Both reproduced from Visconde de Santarem, Atlas i (Paris, 1845) by permission of the Syndics of Cambridge University Library.

Plate 6. *The eastern section of the thirteenth century Hereford mappa mundi (the Terrestrial Paradise is represented by the island at the top). Reproduced by permission of the Dean and Chapter of the Cathedral of Hereford.*

depiction of eastern Asia and India. The polemical purposes
of these maps, together with the added demands imposed upon
them by the biblical literature upon which they drew, required,
furthermore, that this restricted space be occupied by large
numbers of peoples and places; peoples and places for the most
part outside the ordinary reach of European Christian peoples,
but important to their history and their supposed future. Thus,
as somewhere had to be found for the Terrestrial Paradise of
Genesis, so too did somewhere for the Eli and Enoch who
traditionally lived close to paradise,[20] for instance, for the
perennial dry tree of Ezechiel 17:24, and for the land of Ophir
in the east, which provided gold and "almug wood" and
precious stones for Solomon (2 Chronicles 8:18, 9:10). Land
was needed also for the followers of Gog and Magog (son of
Japhet in Genesis 10:2) whose "number is like the sand of the
sea" (Apocalypse 20:8), who peopled "the uttermost parts of
the north," and were expected to burst out of them at the end
of the world "riding on horses, a great host, a mighty army"
(Ezechiel 38:15). Legend had Gog and Magog securely shut up
behind gates of brass for now. They had been shut up by
Alexander the Great, no less; but there was no knowing quite
how long the gates would hold, nor, more importantly perhaps,
exactly where Gog and Magog were. Mappa mundi makers
loved to depict Gog and Magog and distributed them quite
liberally over the globe; but by the later Middle Ages they seem
firmly to be placed in Asia, and to the far east of that
continent.[21] Yet more eastern land was required for the ten lost
tribes of Israel, for God had allowed the King of Assyria to carry
them away for their wickedness and place them "in the cities
of the Medes" (2 Kings 17:6). The ten tribes are, in the

20. On Eli and Enoch, see Chapter 5, this volume.

21. For Gog and Magog and the Alexander legend, see A. R. Anderson,
Alexander's Gate, Gog and Magog and the Inclosed Nations (Cambridge, Mass., 1932),
esp. 87–90 for the placing of Gog and Magog on maps.

corruptness of their lives, sometimes associated in legend with
Gog and Magog, and, through a liberal interpretation of the
extent of Media, occasionally physically placed with them.[22]
Turning to New Testament times, the Magi of Matthew 2:1–12
came from *somewhere* in the east. Then, lastly, there was the
legendary Prester John. The apocryphal *Acts of Thomas* had long
given a quasibiblical basis for a belief that the apostle Thomas
had evangelized India. From the twelfth century onwards a
dimension was added to this, namely the story that there
survived beyond the lands of the infidel a Christian kingdom,
whose priestly ruler (possibly descended from the Magi of
Matthew) might come to the help of the west. The legend of
Prester John went through many vicissitudes, and the kingdom
itself was very variously located, from, at first, the depths of
India and Asia, to Ethiopia or even Africa as a whole. The
possibility that his kingdom and that of his descendants was in
the east, and perhaps in the Indies, remained open, however,
well into the time of Columbus and beyond, despite a growing
skepticism and the disappointments of eastern travellers anxious
to meet him. Thus Prester John too tended to find a place in
the eastern sections of world maps, together with all the
expectations that accompanied his presence there.[23]

Such vivid sections of the Bible and of the apocryphal
scriptures encouraged imaginative elaboration, and the chance
for imaginative elaboration was, of course, a gift to the
illustrators of maps such as these.[24] The vivid sections invited
also, and perhaps precisely because of this encouragement to

---

22. Ibid., 65–74.

23. Behaim's globe has Prester John in both Africa and India; Ravenstein,
Martin Behaim, 95.

24. Further illustrations will be mentioned in the chapter on sea stories. See
also the great number of inhabitants of the east depicted by the Hereford Map
(Plate 6).

extreme imaginativeness, validation where possible from detached and supposedly "scientific" observers. I have mentioned in passing the support which could be drawn from Pliny and Isidore. Mapmakers plundered as many histories, human and natural, and as many encyclopedias and geographical and scientific treatises as they possibly could for supporting evidence. Only those writers whose effusions *did* support the scriptures, of course, were selected. The application of this criterion necessarily limited the area of choice; and that of a second one refined it still further. In addition to their conforming to the teaching of the Bible, the works chosen should (and this is especially important) actively assist in that attitude of wondering amazement which God's work of creation must never cease to inspire in true Christians.[25] This requirement could make the distinctions between history and legend, and instruction and inspiration, as hard to draw as those between fact and fantasy. To a "scientific" age such as our own, each of these requirements might seem a little curious; but they were stringently applied for all that, and, like so many stringent requirements, including those of today, they endowed those who met them with great prestige. Thus, through passing these twin tests of conformity to the Bible and the capacity to excite reverent wonder, certain works became positive authorities for the mappa mundi maker, and essential to his stock-in-trade. So indispensable were they, indeed, that they might be allowed to bring in peoples and places of their own.

---

25. Augustine supported this attitude with vigor in his *City of God*; indeed, he came close to asserting that it was the distinguishing feature of the true Christian. Important passages to this effect are to be found for example in his *City of God*, Book XXI, Chapter iii, *Transl.* W. H. Green, *Saint Augustine City of God* vii (Loeb, London and Cambridge, Mass., 1963), 24–29. One must marvel at the right things and in the right way, certainly; but there was no doubt that the capacity to marvel was essential to a Christian. It is well to bear this in mind for it will be argued that it played an essential part in Columbus's own attitude to his work.

In eastern affairs the *Natural History* of Pliny the Elder, the *Collectanea Rerum Memorabilium* of the late third century writer Solinus, some of the writings of the Fathers of the Church (particularly those of St. Augustine and St. Jerome), the *Etymologiae* of Isidore, the *Imago Mundi* of the twelfth century writer Honorius Augustodunensis, and the *Imago Mundi* of Cardinal Pierre d'Ailly, produced in 1410, were among the more prominent of the independent treatises upon which the mappa mundi makers depended. Thus it happened that, largely as a result of the popularity of Pliny, Solinus and Isidore, and the enthusiasms of those who delighted in copying and embellishing them,[26] the biblical tribes of Gog and Magog, the ten lost tribes of Israel and even Prester John were almost submerged beneath a flood of semihuman monsters which they released into eastern lands. The monstrous races were to become dear to illustrators in general.[27] India was spectacularly rich in them, for Solinus and his embellishers placed an exceptional number of these monsters there. He ascribed to India creatures with the bodies of lions yet the wings and claws of eagles, and (and this is one of the many passages especially relevant to the observations of Columbus, as I hope we shall see) persons who considered it a reverent act to make meals of their aged relatives. Many Indian peoples, he says more mildly (and possibly with a greater accuracy), declined to kill animals or eat their meat, but lived by the sea on fish. There were dog-headed people who barked, and had talons for fingers, and women who gave birth to dogs. There were people whose feet faced backwards and had eight toes per foot; there were Sciapods, or persons with one huge foot, which they used either as a sunshade or to take tremendous

---

26. Perhaps the best known embellisher is the author of the fourteenth century *Travels of Sir John Mandeville*, but, contrary to popular opinion, he may not have been the one closest to Columbus. See Chapter 3, this volume.

27. The best general study of the monstrous races is that by J. B. Friedman, *The Monstrous Races in Medieval Art and Thought* (Cambridge, Mass., 1981).

leaps; there were persons whose eyes, noses and mouths were in their chests, and persons who could live only when within reach of the scent of a special apple. India might have pygmies too (and then what better for good measure than to place in India the giants of the Vulgate Genesis 6:4?). India was also, according to Solinus, the home of a tribe of women founded by the daughter of Hercules who, like Amazons, forswore the rule of men.

There were monstrous beasts in these parts also; the man-eating Mantichore (perhaps based upon the cheetah), with a triple row of teeth in his human head, a lion's body, a hissing voice like that of a serpent, a scorpion's tail and a tremendous speed of movement; the giant black eel; the huge swimming snakes capable of devouring stags; the bulls with turning horns; the Monoceros, rhinoceros or unicorn, with his great front horn and elephant's feet; the two-armed sea serpents that pull elephants under water; whales that cover four acres; the giant turtles with shells large enough to provide roofs for houses. India, according to Solinus, provided parrots too; the "psittacum" with his gorgeous plumage and hooked beak. Some of the fabulous beasts of India found secure refuge in the *Medieval Bestiary*; others roamed across mappae mundi. India was renowned also for pepper, having a great pepper forest on the southern side of the Caucasus mountains, and, of course, it provided many precious metals and infinite numbers of jewels.[28]

The Corpus and Hereford mappae mundi, and the Psalter Map, illustrated here (Plates 1, 6 and 2, respectively), are excellent examples of the general principles upon which such maps of the habitable earth were constructed. They provide us

---

28. The relevant passages are to be found in Solinus's *Collectanea Rerum Memorabilium*, Chapter 52; *edit.* Th. Mommsen, *C. Iulii Solini Collectanea Rerum Memorabilium* (revised edn., Berlin, 1958), 183–195. There is as yet no adequate translation of Solinus into English.

also with good summary indications of the expectations of eastern travel which were aroused by these maps. Here is Paradise and its four rivers, occupying a large section of the space above Jerusalem (the Psalter Map accidentally has five rivers). There, near Paradise, is Ezechiel's dry tree. Gog and Magog are securely shut away in the north east, squeezing China and the lands of the Great Khan between the gates of brass which lock them up, and the Terrestrial Paradise. In India, in the Corpus Map, we have the giants of Genesis, Isidore's pygmies and the dog-headed peoples. We have there also Solinus's pepper forest and his parrots, the people who live by the scent of a special apple, a monstrous Sciapod, a rhinoceros *and* a monoceros, the Mantichore, the giant horned eel and the tribe of women warriors.[29] Off the coast of India, near Ceylon (here "Taprobane"), is Ophir, depicted as an island. Here, in short, in the matter of the east, is much of that stock-in-trade of the mappa mundi maker I have attempted to describe.

Some of the maps drawn later than the thirteenth century, bear at least some impress of the adventures of the great thirteenth century travelers to the east. The Caspian Sea, for instance, is no longer an arm of an unnamed northern ocean in the Marino Sanuto map of ca. 1321, as it is in the Corpus and Hereford Maps (some of the travelers had, after all, passed north of it). There are also, in the same map, many more islands off the far eastern coasts of China and India, in deference especially to the reports of Marco Polo. For all the corrections and improvements, however, the bulk of the stock-in-trade remains exactly the same in many of these later examples. In the same Sanuto Map all habitable land is divided between the three sons of Noah, after the Isidorian pattern. Jerusalem is still in the center of the world, and Gog and Magog remain shut up behind the Caspian ranges (though here quite near the islands)

---

29. Many more of the monsters are distributed along the coast of Africa in the Hereford and Psalter Maps.

with Cathay beyond them. Prester John is clearly marked in southern India, and the whole landmass is surrounded by ocean. I have said that it is impossible definitively to decide which "mappemondes" Columbus actually saw and remembered. We do not know where he was when he saw them, and many "mappemondes" have, of course, been lost. Our only real clue here is the number of islands he mentions. This description would allow of the Sanuto Map just mentioned, and many similar ones; but there are two surviving maps which might be especially close, both to his models and to the models for Behaim's globe. One is the mappa mundi of the great Venetian cosmographer and chartmaker Andrea Bianco, a map put together perhaps in 1436 (Plate 7). The second is the Catalan Atlas, usually assigned to the year 1375.

In the Bianco Map the strict proportions of the TO maps have given way a little, seemingly to include more of the east, and the Indian Ocean has been extended so as to include an even greater number of islands than Sanuto allows. They are also enclosed within a gulf, as were the islands Columbus first identified as the islands of the Indies.[30] The deep conservatism of this map is, however, still very evident. Paradise and its rivers remain high in the far east, (though this time on a peninsula),[31] and so does Ezechiel's dry tree. The depiction of Paradise we may remark, moreover, suggests that it is raised up somewhat, on a conical base — an idea to which Columbus would resort in his third voyage.[32] Gog and Magog remain incarcerated,

---

30. Morison, *Journals*, 57, finds it hard to explain how Columbus reconciled the bay islands he saw with the archipelago described by Marco Polo. If we suppose that Columbus had before him or in his head a map like that of Bianco, this difficulty disappears.

31. The rivers of Paradise debouch oddly, two emptying into the inland Caspian, and one into the Indian Ocean.

32. The river of Paradise which debouches into the Indian Ocean does so into a gulf not wholly unlike the Gulf of Paria. This may have helped Columbus to identify the Orinoco with this great river. See Chapter 5, this volume.

Plate 7. *The 1436 world map of Andreas Bianco. Reproduced from A. E. Nordenskiold,* Periplus *(Stockholm, 1897) by permission of the Syndics of Cambridge University Library.*

northeast of Paradise in this map, as they are in Hereford and Corpus. The realms of Cathay and the Great Khan are compressed below them and adjacent to India. India has in it a monster with eyes in his chest, surely an echo of Solinus. Prester John is still present (though now firmly in Africa).

The Catalan Atlas is, of course, earlier in date than the Bianco Map and it has none of the latter's vivid depiction of Paradise. These drawbacks apart, however, it can lay a claim to being particularly closely related to the kind of mappa mundi which impressed Columbus. The Atlas we have now was specially commissioned by "Pedro el Ceremonioso" of Aragon as a present for King Charles V of France. It was made in Mallorca, and had certainly reached Charles by 1380. It has been kept in Paris, first in the Bibliothèque Royale, now in the Bibliothèque Nationale, ever since. It is more than worthy both of the delight its donor clearly had in making an impression, and of the rank of its recipient. Beautifully illuminated, and provided with multifarious explanatory texts in Catalan, the world map section of this Atlas is remarkably full.[33] My reason for suggesting that Columbus may have had access to a world map similar to this one, stems from my conviction that the Aragonese court must surely either have had the original models for, or kept a copy of, so spectacular an Aragonese treasure.

The Catalan Atlas is the first of the surviving world maps to give evidence of an attempt to keep up with recent discoveries. In the Atlantic it places the Canaries, the Madeira group and even the Azores with a tolerable accuracy, and it commemorates the progress of Catalan sailors to Cape Bojador in Africa in 1346.[34] It knows, and cites, the travels of Marco Polo. It gives Cathay its proper position in the extreme east and southeast (rather than assigning it to the northeast, near Gog and Magog, as other maps, including that of Bianco, had done) and describes at some length the Great Khan's city of "Chambalech"

---

33. The world map has with it a planisphere, astrological observations and illustrations, a magnificent calendar, and a written cosmology and geography. A facsimile, commentary, and translation into German of the Catalan cosmology, geography and inscriptions is to be found in H.-C. Freiesleben, *Der katalanische Weltatlas vom Jahre 1375* (Stuttgart, 1977). I shall draw upon this work greatly here. Though the accepted date for the Atlas is 1375, Freiesleben, 7, suggests 1374–1376. The facsimile is presented both in color and in black and white, but the representation in Santarem, *Atlas*, ii, 32–33, is in fact easier to consult.

34. This was the voyage of Jacme Ferrer, which started from Mallorca. See Beazely, *The Dawn*, iii, 19–20, 420, 429–430.

(Peking), and the Khan's enormous riches.[35] India is clearly a peninsula, and some of the larger islands in the Indian ocean and its neighboring seas are marked. The eastern seas are full of islands, again in tribute to Marco Polo's narrative and as Columbus, too, described them (Marco Polo gives their number as 7448, the Catalan Atlas as 7548). The mapmaker stresses again the great wealth of the area as a whole. "Illa Jana" has aloes, camphor, sandalwood, fine spices, cinnamon, and nutmeg; "Taprobane" has two crop-bearing seasons a year, and is full of gold and silver and gems. Particularly striking, however, is the firm retention, together with these recent inclusions, of so much of that biblical, wondrous and "inspirational" material which distinguished the mappae mundi. Gog and Magog are enclosed behind their walls by Alexander, in much the same place as the Hereford Map assigns to them. The Magi of Matthew ride in from the far east of Persia, just north of India. Two Christian kings are placed in India, "Colobo" and Stephen, whose kingdom guards the body of the apostle Thomas. In India too there is a monastery of Armenian Christians, in which, the commentator declares, the body of St. Matthew lies. India and its islands have many of the strange peoples of Solinus and his followers. There are pygmies who fight with cranes there, and on "Illa Jana" (perhaps Ceylon) there is a "Regio Femnarum", a region that is ruled solely by women. In the ocean there is another island, whose peoples cover themselves only with single leaves, before and behind. On "Taprobane" (usually the name given to Ceylon, but here perhaps Sumatra) there are great black giants, whose favorite dish is white visitors. This particular image is reminiscent of the stories of the voyages of Sinbad the Sailor, to be found in

---

35. After Freiesleben's scrutiny, however, the Catalan Atlas hardly deserves Beazely's claim that "Here . . . we have something like the sketch of Kublai's realm which Marco himself would have made, if he had turned cartographer"; ibid., 19.

the *Thousand and One Nights*.[36] On other islands there live wild men, who are naked, live on raw fish and drink seawater. Pearl fishers cast spells to drive away the man-eating fish which infest the waters. In the Indian Ocean swim creatures called "Sarenas," half woman and half fish, or half woman and half bird.

Real discoveries have touched these mappae mundi very little; indeed, it almost seems as though the further back the boundaries of geographical knowledge are driven, the more zealous are makers of such maps to preserve the sense of the marvelous. The distinguishing feature of the world map is still its faithfulness to its biblical roots, and to its mission to inspire hope and fill with wonder in the cause of Christianity. The fact of the tremendous continued representation of this early medieval and Christian illustrative material needs constantly to be stressed. The further fact that Columbus set great store by it is of the first importance to our understanding of his imaginative vision of the east.

In "mappemondes" of the type we have been discussing, the landmass of the habitable world was surrounded by a circle of ocean (2 Esdras 16:58). The circular outline within which such maps were in general contained was, as I have said, customary rather than obligatory, but water did, in them, always encompass the landmass on all sides. We might remark, whilst speaking of this encircling ocean, that there was no doubt in the heads even of semieducated persons in this period that the world was sufficiently round to be traversable.[37] Thus, as far

---

36. In his third voyage Sinbad tells of great black giants who eat up some of Sinbad's larger companions; *transl.* R. F. Burton, *The Book of the Thousand Nights and One Night* iv (London, 1894), 366–367. Freiesleben, *Der katalanische*, 23, 32, draws attention to another reference in the Atlas to Sinbad, but misses this one. The Sinbad stories will be discussed in Chapter 3, this volume.

37. There is a fine summary of the "flat earth" theory and its proponents, together with the theories of the "sphericists" in C. R. Beazely, *The Dawn*, i,

as the provision of water went, such representations of the position of the ocean made the sea passage *round* all the known lands, west to east from the Straits of Gibraltar round Africa to the Indies, that is, or north past the schismatic Ruthenians (marked clearly by Sanuto) to the lands of the Great Khan, appear perfectly possible. These maps, supplemented by a well-known passage from the *Natural History* of Pliny (VI, xxxiv, 175) which suggested that Africa might be circumnavigable,[38] and usually supplied accordingly with a conveniently foreshortened African continent, as Ham's portion, acted as an inspiration to those who tried to sail the southerly route, and this, of course, the Portuguese were attempting to do precisely as Columbus pondered his own world maps.

More importantly for our own purposes, these representations also made the passage by sea round the back of the world map, as it were, seem, at the least, to be conceivable. Nor might it be excessively long. The prophet Esdras, after all, had declared that:

> On the third day thou didst command the waters to be gathered together in the seventh part of the earth; six parts thou didst dry up and keep so that some of them might be planted and cultivated and be of service before thee. (II Esdras 6:42)

The seas could, then, occupy on this reckoning only one-seventh of the surface of the earth, and, on the basis of these maps as they appeared before the onlooker, one could perfectly well envisage a habitable earth's surface which stretched well round

---

274–281. Effectively, support for the flat-earthers was dead by the end of the sixth century, and the view that the earth was spherical in shape became general from the seventh century onwards with the spread of the *Etymologies* of Archbishop Isidore.

38. *Edit.* H. Rackham, Pliny, ii, 468–469.

the globe, leaving only a relatively small stretch of ocean to be crossed from so-called west to so-called east. Roger Bacon (d. ca. 1292), who had constructed a world map himself (now sadly lost), supported forcefully this interpretation of the prophet Esdras's remarks,[39] and his views were passed on (without acknowledgment) by Pierre d'Ailly, and so to Columbus.[40] And even if Shem's and Ham's and Japhet's portions did not make up absolutely all of the land there was, the rest might either be too small in extent to afford a serious obstruction, or be so distributed as still to allow of a direct sea passage through.

Such optimistic views did, in fact, find favor with certain of our makers of medieval world maps. To explore the quality and the credibility of their support we must pass now from the primarily biblical mappae mundi of which Columbus seems to speak in his journal, to the equally Christian zone and climate maps which often accompanied mappae mundi of the type we have discussed, and which Columbus certainly also knew. These zone and climate maps somewhat modified the happy picture the biblical and geographical mappae mundi conveyed of the traversability of the ocean—but they modified it in ways that could only fortify Columbus's particular ambitions, and, indeed, strengthen his attachment to mappae mundi in general. I have begun already to suggest, and I hope later to argue with some firmness, that this attachment was extreme, and that it accounts for a surprising number of apparently innocent observations on his part, as well as for some of his more extraordinary

---

39. In his *Opus Maius*; *edit.* J. H. Bridges, *The Opus Maius of Roger Bacon* i (Oxford, 1897), 290–294.

40. *Imago Mundi*, viii. They were referred to in a famous passage in Columbus's letter of 1498 to Ferdinand and Isabella, see below. They seem also to have made an impact upon Hieronymus Münzer. He wrote from Nuremberg on 14 July 1493 to attempt to persuade King John II of Portugal to support the westward voyage to the Indies, and clearly knew these sections from Bacon or d'Ailly. Morison, *Journals*, 16. On Münzer's interventions here see Goldschmidt, *Hieronymus Münzer*, esp. 46–49.

deductions. We should now pause over this second category of map in order to form some general idea of the encouragement it afforded.

One stream of tradition in the matter of zone and climate maps reached back at least to Eratosthenes in the third century B.C. It was transmitted to medieval Europe first of all by Pliny, once again, and then by means of the fifth-century works of Martianus Capella and Macrobius, especially by the *Commentary on the Dream of Scipio* of Macrobius. This tradition divided the globe into five climatic zones; a northern extremely cold one, a temperate habitable band further south, a central uninhabitable torrid zone around the equator, and two further zones to the south, first an echoing temperate zone and lastly an echoing frozen one (see Plate 5B). Conventional mappae mundi of the type we have been examining gave, at first sight, the impression that the lands they described fell largely within the northern temperate zone. The true torrid zone in maps such as the Hereford and Corpus Maps was not marked. It was, indeed, very hard exactly to place; but it looked as though it might be found somewhere within the all encircling ocean. The heavily foreshortened Africa, India and Asia they sketched out, therefore, might appear to be safely on the northern side of it. This impression could well, once again, encourage southern explorers; but some zone and climate maps added refinements which, to look ahead for a moment, in the end gave more heart to those who looked to a westerly route.

They did this in three ways. Firstly, they firmly extended the arctic zone and the uninhabitable torrid zone over the lands of the sons of Noah, making the northerly sea passage appear to be impossibly cold and the southerly one impossibly hot. Secondly, they placed Ezechiel's six parts of land upon the circle of the globe in such manner as to substantiate the notion of a clear western seaway. Thirdly, they treated the vexed problem of the existence of an inhabitable southern continent or continents (the problem, that is, of the Antipodes) in such a way as actively to discourage attempts to sail through the equinoctial or torrid zone. In this way they seemed purposely to advocate the route Columbus finally chose, even in the face of the survival and imminent success of explorers south of the equator.

For an example of the type of zone and climate map Columbus surely knew, one which reaches back to Macrobius but which adds many later refinements, we can hardly do better than to turn to that which usually accompanied the *Imago Mundi* of Pierre d'Ailly (Plate 8). This still deals primarily with the world of the sons of Noah, but places the north this time at the top of the map. It refines the distribution of habitable and uninhabitable climates across the landmasses; and it has a little to say about the question of the Antipodes.

Within the larger framework descending from Eratosthenes, the zone map of Pierre d'Ailly numbers and describes the climates of the known world, starting just above the equinoctial or torrid zone of Eratosthenes, Pliny, and Solinus.[41] There are seven such climates in all. The first (after a passage in Pliny, *Natural History* VI, xxxix, 211–218)[42] begins in northern India, in the east, and reaches across to Mount Atlas in the west. The second zone again crosses north India, but ends in the west on the latitude of Carthage and Morocco. The third takes in the Mediterranean and reaches across the Tigris and Euphrates to north of the Indus, the fourth stretches from south Spain to southern Armenia, the fifth, taking in Rome, from north Spain to northern Armenia, the sixth across central Europe (taking in Greece) to the Caspian, and the seventh from "Francia" to "Hyrcania," that is northern Russia. Southern India and southern Africa, according to this delineation of zones, appear to be uninhabitable and possibly impassable by way of a

---

41. Solinus speaks of burning waters beyond Ethiopia. *Collectanea* 56, 6; *edit.* Mommsen, *C. Iulii*, 206.

42. *Edit.* Rackham, *Pliny*, ii, 494–501.

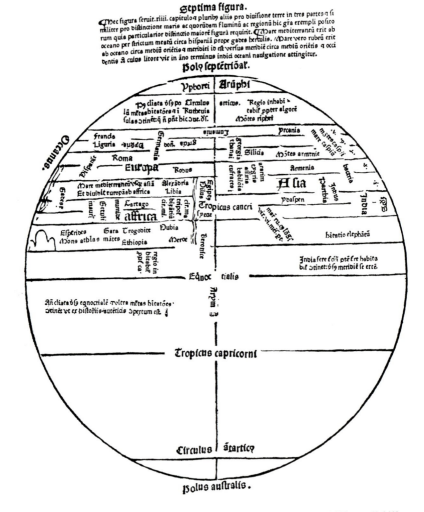

septima figura.

Hec figura feruit.riiii. capituloq pluriby aliis pro diuifione terre in tres partes q fi militer pro biftinctione maris ac quorübam fluminü ac regionü hic gra erempli pofito rum quis particularior biftinctio maiorê figurâ requirit. Mare mediterraneü erit ab oceano per ftrictum meatü circa hifpaniâ prope gades bertulis. Mare vero rubrü erit ab oceano circa mediü orictis q meridiei ió eft verfus meridiê circa mediü orictis q occi dentis A cuius litore vir in âno terminus inbid oceani naulgatione attingitur.

polo fceptêtrióal.

Ypborti | Arüphi

Pg cliata öfg po Circulus
lä mteabitatoreq i Rutheuis
fulaaotinêt:q ñ pñt bic one.öf. | orticus. Regio inhabi ‑
tabif ppter algorê
Mótes ripbei

franda | Proenia
Liguria ·puuda | boñ. epaud | meant | mare cafpia
georgia
thamia | mófcouia
Roma | Silicia | Móstes armenie
Europa | Robus | Armenia
Mare mediterraneü vfq alia | Alexabria | arenü | H lia
Et biuibit europâ ab affrica | Libia | babiloia | Phafpen | pathia
mauric | Cartago | Egipto | Tropicus cancri | mar rubru lafs | India
Efperides | Gara Trogobite | Dubia | spcae
Móns atblao mátes | Ethiopia | Meroc | hitatio elephâtü
regio in
bitabil
ppt ca | India fere cóñ pteâre habita
bif otinet:öfg meribiê fe ertê.
Eqnoc tialis

Añ cliata öfg eqnoctialê mltra mêtas hicatóes·
otinêt vt ex biftoñiis euteticis spertum eft. ᶘ

Tropicus capricorni

Circulus | ãtarticç

polus auftralis.

Plate 8.   Climate map from the Imago Mundi *of Cardinal Pierre d'Ailly. Reproduced from Visconde de Santarem,* Atlas ii *(Paris, 1845) by permission of the Syndics of Cambridge University Library.*

southerly sea route. The northern sea route is equally unattractive to travelers, falling as it does in part within the frozen arctic zone. But a route westwards at the latitude of Spain might, on this reckoning, be quite another matter.

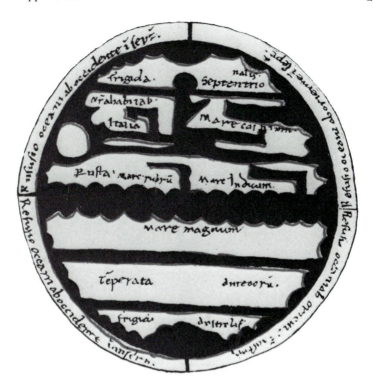

Plate 9. *Macrobian zone map. Reproduced from Visconde de Santarem,* Atlas *i (Paris, 1845) by permission of the Syndics of Cambridge University Library.*

D'Ailly's zone map also allows that there might be habitable land south of the equator. Many medieval mappa mundi makers, as we have seen, allowed the onlooker to assume that the reverse of the globe (the section, that is, they did not describe) was filled with water, and that the three parts of the northern habitable world constituted the only landmass there was; but the zone maps often inspired doubts in others. We now approach the great medieval, and indeed modern, problem of the Antipodes. Macrobius suggested that a great southern continent might well exist, opposite the known northern one (Plate 9), and one of the distinguishing features of the Beatus Apocalypse tradition of mappae mundi lies in the fact that such maps for

Plate 10. *The Beatus Map of St. Sever. Reproduced from K. Miller, Mappae Mundi. Die ältesten Weltkarten by permission of the Syndics of Cambridge University Library.*

the greater part actually depict this southern continent, cut off from the northern world by its encircling stream of ocean (Plate 10). This same zone-map tradition suggested, furthermore, that there might be land on the back of the globe, divided in much the same way as the land on the front, and experiencing the same climates, with their temperate zones, as those described by d'Ailly. Thus, so-called Macrobian world maps gave warning of a great unknown landmass in much the same position as our present North and South America, and exactly where Columbus struck it, but (and we shall come back to this shortly) crucially divided, as on the forefront of the globe, by a stream of ocean crossing, approximately, the isthmus of Panama. The so-called "Cotton Map," the rectangular *mappa mundi* which accompanies the *Periegesis* of Priscien in the tenth century manuscript B.L. Cotton Tiberius B.V. (Plate 3), is itself accompanied by a map of this type in which the four landmasses are described, all intersected by ocean (Plate 11).

The four landmass tradition, with the streams of ocean in between them, was afforded the additional boost of being depicted in maps which accompanied Hyginus's *Astronomicon*. This text was enormously popular in the Middle Ages with both amateur and professional scrutineers of the stars, and was one of the more popular quarries upon which geographers, cosmologers and, we might well suppose, navigators drew. The tradition was given further stimulus in the twelfth century, in part by means of mid-twelfth century copies of the *Liber Floridus* of Lambert of St. Omer. Two surviving copies of the *Liber Floridus* contain mappae mundi with, on the front, the lands of Shem, Ham, and Japhet and the great southern continent (the two landmasses being separated by a torrid stream of ocean), and, at the back (indicated by circles on the edge of the inhabited world) two echoing earth-islands. One of these islands is described as Paradise, and appears to be meant to be placed diametrically opposite the Australian continent depicted on the front—an interesting antithesis. It may be that the

Paradise-islands indicated upon the Corpus and Hereford Maps spring from and support the same tradition. The other earth-island included by Lambert is somewhat confusingly described as "our Antipodes," presumably because its position is supposed to be diametrically opposite that of Europe.

There was, then, no great difficulty in the way of speculating about the existence of other habitable landmasses. They might exist. Both Augustine and Isidore had been prepared to admit this,[43] and, if they existed, they might well be distributed and balanced as Lambert had suggested. There is some poignancy in the fact that early medieval monastic mapmakers were far better intellectually and emotionally prepared for the discovery of a truly New World than was, in some respects, the great admiral himself. These great unknown landmasses might perfectly well be habitable too. The commentator upon the Cotton Map (Plate 11) allowed that they were in principle habitable, for parts of them fell, of course, within the temperate zones. But he wisely left open the question as to whether these postulated landmasses were, in fact, inhabited. Being habitable does not involve their being actually inhabited, or not, at least by humans. The maker of this map drew back, then, before the real medieval problem of the Antipodes; the problem to which we may finally turn.

The vexed question of the Antipodes occupied the most agile of minds and aroused the fiercest of passions, and it was not finally resolved until the great southern continent, or those sections of it which were still above the sea, was in fact discovered. It concerned less the existence than the habitation of these lands. The orthodox position was this. If the torrid zone was not merely uninhabitable but impassable, as Pliny seemed to say it was, then the southern land or lands could not be inhabited by humans; for to suggest that they might be so defied

---

43. Augustine, *City of God* XIV, 9; *edit.* and *transl.* Green, *St. Augustine*, v, 49–51. Isidore, *Etymologies* XIV, 5, 17; *edit.* Lindsay, *Isidori Hispalensis*.

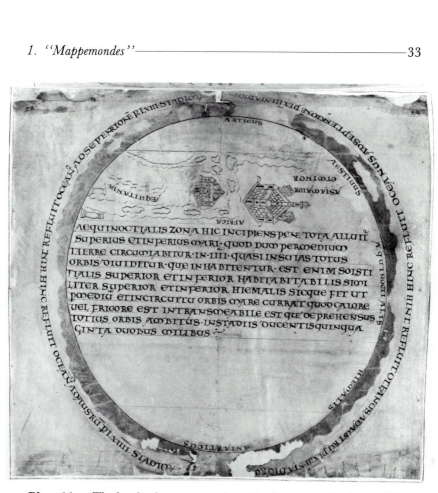

Plate 11. *The four landmasses map, from Ms. London, B.L. Cotton Tiberius B.V., f. 29. Reproduced by permission of the British Library.*

the Bible. The idea of an inhabited Antipodes was irreconcilable with the declaration in Genesis that all men were descended from Adam through the three sons of Noah (Genesis 9:19). It rendered null also Christ's command to the apostles that they go out and preach to *all* nations (Matthew 18:19), and for the same reason; namely, that it was physically impossible for anyone to reach these lands across the torrid zone. There might be a great southern continent, and two more landmasses on the back of the globe; but the southern landmasses were irrelevant to human beings, for they were cut off by a great and burning stream of ocean.

The orthodox solution to the problem of the Antipodes was arrived at in complex and roundabout ways, some of them purely pragmatic. It suited the immediate moral purposes of such pastors as Augustine and Isidore to insist upon the priority of the Bible in such a question, to take Pliny literally and to deny flatly that the Antipodes were inhabited by humans; and they might have been in some sense right.[44] For our own purposes we need only to observe that this solution remained in place for many as the correct moral position when Columbus confronted his own decisions, and the problem of convincing his would-be supporters. Ferdinand, the admiral's son, tells us that Augustine's view upon the matter of the Antipodes was crucial to the Talavera Commission's first refusal of Columbus's request for aid.[45] It was a view which, even at the end of the fifteenth century, was not to be trifled with lightly.

King John II of Portugal, of course, was not troubled by moral delicacy about the Antipodes, and Bartholomew Diaz had actually crossed the torrid zone in his search for the easterly route, as Columbus knew. Columbus himself had sailed to São Jorge da Mina, which he thought lay beneath the equator. Thus, he most firmly declined to subscribe to the traditional view of the impassable torrid zone.[46] But in some ways, and rather by

---

44. I have discussed this question in "Monsters and the Antipodes in the Early Middle Ages and the Enlightenment." In *Ideas in the Medieval West; Texts and their Contexts* (London, 1988), IV.

45. "they all repeated the Spanish saying that is commonly used of any doubtful statement, 'St. Augustine doubts . . .,' because in Chapter 9 of Book XXI of *The City of God* the saint denies the existence of the Antipodes and holds it impossible to pass from one hemisphere to the other. They also used against the Admiral the fables that say that of the five zones only three are habitable, and other falsehoods which they took for gospel truth"; B. Keen, *The Life of Admiral Christopher Columbus by His Son Ferdinand* (London, 1960), 62.

46. He objected openly, for instance, to the support apparently given to the view by Pierre d'Ailly and others; see *edit*. E. Buron, *Ymago Mundi de Pierre d'Ailly* i (Paris, 1930), 196–197, and, more fully, Chapter 2 this volume.

implication than by admission, this view was a help to him in
that which he most wanted to do; travel west to east, that is,
by a westerly route on an encircling stream of ocean. The
tradition of the great all-encompassing, central ocean stream,
attached though it was to unacceptable views about the equator,
could actively assist his plans. This aspect of the orthodox
position on the Antipodes, detached from the others, might
reinforce quite delightfully the thought that both the most
practical and the most Christian of ocean passages might be
found round the back of the globe. Thus, in his annotations
to the *Historia Rerum Ubique Gestarum* of Pope Pius II,[47]
Columbus made a special note of Macrobius's statement to the
effect that the equatorial stream of ocean reached round the back
of Africa, and so around the world. He made this note even
as he himself insisted that he had in fact crossed the equator.
He was well able to select those parts of an argument which
served him and to reject those which did not, and the ocean
part of the Antipodes argument was a useful one. He selected
it accordingly.

Traditions of great antiquity, especially when supported by
the authority of great names among the Fathers, cannot be
removed in a moment. They have immense staying power, as
the Talavera Commission made plain. They should then,
wherever possible, be accommodated. The westerly route might
in fact be both easier and safer. That it could seem, in certain
ways, to be ideologically sounder too was a most welcome
addition. Sadly, residual doubts about the human status of
creatures living beyond this previously impassable zone would,
in the future, offer great excuses for their enslavement. Thus,
in those of its aspects which bore upon the inhabitants of these

47. C. de Lollis, *Scritti di Cristophoro Colombo*, in *Raccolta di Documenti e Studi Pubblicati dalla R. Commissione Colombiana pel Quarto Centenario dalla Scoperta dell'America* i (ii) (Rome, 1894), 294. Again, see Chapter 2, this volume, for a fuller discussion of the *Historia*.

formerly inaccessible lands, parts of the old argument about the Antipodes gained in force, paradoxically, from the very effectiveness with which its geographical supports were now newly breached. It came therefore to be exploited for disastrous ends, and to the dismay, indeed, of the admiral himself. Columbus's medieval map-lore did not all of it give rise to the most beneficial of results. But some of it, delicately adjusted, could turn in his favor. And he was, as I hope to argue fully at the very end of this book, well capable of making such delicate adjustments.[48]

Early in the fifteenth century the *Geography* of the second century geographer Ptolemy was rediscovered. The Greek text of the *Geography* was first brought to the west by Chrysoloras, and it was made generally available through the translation of a version of it into Latin by Jacopo Angelo de Scarperia (often known as Jacobus Angelus).[49] This translation was completed by about the year 1409, and was, through the attentions of Cardinal Guillaume Fillastre, later supplied with maps. Fillastre's body of maps, again translated from the Greek into the Latin, was at first composed of twenty-six regional maps and one mappa mundi. Then, as the fame of the new geography spread, supplementary maps were added.[50] D'Ailly would come

---

48. It may not be wholly fanciful to see, in his comments upon the great heat he encountered in his passage outward on the third voyage, the paying still of a little lip service to those who felt for the old tradition of the torrid zone. This heat burst the wine casks and putrified the meat as they sailed through it; Morison, *Journals*, 264. It was only, after all, the greatness of the seamen and ships of modern Spain which allowed it to be crossed.

49. Helpful introductory words on Ptolemy are to be found in Dilke, *Greek*, esp. 160–66.

50. The most detailed study of Ptolemaic mapmaking in this period is that by D. B. Durand, *The Vienna–Klosterneuburg Map Corpus of the Fifteenth Century* (Leiden, 1952), esp. 24–27, and 252–256. I am grateful for this reference to Professor Michael Reeve, and also to him for letting me read his unpublished paper ''The rediscovery of classical texts in the Renaissance.''

to draw upon Ptolemy and his maps in his compendious *Imago Mundi*, and Columbus's copy of this *Imago Mundi* is the most fully annotated of all of his own books. The admiral was clearly intensely involved in the new outburst of cartographic knowledge. Through the inspiration of scholars gathered at the Council of Florence, and in Rome for the 1450 Papal Jubilee, interest in Ptolemy's *Geography* broke all previous bounds. Prominent among those who contributed to the spread both of the *Geography* and of the "tabulae modernae" (modern regional maps) that increasingly accompanied it, was the German cartographer Henricus Martellus Germanus (fl. ca. 1480–1496). Martellus may have produced one of the prototype maps for Behaim's globe.[51] There is good reason to suppose that Columbus will have known Martellus's work in general, and excellent evidence that he consulted a copy of Martellus's Ptolemaic world map.[52] He may well have done this before he departed on his first voyage. Columbus seemingly also possessed, in addition to d'Ailly's *Compendium*, a copy of a 1478 printed edition of Ptolemy's *Geography*.[53]

---

51. He may have provided a world map graduated in longitude for Behaim. L. Bagrow (revised R. A. Skelton), *History of Cartography* (London, 1964), 107, 259.

52. The world map of Henricus Martellus Germanus survives in a manuscript at present in the British Library; Ms. Add. 15760. This one was drawn after the year 1489, but Martellus may originally have designed such a world map in illustration of the "Descriptio Orbis" of Pope Pius II. A. E. Nordenskiöld, *Periplus* (Stockholm, 1897), 87–88, 128. Columbus possessed and annotated the description of the world Pius II offered in his own copy of the *Historia*; see below, Chapter 2. Columbus was critical, too, in his notes to d'Ailly's *Imago Mundi*, of a certain "pictura" which placed Cathay, in his view, much too far to the north; "Kataium non est tam ad septentrionem ut pitura [sic] demonstrat"; *edit.* E. Buron, *Ymago Mundi de Pierre d'Ailly* iii (Paris, 1930), 747. Martellus places Cathay far up in the northerly regions of Asia. It is possible, then, that his was the map the admiral had here in mind; C. de la Roncière, *La Carte de Christophe Colomb* (Paris, 1924), 35.

53. See the remarks in P. E. Taviani, *Christopher Columbus, the Grand Design* (London, 1985), 82, 148 (translated from *Cristoforo Colombo — la Genesi della Grande Scoperta*, Novara, 1974).

The Ptolemaic world map undoubtedly had a tremendous impact upon, and tempered the dominance of, the medieval mappae mundi; yet it failed most signally wholly to replace them.[54] The earliest printed map (a woodcut, printed at Augsburg in 1472) is a TO map.[55] Still in the mid- and last years of the fifteenth century there survive some spectacular examples of the old medieval mappa mundi tradition. One is the world map of Andrea Bianco we discussed a moment ago. A second is the so-called "Columbus Map" (Plates 4 and 13). This circular mappa mundi, attached to a portolan chart, was long thought to have been one of the maps Columbus took with him on his early voyages.[56] This claim can no longer, alas, be confidently sustained, but the map was certainly drawn up in the last years of the fifteenth century. Yet it still retains an approximate TO form, and includes, in addition, the Terrestrial Paradise, represented as an island, and four other islands taken from the legendary *Navigatio Sancti Brendani*.[57] A third, and even more spectacular survivor is the globe of Martin Behaim itself. Behaim's debt to Ptolemy is clear. It is marked in the outlines he draws of the great known landmasses, and especially in the outlines of the far east. Behaim also gleans and reports much information from Marco Polo's *Travels*, and from the recent

---

54. Durand puts the position well once more; "This process, the modernization of Ptolemy, was complex, tentative and obscure. Nevertheless it can be analysed in sufficient detail to show that the unit of creative innovation at any given point is small, the persistence of tradition great." D. B. Durand, "Tradition and innovation in fifteenth century Italy," *Journal of the History of Ideas* 4 (1943), 5. Cardinal Fillastre himself added pygmies, Sciapods and griffons to the atlas he contributed to Ptolemy's *Geography*; Taviani, *Christopher*, 75.

55. "the printing press was to extend the life of such stereotyped medieval models well into the sixteenth century"; Bagrow, *History*, 91. See also 69–73 for a survey of the persistence of the medieval mappa mundi into the age of Ptolemy.

56. This identification is fully discussed in de la Roncière, *La Carte*.

57. The Columbus Map will be discussed at greater length in Chapter 5, this volume. For the St. Brendan legend, see Chapter 3, this volume.

voyages of the Portuguese. To this extent he could boast that his splendid globe was the very latest thing. But he still includes Havilah from Genesis 2:11 ("where there is gold"), and Ophir to which the fleet of Solomon plied in 1 Kings 10:11, and the realms of Prester John and the Magi of Matthew, and Gog and Magog, and "the trees of the sun and moon which spoke with Alexander."[58] Sirens and sea monsters still prowl the Indian Ocean, and tailed men live in Cathay.[59] Far to the west there is clearly marked the Paradise-island of St. Brendan.[60] Biblical figures, monsters, mythical creatures from the pre-Christian remote past, Alexander, and the Terrestrial Paradise continued to jostle with one another and with Ptolemy for space upon the maps Columbus used.

Much has been made, in studies on Columbus, of the great explorer's rejection of Ptolemy's estimate of the distance by land from west to east; a rejection he made in favor of the longer estimate of Marinus of Tyre.[61] This second estimate shortened, of course, the distance around the back of the world by water, west to east. It was in tune with the observations of Marco Polo, Toscanelli and Behaim, it may have been based in part, as we saw, upon the work of Henricus Martellus Germanus,[62] and it fortified Columbus in his project. It was also, we now know, wrong.[63] This picking about among the authorities which

---

58. Ravenstein, *Martin Behaim*, 94–96.

59. Ibid., 86, 88.

60. Ibid., 77.

61. The most important expression of Columbus's views on this is to be found in his letter to his sovereigns on the fourth voyage; Morison, *Journals*, 375 and notes.

62. Bagrow, *History*, 107.

63. The various reckonings between which Columbus chose are set out clearly in tabular form in S. E. Morison, *Admiral of the Ocean Sea. A Life of Christopher*

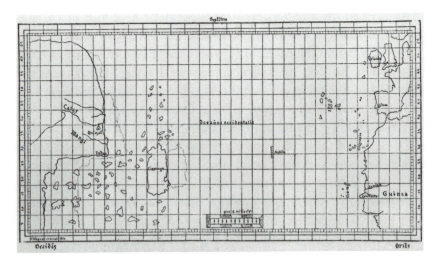

Plate 12. *A reconstruction of Toscanelli's chart. Reproduced from A. E. Nordenskiold,* Periplus *(Stockholm, 1897), 166, by permission of the Syndics of Cambridge University Library.*

suited him can be explained in terms of Columbus's personal and, to some extent self-deluding, ambitions; but this is not the only possible explanation of it. Nor is it the best. Resistance to pre- or non-Christian scientific authority, and, most particularly, to the discouraging aspects of such authority, Christian and non-Christian, has a longer lineage and larger aims than this; and it is not necessarily the easiest option. Resistance to discouragement of this kind is stamped upon the medieval mappae mundi we have surveyed, and with a particular clarity. These very mappae mundi, in their turn, helped this resistance to survive even the shock delivered by the map-corpus which came with Ptolemy. This resistance, this obdurate and optimistic "medievalism", will be imprinted too

---

Columbus i (Boston, 1942), 103. Morison shows how Columbus shortened the length of Marinus's degree to suit his own plans, and so managed to convince himself that Marco Polo's Zaiton might lie a little to the east of present day San Diego, California.

upon many of the other materials we shall come to examine. Columbus's rejection of Ptolemy here is part and parcel of his hopeful and surprisingly complex devotion to a larger, overwhelmingly medieval Christian, tradition. It can only be properly understood from a vantage point within this tradition, and, perhaps most importantly of all, with an eye to those who shared it and revered it.

The same may be said, on a larger compass, of many more of the great admiral's actions and decisions. His rich medieval heritage was a source and emblem of pride to Columbus, and it affected him profoundly. This carrying the medieval tradition on his shoulders as his namesake once did, and this deep belief and involvement in it, may have entailed delusion of a kind. There were indeed certain realities which Columbus appears to have refused to face. Yet, if this was delusion, it was delusion of an order different from, and higher than, that which supports mere selfishness. It was directed to an end beyond, and far greater than, the man himself, and some of the dreams it sought to sustain are dreams which still endure. The enterprise as a whole, it is true, led to blessings which were not unmixed. None of them was long perceptible to the native Americans who first welcomed the discoverer. Equally certainly, however, the blessings were there.

Medieval mappae mundi, through their favored sources, through their attachments in medieval manuscripts, through the answers these sources and commentators gave to controversial problems such as that of the inhabited Antipodes, and through the particular morality and rewards they advocated, acted as both inspiration and support for Columbus's plans. Carefully chosen medieval texts helped him still further. We may next examine these.

Chapter 2

Columbus's Known Reading

Ferdinand Columbus, the admiral's son, and the often equally admiring Bartolomé de Las Casas, historian of the Indies, were in no doubt about the great explorer's powerful intellectual attainments. He was adept at Italian, of course, and Latin; perhaps a little less at ease in Castilian and Portuguese, but capable in these languages too.[1] He wrote well, in an apparently practiced hand. He studied all the arts and sciences necessary to the civilized explorer; astronomy, arithmetic, geography, geometry, history, philosophy, draughtsmanship. He read widely and deeply, as befitted an alumnus of the University of Pavia.[2]

The ascribing impeccable academic credentials to successful public figures is a near-infallible method of attracting the critical attention of scholars. In the case of Columbus it was as blood to sharks, and the waters have foamed accordingly around the question of these credentials. Columbus's association with the University of Pavia sank seemingly without trace at the celebrations of the quatercentenary of his first discoveries. It was argued then, and plausibly, that the admiral had in fact

---

1. Las Casas comments on this comparative inefficacy in, for instance, his abridgment of the journal of the third voyage; S. E. Morison, *Journals and Other Documents on the Life and Voyages of Christopher Columbus* (New York, 1963), 275.

2. B. Keen, *The Life of the Admiral Christopher Columbus by His Son Ferdinand* (London, 1960), 35–36, 40–42.

attended, not the famous university, but a little school set up for the children of wool workers in the *Vicolo Pavia*, in Genoa.[3] Once begun, the destruction of Columbus's reputation as a man of civilized education was continued; by some with an almost unholy glee. Jane, for instance, appears positively to glory in his own decision that Columbus's learning was come by late in life and faultily.[4] He reassures us furthermore that, in that it was still prey to the transports of the admiral's riotous and untutored mystical imagination, his stock of knowledge was not merely small, but was, in addition, of virtually no use to him at all.[5]

Though each of these positions is extreme, and each, too, a little tainted with the distasteful flavor of academic snobbery, the discussion in general still has life in it and is well worth pressing forward.[6] I shall not seek now, however, nor am I qualified, to probe into the finer points of the great explorer's linguistic abilities. Neither have I any new items firmly to contribute to his library (though I do hope later to make one or two suggestions). Instead, something a little different will be

---

3. C. Desimoni, *Questioni Columbiane*, in *edit.* C. de Lollis, *Raccolta di Documenti e Studi Pubblicati dalla R. Commissione Colombiana* iii (2) (Rome, 1894), 29.

4. C. Jane, *Select Documents Illustrating the Four Voyages of Columbus* i (London, 1930), xxxvi, lxxxi–lxxxii.

5. "His assurance that the globe could be circumnavigated . . . appears as being based less upon study and reason, less upon knowledge of any kind and whencesoever derived, than upon his further assurance that he was entrusted with a divine mission. His belief may justly be regarded as evidence of his deep religious fervour; it can hardly be regarded as evidence of deep learning . . . It was rather the product of faith than of science. It was one which might have equally been entertained by a man whose only literature had been works of devotion and who had never emerged from the dim seclusion of a hermit's cell"; ibid., xliii–xliv. See also lii–liii.

6. For a good summary of earlier positions, and a bibliography, see the opening few pages of P. M. Watts, "Prophecy and Discovery: On the Spiritual Origins of Christopher Columbus's 'Enterprise of the Indies,'" *American Historical Review* 90 (1–2) (1985), 73–102.

tried. Firstly, I shall list, and describe the contents and notes of all of those books of which we know, through the presence on them of his annotations, that the great admiral actually read. This will require something of a trudging through, but it is the only way forward to my second purpose; an attempt to show, as a result of this exercise, that Columbus's reading of these books, like his scrutiny of mappae mundi, colored his vision in certain discernibly "medieval" ways; ways which again affected his understanding of the places to which his journeys had taken him, and influenced his descriptions of almost all that he saw. We may follow these influences more closely in Part II of the book. Lastly, it may be possible to see, even at this point, that this, his medieval vision, was guided at least as much by practical considerations as by "mystical" ones—though the proper discussion of this intensely controversial proposition must await the final chapter.

We are now certain that Columbus read, if not widely, deeply and intensely. There survive, in fact, five books that were owned and annotated by the admiral himself.[7] First comes the large

---

7. The pioneering study of Columbus's library and annotated books is that by S. de la Rosa y Lopez, *Libros y Autographos de Cristóbal Colón*, in *Discursos Leidos ante la Real Academia Sevillana de Buenas Letras* i (Seville, 1891), 7–44. The latter part and appendix to this work gave rise to doubts about which of the annotations were made by Columbus himself, which by his brother Bartholomew, and which by an unknown third annotator; doubts which have been by no means yet resolved. The annotations to all five of the books are printed by C. de Lollis, *Scritti di Cristoforo Colombo, Raccolta*, I (ii), but only those parts of the books to which they relate directly are printed with them. The impression this edition gives of Columbus's interests is, therefore, a little deceptive, and I shall try here to give at least equal space to the contents of the works themselves. De Lollis also omitted, sometimes perhaps somewhat arbitrarily, annotations he could not be absolutely certain were by Columbus. I have borne all these doubts in mind but have, in the discussion which follows, generally trusted to Columbus's authorship. Columbus also possessed a copy of Ptolemy's *Geography*, as we saw above, and, technically this is annotated too, for it has two notes, a verse from the Septuagint Psalm 92:4 ("Mirabiles elationes maris; myrabilis in altis Dominum") and the admiral's curious signature. On the latter, see Chapter 6, this volume. There are no notes upon the contents of the *Geography*, however, and Columbus's views on these are adequately indicated upon his other books, notably upon the *Imago Mundi*.

compilation which usually goes under the general name of the *Imago Mundi* of Pierre d'Ailly (1350–1420, Bishop of Cambrai, then Cardinal). This incunabulum, printed ca. 1480–1483 in Louvain by John of Westphalia, incorporates not merely the "picture of the universe" written by the famous Cardinal in about the year 1410, but a whole series of other works, calendrical, astronomical, astrological, polemical and theological, some by d'Ailly himself, others by Jean Gerson (1363–1429), d'Ailly's pupil and distinguished successor to the Chancellorship of the University of Paris. The collection contains some 898 *postille*, or annotations, arguably made by Columbus. The text of d'Ailly's *Imago Mundi* itself clearly commanded a large measure of Columbus's attention, if we are to judge by the number of notes he made on it (475), but each of the other twenty treatises and extracts, save six, seems to have fallen prey to his pen. All of the treatises and the overwhelming majority of the annotations are in Latin.[8]

Second, at least in the number of annotations it can boast as a whole (861), comes the *Historia Rerum Ubique Gestarum* of Aeneas Silvius Piccolomini (Pius II, Pope 1458–1464). The first book at least of this treatise, also in Latin, was read by Columbus in an edition printed in 1477. Thirdly, Columbus possessed a version of Marco Polo's account of his travels, the Latin *De Consuetudinibus et Conditionibus Orientalium Regionum* produced by the Dominican Friar Pipino of Bologna (perhaps between the

---

8. A facsimile of the incunabulum has been published; *Imago Mundi by Petrus de Aiaco with Annotations by Christopher Columbus* (Massachusetts Historical Society, Boston, 1927). The Latin texts of d'Ailly's *Imago Mundi*, *Epilogus Mappae Mundi* and *Compendia Cosmographiae Ptolomaei* (the *Imago Mundi* written ca. 1410 and the *Cosmographia* after d'Ailly had acquired a copy of Angelo's translation of Ptolemy, perhaps in 1414) have been printed together. They are to be found, complete with a list of the other contents of the incunabulum, Columbus's notes, and a translation of the printed Latin texts into French (with full commentary), in *edit*. E. Buron, *Ymago Mundi de Pierre d'Ailly*, 3 vols. (Paris, 1930). Unfortunately the Latin texts are published still complete with their contractions, and the translation into French is fallible.

years 1302 and 1314). Columbus had this in a printed edition produced at Antwerp, 1485–1486.[9] He contributed some 366 annotations to this collection.[10] In fourth place, and turning away from Latin, comes a translation into Castilian (by Alfonso Palencia, printed at Seville in 1491) of Plutarch's *Lives*. There are 437 annotations to this. Finally, Columbus had an Italian translation (by Cristofero Landino) of the *Natural History* of Pliny, in a copy published in Venice in 1489. This has twenty-four annotations. It will be immediately evident that Columbus was one of the earliest, as well as one of the most important, of those who benefitted from the invention of printing; also, fortunately, that he did not hesitate to deface these now precious books.

The number of notes the admiral made upon a given work is, of course, no firm guide to the true measure of its importance to him. Simple reference to one's own habits may lead one to reflect that a highly annotated page is not necessarily of more interest to the reader than is a page left blank; still less may we suppose that the annotated page was the one which inspired the more trust. Evidence of this sort must be treated, in short, with great caution. Nor, again, may we conclude that a word read early in Columbus's career occupied a higher place in his thoughts, or had a more profound effect upon him, than a work

---

9. A facsimile of a copy of the *De Consuetudinibus* printed at Antwerp (of a copy, that is identical with the one Columbus had), was produced, under the direction of the Marco Polo scholar Shinobu Iwamura, by Otska Kogaisha Ltd. of Tokyo in 1949. I shall use this facsimile, number 371 of the limited edition of 800, for my examination of the contents of this work. Unfortunately some of these valuable copies (and 371 is one of them) have been misbound, and the contents arranged in the wrong order, so the reader must be very wary.

10. Columbus's Latin postille to this edition, together with an introduction and translation into Italian of the text of the *De Consuetudinibus*, have been published by L. Giovannini, *Il Milione con le Postille di Cristofero Colombo* (Rome, 1985). There is as yet no translation into English of Pipino's Latin version, and this Latin version differs, in some places widely, from all the English translations of the *Travels* we have. My own references will be, therefore, solely to the book and chapter numbers of the Latin text (which is unpaginated) and, for the postille, to Giovannini.

read late. This last caveat is a cheering one, for it is extremely hard to decide upon the dates at which, or the order in which, the admiral acquired and annotated these volumes. It is probable, in any case, that he read and reread, and annotated and reannotated them several times.[11] It does seem possible to suggest, however, that at least two of them, the *Imago Mundi* collection and the *Historia Rerum* of Pope Pius II, that is, were first read before Columbus set out on his first voyage. He seems to have had the former under his eyes in 1491, and in Spain.[12] His own copy lacks, too, those additional and perhaps contradictory or confirmatory remarks one would expect to find on it had he read the work with enthusiasm *after* his journeys. The admiral may perhaps have completed one reading of the *Imago Mundi* before he read Pius II's *Historia*, but have dealt with the latter immediately afterwards.[13] Such possibilities are possibilities only; but they are significant ones, for they mean that these two treatises as a whole could, at least, have constituted a vital part of Columbus's mental cargo from the very beginning. His version of the *Travels* of Marco Polo, in that it bore so closely upon the explorations Columbus had in

---

11. Buron points to a place in the *Imago Mundi*, for instance, in which Columbus came back to a chapter, and annotated it after reading a later one (on "Taprobane"); Buron, *Ymago*, i, 232–233.

12. P. M. Watts, "Prophecy and Discovery," 85–86. And see Buron, *Ymago*, i, 262–263 for a note, seemingly in his own hand, which suggests that Columbus was in Spain when writing it.

13. Columbus adds to his notes on Chapter XLIV of the *Imago Mundi* a little information from Pius's *Historia* about the Sultan of Egypt (and the Colossus of Rhodes). Buron, *Ymago*, ii, 402–407. But he could, of course, simply have come back to make this annotation later. Also, he seemingly transfers information from the *Imago Mundi* VII to his copy of Pius. In a complex argument, Buron assigns to Columbus's first reading of the *Imago Mundi* a date before 1481, and his first reading of the *Historia* to 1481; ibid., 28–29. Columbus certainly annotated the *Historia* later, however, and after his return from Hispaniola, as we shall see below. The problem is incapable of final resolution.

mind, may have claimed his attention early too. I shall therefore give these three treatises priority here.

The *Imago Mundi* of Pierre d'Ailly was devised, it seems, as a bestselling popular cosmological encyclopedia. As such it owed much to the great cosmological encyclopedias of the past; such, for example, as its twelfth century namesake, the *Imago Mundi* of Honorius Augustodunensis.[14] It aimed to bring such compilations up to date, and it was, in this, enormously successful. Like its most obvious ancestor, the encyclopedia of Honorius, it owed its success in large measure to its author's capacity to identify good passages in denser and less accessible works, and to copy them out clearly (often without acknowledgment of any but the most impressive of sources). Such a treatise both did the more strenuous of the reader's work for him, and reassured him that he lacked nothing in the way of arcane or up-to-date information—an enormous double bonus, and one understandably much to the taste of busy persons of the world. Again like Honorius's *Imago Mundi*, d'Ailly's was devised to accompany, and explain the contents of, mappae mundi, as a sort of gazetteer. It came fully equipped, too, with maps, figures and planispheres of its own, one of which we touched upon in Chapter 1. Martin Behaim knew it, and large chunks are inscribed upon the so-called "Columbus Map."[15] Its imprint can also be seen in the correspondence of civilized persons interested in geography.[16]

---

14. Far more is in fact copied verbatim from this than Buron has identified.

15. E. G. Ravenstein, *Martin Behaim, His Life and His Globe* (London, 1908), 70. For a comparison between the extracts from d'Ailly on the Columbus Map and the annotations to this work by Columbus himself, see E. D. Fite and A. Freeman, *A Book of Old Maps* (Cambridge Mass., 1926), 7–8. For further discussion of this map see Chapter 5, this volume.

16. Hieronymus Münzer quotes from d'Ailly's *Imago Mundi* in his letter to King John of Portugal; Morison, *Journals*, 16.

After illustrative figures, tables of times for latitudes north of the equator and the movement of the sun through the zodiac, and an editor's preface introducing the printed edition, the treatise deals with the whole universe in short order, and in 60 chapters. First we have fourteen dealing with the earth in relation to the heavens, with the arrangement of the elements, the order and movement of the planets, the climates of the earth and its habitable and uninhabitable regions. The Terrestrial Paradise is mentioned as among the habitable lands beneath the equator, close to it, and raised up on a neighboring mountain towards the east.[17] We then turn to a relatively detailed description of the varied continents and countries distributed upon the earth's surface, beginning with the east, and Asia, as seemingly the most interesting and important of them, and journeying westwards. We travel through India, Parthia, Mesopotamia and Syria, pausing to assess the extent of the Promised Land (very small).[18] We traverse Egypt and its neighboring kingdoms, eventually reaching Europe's more barbaric regions (XXVI), via Asia Minor. After the Danube Provinces, Greece, Italy, Gaul and Spain, comes Africa, which is given five chapters. The rest of the treatise is devoted to particular features of the earth; famous mountains, promontories, and, especially, islands. Islands have nine chapters, and seas and gulfs and lakes and rivers another eleven, a balance which perhaps reflects the overwhelming importance of, and interest in, travel by water.

The general introductory chapters set out a form of the stock medieval geocentric universe. Chapter I treats of the roundness of this universe, and we have a long *postillum* here from Columbus, in which he comments upon the etymology of *spera*

---

17. VII; ibid., 198–199.

18. XX; Buron, *Ymago*, i, 284–287.

and emphasizes how appropriate the word is to the roundness it seeks to describe.[19] The spheres of the seven planets reach up from the earth to the eighth sphere of the firmament and the ninth of the *primum mobile*, with perhaps a tenth sphere behind this (a description seemingly drawn from Sacrobosco). The ninth sphere turns uniformly and regularly round the earth from east to west in the course of a day, acting as a drag or brake upon the eighth sphere, or firmament, in which the fixed stars (1022 in number) are set, and which moves at an angle ''quomodo declinando'' in the opposite direction, west to east. The firmament takes 36,000 years, the Great Year, to complete its own revolution. Beneath this firmament, and lying as a belt across it, is the zodiac, and then come the planets, also moving from west to east (within the latitude of the zodiac), and, like the firmament, feeling the drag of the primum mobile as they turn against it through their different circles. All of this movement affects time and the seasons, and so does the balance of the four elements, fire, air, water and earth. These elements take turns to hold pride of place in the atmosphere as we come down to earth from the primum mobile, fire predominating in the upmost level, then air a level lower, then water, then earth. Beyond all the elements, the turning circles and the conjectural tenth heaven, stands, highest of all, the crystalline sphere and the Empyrean, seat of God.

This picture is that of a universe whose creator has completed his work — as, of course, Genesis had said he had. This universe is not, to be sure, without its intricacies and inner complications and opportunities for development, but its contours are clear, and it can now be taken for granted as a backcloth to more important considerations. The prevalence of set introductory chapters such as these in general works of cosmology and geography allows us the better to appreciate the horror with

---

19. Ibid., 166–167. Buron identifies the source of Columbus's *postillum*; the *Catholicon* of John of Genoa.

which the theories of Copernicus were greeted. He threatened assumptions which were not merely traditional, but extraordinarily widely taught, and, in their proper place as an introduction to more earthly concerns, both convenient and freeing. Reinforced here as they are, they continue to play this role.

Columbus pays this general picture little attention in the matter of notes,[20] beyond singling out statements which specially interest him, such as those on the roundness of the universe and the earth (he notes these twice more) and d'Ailly's remark that the size of the earth is that of a mere dot besides the magnitude of the whole.[21] There are signs, however, of increased acuity on Columbus's part when the *Imago Mundi* comes to the earth's habitable and uninhabitable zones. He is clearly interested in the variety of opinions d'Ailly advances in Chapters VII and VIII upon the matter of the habitability of the Antipodes, and the possibility of crossing the torrid zone. Contrary to d'Ailly's own view, that this zone, penetrable or not, is uninhabitable, Columbus advances against these chapters his famous erroneous statement that the Portuguese fortress of Mina lies below the equator.[22] An enormous note then tells of the voyage of Bartholomew Diaz to the Cape of Good Hope, and Diaz's report to the King of Portugal in December 1488, establishing that the southern sea is navigable, despite the torrid

---

20. He is not troubled, for instance, by anxieties about the variable position of the crystalline sphere that a close reading of Ptolemy might have aroused in him.

21. Ibid., 170–171, 186–187, 190–191. Columbus's emphasis here on this roundness makes it all the more easy to understand his amazement and excitement when, owing to mistaken readings from the Pole Star (as we now know), he believed himself, in the third voyage, to be travelling uphill on an unexpected protuberance. See Chapter 5, this volume.

22. Ibid., 196–197.

heat.[23] This note too may begin the argument about the smallness of the distance westwards from Spain to the Indies, (a recurrent theme in these annotations),[24] and about the proportion of sea to land, an argument Columbus was to prosecute later with such energy, especially in his letter to his sovereigns during the third voyage. Columbus, of course, favored the view of the Prophet Ezra, that land covered six of the seven parts of the earth (2 Esdras 6:42, *Imago Mundi* VIII). This particular annotation may also sign the start of Columbus's preference for Marinus of Tyre over Ptolemy; though the possibility remains, of course, that he came back and put the whole into the margins of his copy much later in the story. Whether he did this or not, this note shows signs of considerable independent research on its writer's part among works other than those cited by d'Ailly.[25] Columbus adds references to the letters and the *De Spiritu Sancto* of St. Ambrose, the *City of God* of St. Augustine, the *Historia Scholastica* of Peter Comestor, the *In Veritatibus* of Francis of Meyronnes (1285–1325) and the *Postillae* of Nicholas of Lyra (1270–1305) in support of his views on the authenticity of the writings of the Prophet Ezra, and his conclusions about the extent of the lands of earth. The *Imago Mundi* here offered possibilities which were seized upon by Columbus with great enthusiasm.[26]

---

23. Ibid., 206–215. Columbus reports the voyage of Diaz in his *postille* to the *Historia* of Pius II as well. Comments are frequently made in the margins about the habitability of the land below the equator; ibid., 230–233, 340–345. Columbus returns to the theme in his notes to d'Ailly's *Epilogus Mappae Mundi*, ibid., 522–529.

24. See, for instance, Columbus's notes to d'Ailly's Chapter XLIX, on the Ocean, and to the *Epilogus Mappae Mundi*; ibid., 424–427, 524–527.

25. And other than those cited by Roger Bacon, too, from whose *Opus Maius* the Cardinal copies much of this part of the text, without acknowledgment.

26. He refers back to these notes upon Chapter VIII when emphasizing the same points in his comments to the *Epilogus Mappae Mundi*; Buron, *Ymago*, ii, 534–535.

D'Ailly's following geographical chapters are full of information about Columbus's expectations of the areas he hoped
to visit, from the tentative placing of the Terrestrial Paradise
in southern and distant temperate climes, raised above the
lower air (d'Ailly speaks of this paradise in Chapters VII,
XI, XII, XLI and LV),[27] to the descriptions of the peoples,
customs and produce of all the other regions of the earth which
interested him. D'Ailly was ready with reasons for the behavior
and special capacities of human eastern creatures. In a passage
as revealing about fifteenth century medical practice as it is about
the methods of social geographers, he tells us that to understand
earth's human inhabitants, one must proceed as would a doctor
when trying to understand a single human body.[28] One must
first scrutinize the dispositions of that superior source of
influence, the sky, and then deduce from it the constitution and
state of the given individual. The influence of the sun is
perceptible upon the achievements of the peoples of the east,
for the sun rises over them. They are thus quicker by nature
than other peoples, and inclined to high enterprise and to
astrology.[29]

We might remark at this point that, for his knowledge about,
and interest in, the monstrous creatures of the east, Columbus
had no need to turn to Sir John Mandeville's fantastic accounts

---

27. Columbus marks d'Ailly's statement that the ancients were in error in
identifying the Terrestrial Paradise with the Fortunate Islands (now the
Canaries), XLI; ibid., 392–397. In Chapter XII he had merely referred to this
equation as a possibility (Buron mistranslates the Latin of Columbus's note);
Ymago, i, 240–241.

28. The passage occurs in Chapter XII.

29. XIII; ibid., 246–247. Those in the west, on the other hand, live under the
influence of the moon, and are quarrelsome—like women. D'Ailly adds that
the English and French are none too good at astrology, and Columbus makes
a special note of this. He also notes d'Ailly's suggestion that, whilst every place
has its own east and west, the truest east is to be found at the outermost ends
of India, and the truest west at the extreme edge of Spain; ibid., 248–249.

of his travels. D'Ailly provides more than enough. Extremes of climate tend to produce deformities he says; Columbus adds promptly that the tendency to eat human flesh may well be among these deformities. This interest in cannibalism pervades the admiral's writings, and here seemingly invades his observations from the very first. Chapter XVI of the *Imago Mundi*, on the marvels of India,[30] immediately then supplies us with an absolute plethora of wonders, including pygmies two cubits high who do battle with cranes, Macrobians of twelve cubits who fight griffons, and (again to be important later) persons who kill their parents and eat their flesh. Columbus makes solemn notes upon all this information in the margins, and underlines sections of it in the text, such as the remark (XVI) that the Ganges is full of enormous eels.

The produce of these regions is quite as startling as are its monstrous inhabitants. Gold, silver, precious jewels, spices, unguents and elephants abound in them. Predictably, Columbus's notes show his interest in all of this produce;[31] but they show too his concern for particular items of it. Thus, whilst d'Ailly speaks in general terms of the gems and precious stones in and about the islands off the coast of India, Columbus adds a reference to pearls. He adds too that, as well as its spices and jewels and elephants, India has mountains of gold.[32] There is an especially large note on the placing and products of Tarshish. D'Ailly mentions Tarshish somewhat vaguely (XXIV) as on the

30. Taken straight from Honorius's *Imago Mundi* I, 10 (unnoticed by Buron), a chapter equally remarkable in its contents, position and seeming importance to the treatise as a whole. The good Christian was obviously supposed to be convinced that the east was filled with marvels.

31. He seems to have an abiding interest in gem stones for he picks out d'Ailly's remarks that crystal and gem stones are to be found in Germany too and agates and pearls in Britain (XXVI, XL).

32. XV; *Ymago*, i, 260–261. This note may have come from his reading of Pius II, see below.

western borders of Cathay.[33] Columbus insists that Tarshish
is on Cathay's easternmost frontiers, at the very ends of the east,
that is, and he equates it with that Ophir from which Hiram's
fleet brought loads of gold and silver and elephants teeth to
Solomon every three years. He cites (correctly) 3 Kings 9 and
2 Chronicles 9 in support of this, and also Nicholas of Lyra's
Postillae in Libros Regum and St. Jerome's *Liber de Situ et Nominibus
Terrae Sanctae.* It took the fleet one and a half years to get back
to Ophir from the Red Sea, he notes, a reckoning that clearly
supported most satisfactorily his belief in an extended eastern
landmass.[34] This preoccupation recurs in the notes to Chapters
XLII and LI and to the *Epilogus Mappae Mundi.*[35] A little before
this (XVIII) Columbus had been careful to comment upon
d'Ailly's mention of the biblical Magi. The Magi of Matthew
were often equated with the Psalmist's kings of Tarshish and
the Isles, and of Sheba and Seba (or Saba), in the Vulgate Psalm
71:10. Columbus notes here d'Ailly's statement that these Magi
did not come from the Ethiopian Saba, but from a Saba far to
the east of this.[36] He comes back to this point again later, in
his notes to the chapter (XXXVII) upon Ethiopia itself. All of
these comments, observations and placings will be highly
relevant to his later identification of some of the Caribbean
islands he discovered, and especially to his anxieties about which
one of the islands of the Indies Hispaniola/Haiti must be. The

33. Buron points out how close d'Ailly is here to the description of these regions
Marino Sanuto included in his *Liber Secretorum Fidelium Crucis*, where they were
designed to illustrate a world map; ibid., 306, n. 124.

34. Ibid., 304–307.

35. Ibid., ii, 392–397, 434–439, 534–535. To the first, Chapter XVII, he
appends a note independently taken from Pliny, *Natural History* VI, 24, on the
length of the sea voyage from the mouth of the Red Sea to Taprobana. This
chapter is marked by him in his own copy of Pliny, see below.

36. Ibid., i, 274–277.

Imago Mundi occupied a most important place in the formation of Columbus's strong views about the east. It both helped him to confirm in his own mind certain of his predispositions, and it allowed him to sharpen his disagreements with it into independent convictions.

The *Historia Rerum Ubique Gestarum* of Pope Pius II was not among the famous pontiff's major works, and it was not, it seems, quite as popular as was the *Imago Mundi*. Sixteenth century printed copies tend to reproduce it as a work with a prologue, followed by two books, the first treating of Asia, the second, of Europe.[37] Columbus made notes only upon Book I. The work as a whole is by no means easy reading, and it says something for Columbus's persistence, and perhaps a little more about his religious and political convictions, that he pressed on through it at all. Pius II may reasonably be described as a conservative pontiff, and one made especially so by the disunity within the church made evident at the Councils of Basel and Florence (ca. 1431–1449).[38] He had great hopes both of the eventual success of the crusade against the Turks, and of the role of temporal sovereignty in the service of a reunified and triumphant Christianity. These hopes were congenial to Columbus's Spanish sovereigns and, it seems likely, to Columbus himself. In addition to the recommendations of so

---

37. There is no modern edition or facsimile of this work, and no translation of it into English. I shall refer to the *Historia*, therefore, by book and chapter number. I have consulted a copy printed by Henry Stephen at Paris in 1511. For Columbus's notes on this, and on those other books for which there is no more modern edition, I refer to C. de Lollis, *Scritti di Cristoforo Colombo*, in *Raccolta*, i (ii), 291–369.

38. He has been characterized in the following words: "Never a profound thinker, Pius could hardly divest himself of the political tradition of the later middle ages. He had been for some years as much an imperialist as Dante, who could preserve his illusions because he never had to discharge the political responsibilities of high office"; K. M. Setton, *The Papacy and the Levant (1204–1571)* ii (Philadelphia, 1978), 215. The same words might well characterize the early Columbus.

suitable an authorship, and so appropriate an ambition, the
Historia was, furthermore, an excellent text to read as a
complement to the *Imago Mundi*, for whilst d'Ailly wrote
descriptive geography for Christians, Pope Pius wrote, with an
eye to that eventual predominance of Christian society for which
he so fervently hoped, the descriptive history of many of the
regions d'Ailly surveyed. This fact too may have helped
Columbus to struggle on.

In the prologue to his *Historia* Pius evinces his belief in history
as a subject; "Nugas in fabulis; in historia verum quaerimus
et serium" ("we turn to stories for entertainment, but to history
for the solemn truth"). This proposition evidently sprang from
deep conviction, for he advances it again, in different words,
in Chapter XX.[39] The first book of the *Historia*, and the one
upon which we shall concentrate here, contains 100 short
chapters and begins conventionally *De Mundo in Universo*. It then
progresses through Asia from east to west, ending with the
horrifying Turks, "Gens truculenta et ignominiosa." Pius also
clearly felt strongly about the Turks, for he repeats his long,
and hardly complimentary, description of them in the fourth
chapter of Book II.

The introductory section *De Mundo* of the *Historia* is shorter
than that in d'Ailly's treatise, for it misses out the universe of
the heavens and concentrates instead upon that of the earth.
It becomes clear immediately, however, that the Pope, like the
Cardinal, means to set out a variety of opinions and to leave
many doubtful matters encouragingly open; an ambition with
which, we might remark at the outset, Columbus was not wholly
in accord. Thus (I, i), the world *may* have on it four continents,
says Pius, continents separated by two interlocking streams of

---

39. "De Amazonibus multi meminerunt, et apus Graecos, et apud Latinos,
non Poetae solum, qui fabulosa tractant, verumetiam historici, quos a vero
recedere turpissimum est."

ocean, and all potentially habitable.[40] Here Pius's description is very like that given by the Cotton mappa mundi. Others such as Ptolemy, he continues, think there is only one habitable piece of earth above the equator, with possibly another beneath it. Some believe in the five zones, some do not. It may (I, ii–v) be possible to sail around the known earth via the northern frozen zone, or via the southern torrid zone. Here Pius parts company somewhat with d'Ailly, although it is clear that he personally has doubts about many of the more optimistic of the propositions he so faithfully recounts. People certainly live east of Meroe, the eastern limit usually given for the climates. Ptolemy, he adds, tells us that the island of Taprobana, south of the equator, has inhabitants. Lots of people, in any case, think that the Terrestrial Paradise lies close to the equator. There are perhaps tempering influences, seas or mountains or the like, which can cool the extremes of the torrid zone.

Much of this, of course, is greatly to Columbus's taste. Against Pius's discussion of the zones he notes approvingly how the Portuguese have traveled south of the only supposed habitable ones, and the English and Swedes north of them. He adduces the voyage of Diaz in support of these propositions once more. He writes "contrarium," however, against Pius's record of Ptolemy's view that the known world is closed in by a "terra incognita,"[41] and, on occasion, he is a good deal more

---

40. "Sunt qui arbitrantur quatuor eius plagas apparere, quas magnus interfecet [sic] Oceanus: duobus amplissimis fluminibus eas ambiens, quorum alterum zodiaco subjiciatur: alterum ab aurora dextra levaque per polus defluens extra columnas herculeas coniungantur; atque in hunc modum totius terrae quatuor portiones velut ingentes insulas emergere. Quae celo subiectae benigno mortalium habitationes admittunt."

41. Pius writes, "Ptholomeus habitationem nostram a quatuor orbis partibus terra incognita claudit," and Columbus, "A quatuor orbis nostram habitacionem incognita claudit. Contrarium;" de Lollis, *Scritti*, 291.

enthusiastic about the idea of navigability than is his text.[42] He also seems to extend Pius's measured views upon the possible circumnavigability of the known earth in such a way as to have it encompass his own idea of its circumnavigability west to east. It is at this point in the discussion, for example, that he adduces the famous story of the "Chinese" found in Galway in Ireland.[43] Chapter V sees Columbus noting again how there must be habitation beyond the northern range of climates, and how Eratosthenes, Aristotle and Avicenna all declare that there is temperate and habitable land beneath the equator. He remarks particularly that Aristotle is sure this land must be the finest place on earth. Again he adduces the spurious evidence of the Portuguese fortress of Mina; and he marks (twice) the possibility advanced by Pius, as it had been by d'Ailly, that it is beyond the equator, somewhere in the temperate south, that the Terrestrial Paradise is to be found—but, once more, without any reference to the Pontiff's personal doubts.[44]

In China (IX) there are cannibals, and Pope Pius echoes the cardinal's views about the evils contingent upon silk.[45] The

---

42. Columbus writes, for instance, "Auctor docet quod totum occeanum Septentrionalem sit navigatum" (the author teaches that the whole of the Northern ocean is navigable), which is not strictly true. Pius does, indeed, adduce evidence to this end, but he also expresses great doubts upon the matter, doubts Columbus's annotations do not echo.

43. "[Homi]nes de Catayo versus oriens venierunt. [N]os vidimus multa notabilia, et [spe]cialiter in Galvei Ibernie virum et [uxo]rem in duobus lignis areptis ex mirabili [pers]ona" ("men from Cathay have traveled eastwards. We have ourselves seen many notable indications of this, and especially, in Galway in Ireland, a man and his wife who had been taken out of wooden dugouts, and who looked strange and wonderful").

44. Pius writes (Chapter V): "Nonnuli paradisum terrestrem sub ea coeli parte sitam crediderunt quibus sacrarum reluctatur"—"Some believe that the terrestrial paradise is placed beneath these skies, but sacred [learning] is resistent to this proposition."

45. "ex quo potius est ostendere corpora quam vestire, quod primo foeminis, postea etiam viris luxuriae persuasit ambitio" (. . . whose function is rather

effect upon the west of the lascivious lives of eastern peoples is fortunately limited by the inordinate difficulty and expense of getting there. It remains true, however (X et seq.), that these places abound in marvelous things (elephants, jewels, pepper and monsters), extraordinary foods (snakes, and ants like lobsters), and remarkable peoples, above all Amazons. The Pontiff's entry upon the Amazons (XX) is a full one. Following hard upon his second statement as to the veracity of history, he relates Pompeius Trogus's account of them, (found in Justin's *Epitome*), with every sign that he believed this account to be true. The Amazons sprang up in Scythia, he tells the reader, led originally by the wives of two young slaughtered kings. They preferred war to marriage (arguing that the latter spelt only servitude), and so slaughtered everyone else's husbands. Amazons occasionally sought impregnation from neighboring males, but solely to guard against the dying of the line. They put the male offspring of these liaisons to death, and burnt the right breasts from the female children that no obstacle might impede the bowstring. They absolutely forbade the females to take to needlework. Instead, they must show prowess in armed combat, on horseback and on the hunting field. One can understand, perhaps, why the Pontiff was so interested. It took Hercules finally to defeat them.

In all this Columbus seems to be in his element. He notes, once more, the remarks about cannibals ("ubi humana corpora cibum est"), and about that moral turpitude the wearing of silk must inevitably bring in its train. He adds to Pius's description of the quiet serenity of the Chinese people (a description apparently unconnected in the Pontiff's mind with any of his preceding observations) the note that China marks the outermost edge of India, and is opposite Spain, and, in the north, opposite

---

to display the body than to clothe it. Women fell prey first to this luxury, and men then followed them).

Ireland.[46] He indicates the "mirabilia" of India, the eating of snakes and ants, and the monsters. He seems absolutely fascinated, among many notes upon curious customs and great leaders, by Pius's chapter on the Amazons. He draws repeated attention to certain features of this; "wives bore arms," "they killed the men who stayed at home," "men did the weaving and wives the fighting," "young girls bore arms and rode horses," "they subdued the great part of Europe and many of the cities of Asia." Finally he notes, with or without relief we cannot tell, the victories over them of Hercules.[47] He picks up too the Pope's remark that Bohemia favors female rulers. In the remaining chapters of the *Historia* Columbus returns to his usual interest in gold and silver, marking how the Scythians were believed to spurn it. He is interested in the history and rise of the Turks, and in Pius's tale (LXXXVIII) about the dogs of Rhodes who fawn upon Christians but bite Turks on sight. He is understandably delighted by the chapter (LXXXXVII) on Genoese triumphs. And, finally, he continues onto the flyleaves with contributions of the first importance.

He copies out here first of all Toscanelli's letter to Martins; but he copies a great deal more. First comes Isaiah, 24:14–16, in the Vulgate Latin:

> They lift up their voices, they sing for joy; over the majesty of the Lord they shout from the west. Therefore in the east give glory to the Lord; in the coastlands of the sea, to the name of the Lord, the God of Israel. From the ends of the earth we hear songs of praise, of glory to the Righteous one.[48]

---

46. de Lollis, *Scritti*, 297.

47. Ibid., 311–312.

48. Ibid., 365.

The relevance of these verses to Columbus's concerns needs hardly to be stressed. There follows 2 Chronicles 9:21:

> For the king's ships went to Tarshish with the servants of Huram; once every three years the ships of Tarshish used to come bringing gold, silver, ivory, apes and peacocks.

Then we have an entire chapter from the *City of God* of St. Augustine, Book XVII, xxiv. This chapter is devoted to the defense of the authenticity of the writings of the Prophet Ezra, and is the one Columbus cited in his *postillum* to the *Imago Mundi*, Chapter VIII.[49] After this comes an edited chunk from Josephus, *De Antiquitatibus* VIII. This tells first of Solomon's building of his fleet, its sailing (in accordance with 1 Kings 9:21–28 and 2 Chronicles 8:17–18) to the land of Ophir or Land of Gold in India, and its return with 400 talents of gold. Josephus dilates upon the precious stones and pinewood brought back from Ophir for the temple and the palace, and upon the construction of musical instruments. He stresses of what great quality this wood was, and also what a weight of gold came with it, sufficient for the making of 200 shields and 300 bucklers, and drinking cups too. The sea voyage took three years, but everyone was impressed, as a result, with Solomon, and sent him gifts of gold and silver vessels, purple garments, spices, horses, chariots, asses and mules.[50] Western sovereigns hoping to imitate Solomon would, on this reckoning, have a great deal to live up to.

---

49. It may be read in English in E. M. Sanford and W. M. Green, *Saint Augustine the City of God Against the Pagans* v (Loeb, London, and Harvard, 1965), 356–359.

50. An English translation from the original Greek text (a text which fortunately differs here from the Latin only in ways unimportant to us now) may be read in H. St. J. Thackeray and R. Marcus, *Josephus* v (Loeb, London, and Cambridge, Mass., 1966), 658–661, 664–671.

Columbus's next extract came from Ovid. He exercised his editorial talents on this too—but in a most revealing way. The passage Columbus copies out here comes from Ovid's *Metamorphoses* I, lines 32 to 55, supposedly twenty-three consecutive lines—but in fact Columbus misses out seven lines (lines 45–51 inclusive), with no apparent violence to the continuity of the whole as he copies it.[51] Columbus's edited Ovid describes the formation of the universe out of chaos by God or "Nature," and that of the round ball of the earth, within the universe, with all its waters and springs, rivers and mountains and valleys. It includes three lines upon the elements of air, fire, water and earth; but it misses out the portion in between in which Ovid speaks of the five zones later made so popular by Macrobius, the two temperate ones, that is, and the three intemperate and therefore uninhabitable ones. This omission is markedly consistent both with Columbus's often-expressed views upon the habitability of the zones of the earth, and also, perhaps, with his attitude to the uses of written evidence.

Columbus's annotations upon, and additions to, his copy of the *Historia* end with some mnemonic verses upon the planets, and an account, in Spanish, of the various historic ages from the beginning of the world, an account which ends in 1481 (and gave to Buron his ideas about dates). There is also a short note about the divisions of the equatorial circle (apparently made with reference to the marking of a map), and an entry, now famous, about the observations of one "Magister Ihosepius, fixicus et astrologus" (employee of the King of Portugal) to the effect that Sierra Leone lay at latitude 5 degrees north. Attached

---

51. de Lollis, *Scritti*, 367. Neither the editing of Josephus nor the editing of Ovid has, so far as I know, been remarked upon before. The Latin text (one that differs slightly from that of Columbus) may be read in an English translation in *edit.* F. J. Miller, *Ovid, Metamorphoses* i (Loeb, Harvard, and London, 1984), 4–7.

to this is a note upon Columbus's own conviction (fortified, he claims, by the same Master Josephus) that the fortress of Mina lay below the equator.[52] Finally, there are two recipes, (one for quick growing of parsley, and a second, involving sulfur, ammonia and "goldworker's powder," seemingly for cleaning), and a note about the psalm to be said at Mattins on Thursday.[53] The psalm prescribed is in fact the Vulgate Psalm 73, the lament for the sacking of the temple and the call for God to avenge it. It is a psalm peculiarly appropriate to the mental state of one who feels himself unloved, and if, as I suspect, the *Historia* formed part of Columbus's shipboard library, then this psalm may have helped to anneal many of the disappointments he suffered.

Marco Polo's book about his travels to Cathay had one feature which recommended it to Columbus quite independently of the information it contained. Its author's experiences were committed to writing, with the help of a fellow-prisoner, Rustichello of Pisa, whilst both were in prison in Genoa, booty from the late thirteenth century wars between the rival trading cities of Venice, Pisa and Genoa, and evidence of Genoa's successes. Marco Polo (1254–1324) and Rustichello produced their original account, it seems, in a Franco–Italian dialect, but the original has not survived and the work is known only through translations. The translation into Latin by Friar Pipino, the one

---

52. See below, Chapter 5.

53. "ut subito nascatur porsimolium pone in remolio semine in aceto per spacium .iii. dierum, postea fere ipsa sub aselis dies tres, et quando . . . volueris semina ipsa et subito in hora .i. nascatur et comedatur . .. acipiunt pulver solphari, quem ponunt super eum, et co[m]busta recedit; ipsum moliunt et fondant cum salmoniaco et se . . . et aliquando ponunt de pulvere aurifabris cum qua solidant reduntur [reducuntur?] albis cum sale et aceto." I am much indebted to Professors Isabella and Giovanni Orlandi for their help with this puzzling passage: "Por la matinada de jueves el .6. salmo que comienca: 'ut quid, Deus, repulisti' in finem, et sequitur: 'operatus est salutem in medio terre.'" de Lollis, *Scritti*, 369.

Columbus had, was one of the most popular and was the first to be printed. Marco and Rusticello, like Pierre d'Ailly, had a good eye for a bestseller, and Friar Pipino an equally deft hand at producing a sort of Reader's Digest version of one. Thus, this particular condensed rendering of their efforts was widely read from the first, and this published version no less so, despite a quantity of typographical errors in the printing. Columbus himself read and annotated it at several different times.[54]

Pipino's version of the *Travels* is in three books comprising 186 short chapters in all. The first book (of 67 chapters) is concerned with the initial adventures of the two brothers Nicholas (Marco's father) and Matthew Polo, their journey to the court of Kublai Khan, their return to the Pope to report the Khan's interest in Christianity (1269), and their journey back to the Khan at Xanadu, this time with Marco, to stay for seventeen years (ca. 1275–1292). Books II and III report the experiences of Marco, who found favor with the Khan, and became his ambassador. They give an account of Marco's famous travels eastwards from the Khan's court, then southwards along the coast of Cathay from Fuchu to Zayton, through Mangi. They report the knowledge he gained about, and his voyages among, the islands of the Indies, from "Cipangu" to "Seylan," and they describe his journey back (via the shrine of St. Thomas) through India itself, to reach Venice in 1295 in time to become war-booty and to write. These last two books are the crucial ones for us, for they provide us, as they did Columbus, with

---

54. L. Giovannini, *Il Milione*, 36. In a recent and convincing article, the idea that the *Travels* was meant to describe a real journey has been doubted, and the work ranged instead among "encyclopedic treatises" of the kind d'Ailly and Pius II compiled. J. Heers, "De Marco Polo a Christophe Colomb: comment lire le *Dévisement du Monde*," *Journal of Medieval History* 10 (1984), 125–143. If Columbus understood it to be such a treatise, that would explain his extreme interest in it. Heers also (pp. 140–141) makes the point that Columbus did not turn to Marco Polo, as he had to the other two, for support for his optimistic views on distances. This may indicate that Columbus actually read the *Travels* a little later than he did the *Imago Mundi* and *Historia*.

information of the first importance about the lands to which he proposed to sail, remote as they are from the actual period of his discoveries.

The text of the *De Consuetudinibus* provided tremendous support both for Columbus's proposals and for his sovereigns' hopes. The distances the Polos traveled overland were clearly enormous, the sea voyage from Cathay to Cipangu too great even for the merchant ships of the Great Khan to have secure and permanent access to Cipangu (III, ii). The inhabited lands and islands of the east, then, stretched out towards Spain. There was no doubt at all about the riches of the realms of Kublai Khan. On the mainland of Cathay, Cambaluc (II, xi) Quinsay (II, lxiii) Fuchu and Zayton (II, lxix–lxx), to name only a few of the great cities described, burst with ships, jewels, pearls, pepper, spices, cottons, silks and general merchandise. The Khan himself, by means of his extraordinary use of paper currency with which to buy it, has treasure beyond the dreams of avarice (II, xxi). The Khan and his subkings have always been inclined towards friendship with Christian rulers, and show great respect for the wealth and prowess of Prester John (II, xxx). The Khan is a great huntsman too, an item perhaps especially to the taste of western sovereigns. Columbus notes with admiration his reported ability to train eagles (II, xvi).[55] This information could be absorbed together with the evidence of his riches, and with at least an equal delight. Everything said of Cathay and Mangi, in short, seemingly reinforced the prospect of the profits, material, convivial and religious, which might accrue from an established and workable alliance with these regions. The Indian mainland, too, boasted pearl fishers along its coasts (III, xxiii), rubies, sapphires, emeralds, and diamonds (again collected by eagles, III, xxix) within, and also pepper, parrots, brasil wood, ginger, and indigo,

---

55. Giovannini, *Il Milione*, 162.

not to speak of the body of the Apostle Thomas (III, xxiiii–xxxvi).

Marco Polo's descriptions of the islands off the coast only enhanced these hopes. Cipangu is full of gold and pearls and gemstones, in part because the ships of the Khan find it so hard of access, in part because it is a frightening place, full of idols and cannibals (III, ii, vii). The other islands, of which there are 7,378 (III, viii), many lying well off the coast of Cathay and encouragingly in the direction of Spain, are all of them full of wonders of some kind; valuable woods and spices, black and white pepper, gold and precious stones. Java the Greater (III, x) has nuts and musk and cloves. Java the Less (Sumatra, III, xiii) has treasure, lign-aloe, spikenard, "and many other spices never seen in Europe" (this gave Columbus scope, and he noted it).[56] Its inhabitants produced a remarkable wine by tapping trees. They also used a type of sorcery to predict the eventual fate of a sick man, a practice which Columbus will remark that he found in his own "Indies."[57] Tailed men are also to be found on Sumatra (III, xviii), and unicorns, and on the nearby island of Angemain (III, xxi) there are dog-headed peoples, as well as more cannibals (III, xxi). Off the coast of India there are two islands populated, respectively, only by men and only by women (III, xxxvii).

The *postille* to the *De Consuetudinibus* give overwhelming evidence of Columbus's interest in the gold, silver, spices, medicines, and animal and material produce of the east. Certainly he has an eye for marvels in general,[58] and for

---

56. "Aromatum copia, de qua nunquam visum fuit ultra equinoctiali"; ibid., 245.

57. See below, Chapter 4.

58. He writes "miraculum," for instance, beside the story of the moving mountain in I, xviii, and against that of the moving pillar-stone in the church of St. John the Baptist in Samarkhand, I, xxxix.

innocent items of information,[59] but, clearly, as he annotates the book it is the riches of the east which occupy the forefront of his thoughts. There are innumerable entries of "aurum, argentum, lapides preciosas," of silk and golden cloth ("panni serici," "panni aurei," but noted here without disapproval), and pearls. He is careful to mark ginger ("zinziber"), amber and ambergris, pepper, musk, cloves, camphor, aloes, brasilwood, sandalwood, cinnamon, rhubarb, sugar, cotton, numbers of ships and of horses. He remarks on the gold teeth of the men of "Zardandon" (near Mangi) and how gold can be had there in exchange for silver.[60] He notes too the lengths of the canes reported in those parts, and their use in ropemaking; vital information for a shipmaster.[61] He singles out, again understandably, places and islands reputed to be cannibal islands, the tailed men of Sumatra, the male and female islands.[62]

Copies of Pliny's *Natural History* and Plutarch's *Lives* were, in the late fifteenth century, standard works for the library of any cultivated gentleman. The first was the source for all, or almost all, a gentleman needed to know about the world of science. Pliny claimed, in his preface, to offer his readers no fewer than 20,000 matters of note, and although perhaps few of them have tested this statement to the end, the 37 books of the *Natural History* do suggest that their author's claim has substance. The work contains information on seemingly every aspect of creation, from the shape and contents of the universe,

---

59. He underlines, for instance, the information that it was Pope Clement IV who finally sanctioned the expedition of the Polos. Pipino's version is the only one to be as specific as this. Others either leave the space blank or merely enter "Clement"; see H. Yule, *The Book of Ser Marco Polo* i (London, 1903), 18. This fact suggests that Columbus was aware of the discrepancies.

60. Giovannini, *Il Milione*, 192–197.

61. Ibid., 213 and 219.

62. "Carnes humanas comedunt," "homines comedunt," "homines cum cauda," "Duas insulas, Masculia, Femenina;" ibid., 225, 249, 250, 271.

through all that lives and grows, to medicine, gems, and minerals. It includes also a deal of geographical information. A very large portion of Pliny, perhaps more than we have previously suspected, was directly relevant to the ambitions of Columbus.

The geographical information is concentrated in Books III to VI, and Book VI contains the more important of the passages upon the Far East and India. The Chinese are singled out as producers of silk, a material Pliny clearly feels has disgraced the matrons of Rome. His passage on this substance encouraged both d'Ailly and Pope Pius in their disapproval—though they may have managed without it.[63] Pliny's description of Chinese traders as persons with no small talk, and who waste no words in trading, was taken up too by both.[64] Of India, we are told that the country subdued by Alexander contained 5,000 towns and nine nations, was filled with tremendous standing armies and huge numbers of elephants and horses, and covered one-third of the surface of the habitable earth. It has mountains made of gold. Off its coasts stand the islands of "Patale," "Chryse," "Argire," and "Taprobane," rich in gold, silver, pearls and precious stones.[65] We are told too about sea voyages eastwards

---

63. "the Chinese . . . are famous for the woollen substance obtained from their forests; after a soaking in water they comb off the white down of the leaves, and so supply our women with the double task of unravelling the threads and weaving them together again; so manifold is the labour employed, and so distant is the region of the globe drawn upon, to enable the Roman matron to flaunt transparent raiment in public"; VI, xx, 54–55. In XI, xxvi, 76 he attributes the invention of the process to one Pamphile, "who has the undeniable distinction of having devised a plan to reduce women's clothing to nakedness." *Edit.* H. Rackham, *Pliny Natural History* ii (Loeb, London, and Cambridge, Mass., 1961), 378–379, iii (1967), 478–479. My references will be to this edition, rather than to Landino's Italian version, for the edition is accompanied by an English translation.

64. *Imago Mundi* XLII; Buron *Ymago*, ii, 392–397. *Historia*, IX. It was a trait unfamiliar, perhaps, in medieval traders.

65. VI, xxi, 59, xxiii, 74–75, 80, xxiv, 81; Rackham, *Pliny*, ii, 382–383, 392–395, 398–399.

from Arabia to India, an account encouraging to Columbus in its emphasis on their length and hazardousness, and in the evidence it gives of the vulnerability of such voyages to pirates.[66] Columbus in fact refers to this very section of Pliny in a postillum to *Imago Mundi* XLII, when he comments upon the length of the voyage from the Red Sea to Taprobana (Ceylon).

Columbus's comments upon Pliny are, as we might perhaps expect, much concerned with the information Pliny provides about India and the Far East, and so with Book VI of the *Natural History*.[67] He draws special attention to Pliny's reference to the mountains of gold in India, and to the gold and silver in Chryse and Argire. He points out that there must be many precious minerals there as well. He emphasizes again the length of the sea voyage there.[68] He manifests yet once more his particular interest in the Indies' gold and pearls.[69] It is clear, too, that his attention was caught by the chapter on amber, including Indian amber, Pliny offered in a later book. In the last annotation he made to his copy of Pliny, Columbus compares the amber he has himself had dug out in Hispaniola (the island of "Feyti,"[70] "Ofir" or "Cipango," that is), with the Indian amber Pliny mentions in Book XXXVII.[71] The Hispaniolan

---

66. VI, xxvi, 100; ibid., 414–415.

67. These are printed in de Lollis, *Scritti*, 471–472.

68. This note, "En que tiempo van y navegan los Indios a la mer Bermeja" is written against Landino's translation of Pliny VI, xxvi, 105–106.

69. A note on pearls appears alongside Landino's translation of Pliny VI, xxviii, 110, on the island of "Cascandrus;" Rackham, *Pliny*, ii, 422–423.

70. Feyti is the name from which Haiti developed.

71. "Del ambra es cierto nascere in India soto tierra, he yo ne ho fato cavare in multi monti in la isola de Feyti vel de Ofir, vel de Cipango, a la quale habio

type of amber, though found in large pieces, was evidently less pure than Columbus expected; but, equally obviously, it is related to that which Pliny has in mind. Also, to look ahead a little, Columbus's interest in this differently colored amber, and in its size, may perhaps have been fed by his knowledge of *Sinbad the Sailor*.[72] "Science" and stories may here have acted in tandem as reinforcements of his expectations. Certainly, Pliny supported Columbus's decision that he had indeed reached the Indies here, much as he would in many other places.

The admiral's annotations to Pliny were not, however, confined to the geographical, vegetable, and mineral sections of the work. Some, both funny and a little sad, reveal that the great admiral turned to Pliny for succor in matters of a more domestic nature too. He makes a note, for instance, against the directions for *quelling* the ardor of a woman; and of a means

---

posto nome Spagnola, y ne o trovato pieca grande come el capo, ma no tota chiara, salvo de chiaro y parda, y otra negra, y ve n'e asay.'' de Lollis, *Scritti*, 472. The note is placed alongside Landino's translation of XXXVII, xi, 36–39; see D. E. Eichholz, *Pliny*, x (1962), 190–193, for a translation into English of the passage from Pliny to which it refers. I would render Columbus's note thus; ''Amber is certainly found in India under the ground, and I have had it dug out of several hills in Feyti, Ophir or Cipangu, which I afterwards named Hispaniola. I have found one piece as big as a head, but it is not wholly clear, rather, clear-grey. Another one is black. I now have enough.'' I am grateful to Dr. Miriam Cabre for her help with this passage.

72. In his account of his sixth voyage, Sinbad tells of the ambergris he found near a stream, on a peninsula far in the east (perhaps Pliny's ''Patalis Regio''). This ambergris: ''floweth like water or gum over the stream-banks, for the great heat of the sun, and runneth down to the sea-shore, where the monsters of the deep come up and swallowing it, return into the sea. But it burneth in their bellies; so they cast it up again and it congealeth on the surface of the water, whereby its colour and quantities are changed; and at last the waves cast it ashore, and the travellers and merchants who know it collect it and sell it.'' Transl. R. F. Burton, *The Book of the Thousand Nights and One Night* iv (London, 1894), 399. Pliny speaks of the action of the sun in melting the amber in the passage Columbus annotates. For an account of the voyages of Sinbad and of Columbus's possible knowledge of them, see Chapter 3, this volume.

of increasing the intoxicating effects of wine.[73] He draws attention to remedies for greying hair, and for hair loss.[74] He seemingly advocates Pliny's advice on the refixing of loosened teeth.[75] In all of these prescriptions we might see, perhaps, remedies for afflictions to which the seaman's trade rendered him peculiarly vulnerable, and a concern on the part of the admiral which extended to his men. Remedies for more serious afflictions are marked too; kidney stone, for example. A dead sea scorpion soaked in wine, or the stone in its tail similarly served, are good, and so are cuttlefish eggs, or water snakes' livers, or blenny ash, or sea nettles, also in wine.[76] We might remark here that these cures are all supplied from the sea.

A few selections have a more general application (for instance, "Foxes will not take a chicken which has eaten fox liver" and

---

73. "Com verna en fastidio Venere e el amor a las mujeres." This note appears against the following passage from Pliny XXVIII, lxxvii, 256: "Osthanes says that if the loins of a woman are rubbed thoroughly with the blood of a tick from a black wild bull, she will be disgusted with sexual intercourse, and also with her love if she drinks the urine of a he-goat, nard being added to disguise the foul taste." W. H. S. Jones, *Pliny*, vii (1966), 172–173. Bugloss is the vital addition for wine; XXV, xl; ibid., 194–195 (Columbus's note reads "para leticia").

74. Pliny's prescriptions read: "It is thought that a thicker growth of hair and prevention of greyness are given by an ass's genital organ reduced to ash; this should be pounded with oil in a leaden mortar, and applied after shaving the head. They also think that thicker hair is encouraged by applying the urine of a young ass," and "goat's horn, ground to powder or reduced to ash, a he-goat's being better, with the addition of soda, tamarisk seed, butter and oil, the head being first shaved; this treatment is wonderful for preventing loss of hair, just as goat's meat, reduced to ash and applied with oil, darkens the eyebrows." XXVIII, xlvi, 164, 166; ibid., 112–115.

75. "Loose teeth are made tight by the ash of deer's horn, which relieves their pain, whether used as dentrifice or in a mouth wash. Some consider more efficacious for all the same purposes the unburnt horn ground to powder;" XXVIII, xlix, 178, ibid., 122–123. Columbus's note reads "para los dientes."

76. "Remedio a la piedra." This note appears against Landino's translation of Pliny XXXII, xxxii, 102–104; Jones, *Pliny*, viii (1963), 524–527.

"How to stop wolves coming into a field"),[77] but the parts of Pliny upon which Columbus appears particularly to concentrate seem, understandably, to have been chosen with an eye to the ambitions and pains of himself and his seamen. They throw upon these, then, some welcome further light; and Pliny has certainly even more treasures to offer. For all the curiosities the *Natural History* contained, and despite the fact that it had been both supplemented and surpassed by the time it reached Columbus, nothing had wholly replaced it. Pliny, and, most particularly, many of his medical remedies, may have conditioned Columbus more than we have realized to look for that eastern produce he was so anxious to believe he had found; aloes, for instance,[78] or mastic,[79] or myrrh,[80] or cinnamon.[81] The list could become very long. Pliny is central to our thorough understanding of Columbus's intentions and achievements, and perhaps the medicinal sections of the *Natural History* above all.

Plutarch (ca. A.D. 46–120) was a younger contemporary of Pliny. His *Lives* were written originally in Greek, and consisted of a series of Lives of the Caesars (of which only two, Galba and Otho, have survived), and another of parallel Lives, a Greek paired with a Roman. Of these there are twenty-two remaining. The *Lives* were originally devised to inspire, within the two great empires, mutual (and peace-giving) respect, and to provide

---

77. "La zorra non toma pollo que aya picado en figado de zorre," "Como non entran lobos en una heredad." The notes are against Pliny XXVIII, lxxxi, 265–266; Jones, *Pliny*, viii (1963), 178–179.

78. Aloes can be mixed with Scammony to relieve stomachache, and are marvellous for healing wounds. XXVI, xxxviii, 59, 61, XXVII, v, 14; Jones, *Pliny*, vii (1966), 308–309, 398–399.

79. XXXIV, xxviii, 42–43; ibid., 34–37. Mastic is good for loose teeth too.

80. Mixed with eggs, white lead (or litharge) and wine, myrrh heals chapped feet. XXIX, xi, 40; Jones, *Pliny*, viii (1963), 208–209.

81. Mixed with pepper, cinnamon is good for sprains. XXIX, xii, 55; ibid., 218–219.

models to be followed. Plutarch was long neglected in the Latin West, and his *Lives* remembered only sporadically. They were epitomized in the fourteenth century, but the true revival of interest in him awaited the Italian Renaissance. The *Lives* and their epitomes were translated piecemeal into Latin in the early years of the fifteenth century, and then into Italian. A complete Latin edition was printed for the first time in 1470.[82] Only late in the century did the *Lives* become more widely known in other vernacular languages, and Columbus's possessing a copy of Palencia's translation of them into Castilian is yet one more indication of the admiral's wish to be *au fait* with current fashion in his reading. It may be a sign too of an attitude towards greatness both admiring and shrewd.

Columbus's copy contained the surviving twenty-two parallel *Lives* and four separate ones, including Galba and Otho. In common with other versions, including the Roman printed edition, it was supplemented by extraneous matter, such as the lives of Hannibal and Scipio by D'Acciaiuoli, and by a series of short biographies on persons of general note such as, in this case, Evagoras, Pomponius Atticus, Homer, Plato, Aristotle— and Charlemagne. Columbus annotates twenty of Plutarch's parallel lives, Acciaioli's supplements to them, and the separate final series.[83]

Columbus and Plutarch would readily make a separate study in itself; here we can touch only upon a little of the subject. The great admiral was clearly interested in historical biography as well as in pure history, and in a way which would again have

---

82. D. A. Russell, *Plutarch* (London, 1973), 148.

83. Thus, at Columbus's hands, Plutarch's *Lives* escaped from the world of the scholar and entered that of "men and women of the world" at an earlier date than Russell assigns to this process; ibid., p. 108. Columbus here also joined a company which included Shakespeare, Queen Elizabeth of England, and Benjamin Franklin. The annotations may be found in de Lollis, *Scritti*, 473–522.

pleased Pope Pius II. Columbus's annotations show that he meant to draw upon the whole range of his material, from simple information to the sort of deep truth the Pope insisted was there in history. He was looking also for models to be followed (or shunned). Much in the *Lives* touched him personally, and we might learn from them about the admiral's own concerns. Teeth surface once again, we might remark, and so do cures,[84] and so do Amazons.[85] He dislikes homosexual practice.[86] He constantly marks stories about dreams and auguries and marvelous portents,[87] an interest which is consistent with that larger one he manifests in his Book of Prophecies. And there are signs of an even more profound involvement, signs which may perhaps give us a clue as to the date at which some of the

---

84. In Pyrrhus iii, 4, Plutarch says this of Pyrrhus; "He had not many teeth, but his upper jaw was one continuous bone, on which the usual intervals between the teeth were indicated by slight depressions. People of a splenetic habit believed that he cured their ailment; he would sacrifice a white cock, and, while the patient lay flat on his back, would press gently with his right foot against the spleen. Nor was any one so obscure or poor as not to get this healing service from him if he asked it;" *edit.* B. Perrin, *Plutarch's Lives* ix (Loeb, London, and Harvard, 1968), 352–353. There is no translation into English from the Castillian version. My references will be, therefore, to this one, from the Greek. Columbus comments both upon the teeth and the cure; de Lollis, *Scritti*, 492.

85. Pompey, xxxv, 3–4; ibid., v (1961), 208–209. Ibid., 499.

86. He describes it as "nefas" and productive of cruelty, see Alcibiades iii, Cato, xvii, 1–4 (of Lucius Flamininus), and his notes upon the affairs of the young Demetrius, Demetrius, xix, 5–6, xxiv, 2–3; ibid., ii (1968), 8–9, 350–352, ix (1968), 44–45, 54–57. Ibid., 476, 485, 511.

87. For example, his marking the appearance of the stars Castor and Pollux on either side of Lysander's ship as he sailed out to victory, or the falling of the great stone from heaven at Aegospotami; Lysander, xii, 1–2; ibid., iv (1968), 260–236. Ibid., 489.

annotations were made. The admiral seems to be particularly interested in public-spirited forbearance in the face of sufferings, in treachery, and in wrongs done too late to be requited. Against Pericles, for instance, he notes how Pericles never gave way beneath his adversities, nor even wept until the death of his last son,[88] and how Brutus gave up his sons for treason, and watched their executions without pity.[89] He draws special attention to the unjust accusations against, and death of, Phocion, and how he was treated with honor only after his death, when the truth was known.[90] He points also to the treachery of the Syracusans against Dion, after the latter had brought them wealth and freedom, and he is clearly affected by the fate of Demetrius, betrayed, captured and held under house arrest until he died of a surfeit of inactivity, good food and wine.[91] It is tempting to see in these preoccupations the reflection of Columbus's own sufferings and sense of injustice, especially, perhaps, those which followed the third voyage.

The true interest of Columbus's annotations to Plutarch's *Lives*, however, may lie in a field we have not yet discussed. This is one reason for my placing this text last in line. In contrast with the preceding books, the *Lives* tell us little about Asia or about the admiral's expectations of his discoveries; but they tell us a very great deal about the settlement and ruling of societies. They may best be related then, I suspect, to the admiral's plans for his colonies. Read with such plans in mind, they are, indeed, most informative. The admiral's views upon the appropriate place of riches seem to be strong. Excessive

---

88. Pericles, xxxvi, 4–5; Perrin, *Plutarch's Lives*, iii (1967), 104–107. De Lollis, *Scritti*, 480–481.

89. Publicola, vi, 1–4; ibid., i (1967), 514–517. Ibid., 476.

90. Phocion xviii, 1–3; ibid., viii (1959), 184–187. Ibid., 504.

91. Dion, xxxviii, 2, Demetrius, 1, 5–6, lii, 4; ibid., vi (1961), 82–83, ix (1968), 128–129, 132–133. Ibid., 506, 512–513.

public display is wrong,[92] and he appears to think it admirable to lack a greed for gold.[93] He marks how Cato's care for the public good was great enough for him to eschew all patronage of family.[94] He notes instances of liberality and openness,[95] and also prescriptions to induce fellow feeling among citizens.[96] Of course, some of these notes may simply mark Columbus's amazement at such paragons of virtue; but if, instead, they bear witness of intentions towards his colonies, then the early American colonies, and the native Americans especially, were very grievously deprived.

The amount of reading material which bears Columbus's notes is by no means negligible. Pliny and Plutarch alone would have occupied many rainy days on land or weeks at sea. Also, as we have remarked, some of his annotations show that Columbus had read more widely still. Yet, even with all this, we are far from reconstituting the whole of the admiral's inner medieval universe. We have surveyed so far a little of that which he had in pictorial or written form; but sailors, proverbially, love stories. Stories help to while away the long hours at sea; and they don't get wet. They love to hear them and they love to tell them, and Columbus and his sailors, it seems, were no exception. The stories the admiral heard, and which were perhaps retold among his sailors and among others, might, indeed, have been among the most important supports to him of all.

---

92. Publicola xxiii, 2–3; ibid., i (1967), 562–565. Ibid., 476. Porsenna was generous, but the expenditure upon his funeral was outrageous.

93. Solon despised riches, Columbus notes, and Phocion actually refused the gold of Alexander, considering it wiser not to need it than to have it. Solon, i, 2, Phocion, xviii, 1–3; ibid., i (1967), 406–407, viii (1959), 184–187.

94. Ibid., 505.

95. Crassus could be "franqueza," Crassus iii, 1; ibid., iii (1967), 320–321. Ibid., 496.

96. Allowing anyone to take up another's cause seemed to help under Solon. Solon xviii, 5; ibid., i (1967), 452–453. Ibid., 475.

Chapter 3

Sea Stories

The Atlantic seaboard which Columbus traversed as a young man, from the west of Ireland to the Guinea Coast, was studded with stories of the sea. Some of these had passed northwards and westwards from the Mediterranean and were of great antiquity, though their origins and age in no way diminished the excitement and the popularity they still commanded. Some were of more recent invention; and many were Christian, or adapted, and put to Christian uses, gaining in force as the infant Christian church pressed to the outer edges of European settlement, and as preachers recognized the roles such stories might play. The account of St. Christopher's own perilous crossing of the waters with his sacred burden was itself such a story. James of Voragine (Dominican Archbishop of Genoa, 1292–1298) tells of the exploits of St. Christopher in his *Golden Legend*, printed in 1470.[1] This story told, it might be recalled, of how the pagan giant Reprobus wanted a strong king to serve. Convinced at last that the only true king was Christ, he set out in search of him, and was ordered to place himself by a raging torrent and carry across whoever wished to go. One peculiarly

---

1. We can reasonably suppose that Columbus was familiar with the *Golden Legend*, both because of its author's Genoese connections and because the work was so widely popular in the later Middle Ages. The *Golden Legend*'s rendering of the St. Christopher story may be read in translation in G. Ryan and H. Rippenberger, *The Golden Legend of Jacobus de Voragine* (London, 1941), 377–382.

deceptive burden, first child-like and light, then dauntingly heavy, turned out to be Christ himself. Reprobus thus found his king and was baptized as Christopher, the Christ-bearer.[2] This motif of carrying strange persons over stretches of water was ancient in origin, and came to be very widely employed in company with other early wonder and adventure stories.[3] The St. Christopher story had certainly captured the attention of the medieval traveler by the time his namesake attempted to imitate the saint upon a rather larger scale;[4] but there were many more.

As in the preceding chapter we attempted to explore the contents of some of Columbus's reading, so here we shall try to follow in outline the stories of water and sea crossings he knew, or might have known—and to the same end. Columbus's

2. "Before his baptism, Christopher was called Reprobus, but after his baptism he was called Christopher, which means Christ-bearer, because he bore Christ in four ways: upon his shoulders when he carried him, in his body by his mortifications, in his mind by his devotion, and in his mouth by professing and preaching him;" ibid., 377. The Latin speaks of St. Christopher as "Christum ferens;" *edit.* Th. Graesse, *Jacobus a Voragine Legenda Aurea Vulgo Historia Lombardica Dicta* (Leipzig, 1850), 430. This phrase is, of course, echoed in Columbus's famous signature, see Chapter 5, this volume.

3. The motif is a double one. The saint-hero is to carry anyone, however unattractive, across a difficult stretch of water. The heaviest and most daunting burden turns out in the end to be the saviour and the lightest. The *Golden Legend* version includes features common to many other such stories. It is a hermit, for instance, who gives Christopher the crucial direction which leads him to Christ. The same is true of St. Brendan, see below. See on the St. Christopher story's antiquity, and its especial association with Irish sea stories, the important article by Kathleen Hughes, "An Irish Litany of Pilgrim Saints Compiled c. 800," *Analecta Bollandiana* 77 (1959), esp. 328–329. In the earliest known codex containing the curious treatise *Marvels of the East*, the British Library Ms. Cotton Vitellius A xv (of about the year 1000), the *Marvels of the East* and the legend of St. Christopher are bound together.

4. The early fourteenth century Franciscan Friar Odoric of Pordenone, for example, in Chapters 18 and 30 of his account of his own travels, draws attention to the resemblance of the huge idols of the east to western representations of St. Christopher—"as big as St. Christopher is commonly represented by the painters;" H. Yule, *Cathay and the Way Thither* i (London, 1866), 81, 109.

reading of these stories, his listening to them, and his engagement in some of the sacred and secular dramatic entertainments that involved them, made for an extremely formidable freight of expectation. It was a freight trimmed into place by many different but complementary mental influences, from the intellectually most respectable to the imaginatively highly agreeable; and it was a rich one. It was also profoundly medieval; more so perhaps than anything we have looked at so far, in that it drew so very deeply upon the resources of the spoken word. This freight of stories was carried on Columbus's western voyages to the very end, and it seems to have made upon the great admiral an impression of a kind from which he neither could, nor would, escape.

The *Odyssey* of Homer, in its Latin rendering, the *Iliad*, and the adventures of Aeneas in his voyage to the Italy of his forefathers from fallen Troy (especially as told by Virgil in his *Aeneid*), were perhaps the most impressive of the classical sea stories, and the ones which captured the widest of audiences. Lucian, in his *True Histories*, added his tales of the Isles of the Blest (in Latin the "Insulae Fortunatae") to those of the Islands of the Phaeacians in Book VIII of the *Odyssey*. All of these more than prepared the palates of readers and listeners for a little ocean-salt. Then, in the later Middle Ages, the full version of Plato's *Timaeus* came to light. This told the story of Atlantis, the great sunken continent in the western seas with its attendant archipelago, the latter perhaps not yet quite submerged. Plato's *Critias* added an account of Atlantis's lost, but ideal, commonwealth. Seneca's tragedies, and his *Medea* in particular, kept alive the memories both of Atlantis and of that Thule the navigator Pytheas had placed far in the northern seas. The tragedies spoke of many of the great heroes of the ancient seas; and they did more even than this. The very fact that they were tragedies meant that such stories were conveyed within a tradition both of the most entertaining and of the most dramatically intense. The rehearsal and enactment of tragic drama is a powerful means of inciting to high adventure, perhaps one of the most powerful we have.

Then, added to those of Aeneas and Odysseus, there were the seaborne triumphs of the Greek Heracles (romanized as Hercules), and of Jason and the Argonauts (sometimes combined with the Hercules cycle). Seneca, together with Ovid in the *Heroides* and *Metamorphoses* (VII and IX especially), were the more important of the means by which the Hercules and Jason stories reached the medieval west.[5] Two of the famous twelve labors of Hercules concerned the western ocean. As his tenth labor, Hercules was sent to capture the cattle of Geryon, pastured on the mythical island of Erytheia in the great seas beyond the Mediterranean. He was, of course, successful, and at the end of his journey he erected two pillars, one on either side of the modern Straits of Gibraltar. The pillars of Hercules are often represented, with a somewhat fluctuating accuracy, on medieval maps of the world. In his next labor, the eleventh, the hero was sent to gather the golden apples of the Hesperides; treasures which were again kept at the edge of the world, in a garden overlooking the western ocean, and guarded by a dragon. The dragon suffered the customary fate of guardian dragons on the wrong side, and was killed. The golden apples were carried off successfully to complete the labor.

In a story in some respects similar to that of the twelve labors, a story which, moreover, sometimes includes Hercules himself among the crew of the ship "Argo," Jason and his Argonauts sail to the island of Colchis. The journey is made necessary to avenge a murder, that of Phryxus, and to correct the wrongful usurpation of Jason's kingdom of Iolcus. Jason is to recapture the golden fleece of a ram sacrificed to Jupiter (by Phryxus) from the ever wakeful dragon which guards it. The King of Colchis, Aëtes, lays down terrible conditions for the surrender of the golden fleece.

---

5. The fullest account of Jason and the Argonauts is that given by Apollonius Rhodius in the *Argonautica*, but it needed Latin intermediaries.

Jason must tame two bulls with brazen feet and horns, and vomiting smoke and fire. He must harness them to a plow of adamant, and plow two acres. He must sow dragons teeth in the plain, and destroy the armed men which will rise up from them. He must slay the wakeful dragon. All this he must do in one day. Fortunately Medea, daughter of Aetes, falls in love with Jason and, through her magic, enables him to fulfil the king's commands. When this second unfortunate dragon is finally drugged into sleep, and killed, Jason and Medea set sail with the fleece for Iolcus. Some versions of the Argonauts cycle have the victors returning to Greece by traveling along the stream of Ocean, and reentering the Mediterranean through the pillars of Hercules. After a series of adventures, (including encounters with Circe, Scylla and Charybdis, and the Sirens), they reach the islands of Phaeacians, and are married. Medea then is deserted by Jason, and banished; an act which earns him a place in Dante's eighth circle of Hell. The Argonauts cycle was immensely popular and well known, and the love story of Jason and Medea, with its bitter ending, was especially effective in ensuring the whole tale a role in epic tragedy. Through Seneca's *Medea* especially, it gained a wide renaissance audience.[6]

The sum of these stories from antiquity bequeathed to the Middle Ages a western ocean teeming with terrors, it is true, but resplendent too with wonders and rewards for the imaginative and for the brave. When Christianity came to overlay them with stories of its own, the sea would often still play a vital part in the plot, and especially so in regions where the sea was crucial to the livelihoods of the people on its coasts. The use of Virgil's *Aeneid* as a textbook in the schools

---

6. Seneca's Tragedies were printed at Ferrara in 1484.

of early Christian Europe kept the adventures of the latter
especially alive in the imaginations of Christian pupils,
and, as a result, Aeneas's journeyings often left their
mark upon these later Christianized stories. They also lay
ready to support more modern memories of persecution, loss
in battle, exile, and, and this is especially important, hopes of
the subsequent establishment of successful societies and
states. All of these experiences, both the sad ones and the
cheering, were a part of the history of the medieval Atlantic
seaboard, notably so during the invasions of the "Nordmanni"
(who were themselves thought to have come from an island
in the northwestern sea, perhaps Thule), and of the
Moors.

And then again, there was the rather different Christian
pilgrimage–exile story, one in which single figures or groups
set out wholly willingly from their own lands and families in
accordance with the command God gave to Abraham in Genesis
12:1, "Go from your country and your kindred and your father's
house to the land which I will show you." The fulfillment of
such a command might naturally take a seaborne form in
coastal districts, and this species of adventure became
particularly popular in Ireland in the early Middle Ages, and
inspired many a Christianized *Imram* or story of a sea voyage,
in its turn. Thus, saints of Celtic extraction or persuasion,
pursuing their vocations on the coasts of Ireland or western
Britain or Brittany with the aid of the Christian God, seemingly
spent the greater part of their time skimming about on the waves
on wholly improbable vehicles (altar stones were especially in
demand as craft), in quelling ocean storms, overpowering sea
monsters, listening to magical seabirds and finding miraculous
islands filled with good things. In his *De Mensura Orbis Terrae*,
written in the ninth century, the Irishman Dicuil pulls many
strands together when he tells both of multitudes of willing
pilgrim–exiles setting out in their boats for, and building
communities on, lonely islands far out in the mysterious western

ocean, and, in his own day, of people fleeing from the Northmen.[7]

Whether or not Columbus's Latin learning was confined to the Vicola Pavia, he will certainly have read Virgil and Lucian.[8] He knew Homer too, and marks apparently with approval, in his copy of Plutarch's *Lives*, how Lycurgus was instructed by Homer, and how the most precious object Alexander could think of to deposit in Darius's treasure chest was the *Iliad*.[9] Columbus shows himself from the first, indeed,

---

7. "There are many other islands in the ocean to the north of Britain which can be reached from the northern islands of Britain in a direct voyage of two days and nights with sails filled with a continuously favourable wind. A devout priest told me that in two summer days and the intervening night he sailed in a two-benched boat and entered one of them. There is another set of small islands, nearly all separated by narrow stretches of water; in these for nearly a hundred years hermits sailing from our country, Ireland, have lived. But just as they were always deserted from the beginning of the world, so now because of the Northman pirates they are emptied of anchorites, and filled with countless sheep and very many diverse kinds of sea-birds." *Trans.* J. J. Tierney, *Dicuili Liber De Mensura Orbis Terrae* (Dublin, 1967), 74–77.

8. Columbus mentions the story of the "insulae fortunatae" in his notes to the *Imago Mundi*; *edit* E. Buron, *Ymago Mundi de Pierre d'Ailly* i (Paris, 1930), 240–241. In the 1507 map attributed to Waldseemuller, Columbus is himself seen as the fulfillment of the prophecy in *Aeneid* VI, 795–797. A passage on the top left of the map pays Columbus this tribute: "Many have regarded as an invention the words of a famous poet that 'beyond the stars lies a land, beyond the path of the year and the sun, where Atlas, who supports the heavens, revolves on his shoulders the axis of the world, set with gleaming stars'; but now finally it proves clearly to be true. For there is a land, discovered by Columbus, a captain of the King of Castile, and by Americus Vespucius, both men of very great ability, which, though in great part it lies beneath 'the path of the year and the sun' and between the tropics, nevertheless extends about nineteen degrees beyond the Tropic of Capricorn toward the Antarctic Pole, 'beyond the path of the year and the sun'." E. D. Fite and A. Freeman, *A Book of Old Maps* (Cambridge, Mass., 1926), 26.

9. Lycurgus, iv, 3–4, Alexander, xxvi, 1; *edit* B. Perrin, *Plutarch's Lives* i (Loeb, London, and Cambridge, Mass., 1967), 214–215, vii (1963), 298–299. C. de Lollis, *Scritti di Cristofero Colombo*, in *Raccolta di Documenti e Studi Pubblicati dalla R. Commissione Colombiana pel Quarto Centenario dalla Scoperta dell'America* i (ii) (Rome, 1894), 473, 502. Columbus also marks the contents of the *Iliad* and *Odyssey* against the entry on Homer at the end of his copy of the *Lives*; ibid., 519.

susceptible to such sea stories. In his journal of the first voyage, for example, he speaks of the "sirens" he saw off the Rio del Oro, but "they were not as beautiful as they are depicted, for somehow their faces had the appearance of a man."[10] He clearly has in mind here the sirens of the *Odyssey* Book XII, or the half-woman, half-bird sirens of the story of Jason and the Argonauts.[11] He may also, as we shall later see, have kept in his head both the dragon and the golden apples of the Hesperides story, and the story of Jason and the golden fleece; particularly so on the third voyage.[12]

It is likely, too, that Columbus enjoyed tragic drama. Such a taste would certainly not be out of character, and he had, it

---

10. 9 January: C. Jane, *The Journal of Christopher Columbus* (London, 1960), 143. They may in reality have been Caribbean Manatees or seacows; S. E. Morison, *Journals and Other Documents on the Life and Voyages of Christopher Columbus* (New York, 1963), 148.

11. The sirens are not precisely described in the *Odyssey*, but are given the half-woman half-bird shape popular in ancient art by Apollonius Rhodius; R. C. Seaton, *Apollonius Rhodius, the Argonautica* (Leob, London, and Harvard, 1967). 354–355. In the Middle Ages they were depicted sometimes as half-woman and half-fish, and are found in this form, for instance, in the Catalan Atlas, which places them in the Indian Ocean.

12. The story of the islands of the Hesperides persisted to the extent of tempting Oviedo to insist that they (and all islands in the western ocean that could be associated with them, including the Indies) had always belonged to Spain; this because they were a part of the dominions of, and had been named after, Hesperus, twelfth king of Spain. Oviedo asserts that this claim provided Columbus with just motive for the discoveries and annexations he made in the name of the sovereigns; J. M. Cohen, *The Four Voyages of Christopher Columbus* (Harmondsworth, 1969), 31. In his life of his father, Ferdinand Columbus took exception to Oviedo's assertions, for they detracted in his view from his father's achievement; but the story could well have served Columbus in his original request for support. B. Keen, *The Life of the Admiral Christopher Columbus by his Son Ferdinand* (London, 1960), 52–53. Ferdinand tells us, in other places, that the admiral listened to stories of the sea both with enthusiasm and in the expectation of useful information; ibid., 40, 42, 48. Memories of the Jason story may be reflected in place names assigned, for instance the "Bocas del Dragon" and "Jardines" of the third voyage, but this is not the only contender; see Chapter 5, this volume.

seems, his own palimpsest copy of Seneca's Tragedies.[13] He also, as we have seen, knew his Ovid well enough to feel able to edit the latter's *Metamorphoses* to suit his own purposes. There is something to be said, indeed, for the idea that Columbus saw his own first voyage as a species of *Argonautica*, with himself cast as Jason and Queen Isabella as Medea (in the more attractive of her guises). In the Jason story, Jason is recognized as the rightful heir to the Kingdom of Iolcus by the fact that he has only one sandal when he comes, a description prophesied of the rightful heir. Jason had lost his sandal, interestingly, by acting as a type of St. Christopher. He had carried an old woman across a river, an old woman who turned out to be the Goddess Hera in disguise. Queen Isabella certainly overturned the first intentions of a king in Columbus's favor, as Medea did those of King Aetes for Jason. A famous passage often thought to prophesy the finding of the New World, and quoted by Columbus both in his *Book of Prophecies* and in his 1503 "Lettera Rarissima," is taken from Seneca's *Medea* (interestingly, from the passage in which Seneca compares the terrors faced by Jason's ship Argo with the happier prospects of the ships of Seneca's own day).[14] The *Medea* seems, then, to have been

---

13. S. de la Rosa y Lopez, *Libros y Autographos de D. Cristóbal Colon* in *Discurso Leidos ante la Real Academia Sevillana de Buenas Letras* i (Seville, 1891), 21.

14. For the quotation in the *Book of Prophecies* see de Lollis, *Scritti*, 141, and, for a translation into English of the relevant passage in the "Lettera Rarissima," S. E. Morison, *Journals*, 378. Columbus's son Ferdinand also knew Seneca's *Medea*, and he too quoted the famous passage. He certainly saw it as prophesying the discovery of the New World; Keen, *The Life*, 43. The passage reads (in a modern edition):

> Venient annis saecula seris,
> Quibus Oceanus vincula rerum
> Laxet, et ingens pateat tellus
> Tethysque novos detegat orbes,
> Nec sit terris ultima Thule.

F. J. Miller, *Seneca, Tragedies* i (Loeb, London, and Harvard 1968), 260–261. The queen certainly owned copies of Seneca; F. J. Sanchez Canton, *Libros, Tapices y Cuadros que Collecionó Isabel la Católica* (Madrid, 1950), 43–44.

much on Columbus's mind. The idea that Columbus and Isabella so cast themselves can never, of course, be fully tested. If it was ever put forward at all, it will have been so surely in fun. Yet, the capacity to support the most serious and far-reaching of purposes by the judicious use of fun is one of the strengths of stories. Perhaps it is their greatest one. The ability to appreciate and employ this capacity may, in addition, be one of the marks of the great leader.

Columbus was familiar too with many of the early medieval Christian sea stories. Three of them seem to have left especially deep impressions, both upon his thoughts and upon his discoveries, impressions varying of course in their seriousness, as did the tales themselves, but all perceptible. One is of a voyage of escape and settlement, one is a Christianized Celtic *Imram*, and the third is a story of self-renunciation across the sea, and was remembered, I am sure, again primarily in a sense of fun. They are, respectively, the legend of Antillia, the *Imram* account of the voyage of St. Brendan to the Promised Land of the Saints, and the legend of St. Ursula and her 11,000 accompanying virgins — after whom, during the second voyage, Columbus named the Virgin Islands.

Antillia is mentioned in the famous letter of Toscanelli to Canon Martins, the letter in which Toscanelli describes part of his accompanying chart (Plate 12) now lost, and advances his hugely optimistic estimate of the amount of ocean to be covered westwards to the Indies:

> But from Antilia, known to you, to the far-famed island of Cippangu there are ten spaces . . . So there is not a great space to be traversed over unknown waters.[15]

Antillia, as an island to be found along the way, was an important support to that optimism, and Columbus had gained

15. Morison, *Journals*, 14.

possession of the letter and probably of the chart also, at the very outset of his adventures. In the journal of the first voyage, entered under 9 August whilst he was on Gomera, in the Canaries, Columbus recounts, moreover, a tale much believed in by Spanish sailors. These, he says:

> swore that every year they saw land to the westward of the Canaries, which is towards the setting sun; and others from Gomera affirmed exactly the same under oath. The admiral here says that he remembers that, being in Portugal in the year 1484, one from the island of Madeira came to the king and asked of him a caravel, to go to this land which he saw, and that this man swore that he saw it every year and always in the same way. He also remembers that they said the same thing in the islands of the Azores, and that all these agreed concerning the direction and the manner of appearance and the size.[16]

This passage from this journal could have reference either to Antillia or to the extraordinary islands Brendan was held to have visited in the saint's own voyages, and to which we shall shortly come.[17] Columbus certainly had maps with such islands on them, as we have seen, and as we shall see.[18]

The story of Antillia was inscribed in simple outline upon Behaim's globe:

> In the year 734 of Christ, when the whole of Spain had been won by the heathen of Africa, the above island Antilia,

16. Jane, *The Journal*, 8.

17. Morison believes so, and also that Columbus and his crew's mistaking landbirds for seabirds betokened an expectation of St. Brendan's island; *Journals*, 51, 53–54.

18. And as Columbus says, for example, in the entry for 25 September; Jane, *The Journal*, 14. Ferdinand draws attention to the admiral's account of the caravel story too, and notes the appearance of such islands on early maps; Keen, *The Life*, 50. For further discussion of these maps, see Chapter 5, this volume.

called Septe Citade, was inhabited by an archbishop from Porto in Portugal, with six other bishops and other Christians, men and women, who had fled thither from Spain, by ship, together with their cattle, belongings and goods. 1414 a ship from Spain got nighest it without being endangered.[19]

It is more than likely that Behaim took his own information from Toscanelli, for the distance between Antillia and Japan which Behaim sets out on this same globe is startlingly close to Toscanelli's highly idiosyncratic one, and Toscanelli had Nuremberg connections.[20] Ferdinand Columbus knows the legend of Antillia and tells the same story as Behaim, although he changes the date of the escape there from 734 to 714, and attributes the early fifteenth century rediscovery of the island to the Portuguese.[21]

This was a markedly short sea story, for this is almost all we have of it. In this it is unlike those of St. Brendan and St. Ursula, and, again unlike them, it was a persecution story of relatively recent invention, despite the early date attributed to the original settlement. The name "Antillia" may reach back into the fourteenth century, indeed to the chart of Franciscus Pizzigano of 1367, and its formation may well owe a great deal to the mapmaker's memory of the tenth labor of Hercules.[22] The

---

19. *Transl.* E. G. Ravenstein, *Martin Behaim, his Life and his Globe* (London, 1908), 77.

20. Regiomontanus (Johan Müller) in Nuremberg had dedicated a copy of his *De Quadratura Circuli* to Toscanelli, and he might have been the medium through which Behaim had access to Toscanelli's letter and chart; ibid., 64.

21. Keen, *The Life*, 50–51.

22. In an ingenious article, G. R. Crone associates the name Antillia with a *mistaken* note on the chart of Pizzigano. This chart describes certain statues off the coast of West Africa (probably the columns of Hercules) as standing "ante ripas Atuliae." "Ante ripas *Getuliae*," or northwest Africa, was, Crone argues,

legend attached to the name, however, does not appear upon the scene until the early fifteenth century. It may have sprung into being as a result of distant sightings of the Azores before their discovery had been completed (1452 is the date usually agreed for this), or because of renewed hostility towards the Moors. It certainly seems to have played a part in the ambitions of Portuguese mariners anxious to recapture the supposed settlement for the crown, and to claim the support and the rewards due to such a venture.[23] Perhaps the legend was fabricated for these very ends. But once it did come into being, it made its mark, and Antillia is included as an island far out into the Atlantic, sometimes with an explanatory note and sometimes without, on the majority of surviving fifteenth century maps from 1424 onwards, and especially upon maps supplementary to Ptolemy's *Geography*.[24] Ferdinand Columbus is in no doubt that his father took the legend seriously.

---

originally meant, and the transcription "Attuliae" is the result of a scribal error. Later copyists made further errors, and therefore placed the mythical island of Antillia even more firmly upon maps; G. R. Crone, "The origin of the name Antillia," *The Geographical Journal* 91 (1938), 260–262. The name might also have in its makeup a distant echo of the Atlantis legend.

23. Ferdinand Columbus says as much, and emphasizes how disappointed the Portuguese Infante was that the rediscoverers of the island had failed to cement relations, especially as the ships' boys had found gold in the sand they were gathering for their firebox; Keen, *The Life*, 50–51. The incident Ferdinand recounts took place sometime during the reign of Henry the Navigator (1394–1460).

24. Subsequent to its appearance on Zuane Pizzigano's chart of 1424, Antillia is to be found, for example, on Beccaria's map of 1435, on Bianco's regional chart of 1436, as well as (unnamed) on the latter's world map of the same year, on the Pareto chart of 1455, on Benincasa's map of 1463, on Toscanelli's lost chart, and on Behaim. The markedly similar outlines of Antillia and its companion island Satanaxes in some of these maps are reproduced (together with those in the notorious Vinland map) in R. A. Skelton, *The Vinland Map and the Tartar Relation* (New Haven, Conn., 1965), 158.

The story of Brendan is very different, and because it too had arguably a most profound effect upon Columbus's explorations, and especially upon his claim to have found the Terrestrial Paradise, I shall recount it here quite fully, singling out for particular attention the passages that find, in my view, echoes in Columbus's own records of his voyages. Storm clouds still roll threateningly around attempts to date the story of Brendan exactly, to categorize it strictly, and to define its sources fully.[25] Of some few facts, however, we can begin to feel assured. The *Navigatio Sancti Brendani Abbatis* tells of the sea pilgrimage of a mid-sixth century abbot of Clonfert in Galway, in the west of Ireland. Written down in Ireland perhaps about the year 800, carrying memories of a far earlier oral tale or tales, and with help from the *Odyssey* and the *Aeneid*, the Latin *Navigatio* was among the most popular of all stories of this kind. Surviving copies of it span the whole of the later Middle Ages, from the tenth to the fifteenth century (about 120 in all, 29 from the fifteenth century), and it was translated into many European vernacular languages, and quickly printed.[26] Columbus could easily have had access to it. Indeed, to have avoided it would have been far more difficult.[27] Columbus had, in addition, become alerted to the connections between Galway and those eastern lands and islands he meant to find by an incident early in his career. It was in Galway, most probably in 1477, that he

25. The most thorough (and convincing) recent discussion is to be found in G. Orlandi, *Navigatio Sancti Brendani i Introduzione* (Milan, 1968).

26. The best edition of the Latin *Navigatio* available at the time of writing is that of C. Selmer, *Navigatio Sancti Brendani Abbatis* (Notre Dame, Ind., 1959). Good English translations are given by J. F. Webb, *Lives of the Saints* (Harmondsworth, 1965), 33–68, and J. J. O'Meara, *The Voyage of St. Brendan* (Dublin, 1976). My references will be to the latter.

27. The Iberian countries, Venice and Genoa were all intensely interested in the voyage of Brendan. "Some read a famous passage in Dante's *Inferno* [xxvi, 100–142] as referring not only to Ulysses but also to Brendan"; O'Meara, *The Voyage*, xv.

had come upon two corpses which he took to be Chinese.[28] An optimistic interpretation of a story such as that of St. Brendan, then, would thus have been welcome to him from the very beginning.

Brendan, the story relates, was inspired to sail out into the Atlantic Ocean by the visit of a somewhat tearful fellow monk, Barrind. Barrind had himself just returned from an Atlantic sea voyage. In a telling comment upon that attitude of joyous amazement at discovery which was thought proper to true medieval Christians, and of which I spoke in Chapter 1, Brendan, at the very outset of the *Navigatio*, chides Barrind for his current gloominess, urges him to correct it, and tells him how:

> Father, why should we be sad during your visit? Did you not come to encourage us? Rather should you give joy to the brothers. Show us the word of God and nourish our souls with the varied wonders that you saw in the ocean.[29]

Barrind complies. He recounts how one of his monastic sons, some time ago, had sailed westward on a three-day journey, and had settled upon an "insula deliciosa." Barrind had been to visit him, and had found on the island an exemplary Christian community — a community seemingly not unlike that of Antillia but for the fact that it was monastic (the two stories might perhaps both have been part of a related oral tradition of island settlement). Barrind had then joined his son on a second voyage, to find another island of which this son had heard:

---

28. He records this incident in a note in the margin of his copy of the *Historia Rerum Ubique Gestarum*, see above, Chapter 2. Morison presumes them to have been Finns; *Journals*, 23. We have also proof that at least one man from Galway ("Guillermo Ires: natural de Galney en Irlanda") traveled on the voyages to the Indies before 1511, for his heirs claimed compensation for his death there; S. E. Morison, *Admiral of the Ocean Sea* i (Boston, 1942), 197.

29. O'Meara, *The Voyage*, 3.

which is called the Promised Land of the Saints which God will give to those who come after us at the end of time.

At first they got lost in a sea fog. Then a great light revealed to them this very island. They walked about on it for fifteen days without finding its limits and, says Barrind (in words reminiscent both of Ezechiel and of the Apocalypse on the new Jerusalem):

> We saw no plants that had not flowers, nor trees that had not fruit. The stones of that land are precious stones. Then on the fifteenth day we found a river flowing from east to west.

They were not, however, to cross the river; hence perhaps Barrind's tears. A messenger appeared to them in a great light, and explained that the heart of the island was reserved by God for his saints. They were allowed only to glimpse it. So they sailed back to the island of delights, and explained to the brothers there how close they in fact lived to the gates of Paradise:

> Do you not perceive from the fragrance of our clothes that we have been in God's Paradise?

Brendan and his community were immensely impressed, and determined to set out themselves, in confirmation of the fact that they had done as God bade Abraham do in Genesis 12:1. They had renounced their country and their kindred and their father's house; and they were now prepared for even more renunciations. The central excitements of the story then begin. In an incident which recalls the consultation of the priest Anius by Aeneas in *Aeneid* III,79, Brendan and fourteen companions sail off first of all for advice from a holy man, Enda, who himself lived upon an island in the western sea. They receive his blessing, build their discovery-boat, and depart still further westwards. Adventure follows upon adventure. They find an island with a great high cliff and streams flowing down from it, where they are miraculously provided with food in a wondrous house, with:

> hanging vessels of different kinds of metal fixed around its walls along with bridles and horns encased in silver.[30]

One of the monks succumbs to temptation, steals a bridle and, after confessing his sin, dies there. A young man appears and promises them miraculous supplies of food and drink until Easter, after whom the island becomes known as the Island of the Steward.

Next they are blown upon an island equally full of springs and streams and fish, but with, in addition, great white woolly sheep, from which they furnish themselves with meat for the Paschal meal (for it is Holy Saturday). Then comes the famous story of Jasconius the whale, who is first mistaken for a barren stony island on which they land to boil up brine to salt their meat. Only when the island rushes away with the fire still lit upon it do they realize their mistake, and take to the next island, the Island of Birds, or fallen angels in that guise. It is here that Brendan and his company learn that their voyage to the Promised Land must take seven years, of which they have now served almost one. In each of the successive years they must revisit the selfsame islands, celebrating the great feastdays of the liturgical year in identical places.[31] They then find their destination for Christmas and the Octave of the Epiphany, another monastic settlement upon yet another island, supplied this time with "loaves of incredible whiteness and roots of

---

30. Ibid., 5–12.

31. Ibid., 24. The feasts named are Maunday Thursday (Island of the Steward), Holy Saturday (Island of Sheep), vigil of Easter Sunday (Jasconius), Easter until Pentecost (Island of Birds), Christmas to Epiphany (Island of the Community of Ailbe).

incredible sweetness'' (brought to them by "some dependent creature''), and perpetually burning lamps, and a church on a scale again reminiscent of Ezechiel and the Apocalypse, and with crystal altars.[32] There was also a soporific well, from which some of the brothers drank more deeply than was wise.

The cycle repeats itself as the angel–bird had said it would, with some few extra interventions. They encounter a huge sea beast, which is overcome and dismembered by a second sea monster breathing fire. They find an island on which three choirs chant the monastic hours in turn, a perfumed island full of grapes, a griffin, a great crystal pillar wound about with a silver net standing up in a sea of glass, and an island full of fires and smiths' forges, whose unfriendly inhabitants throw coals at them and boil the sea.[33] They see another fiery mountain in the ocean, which swallows up one of Brendan's monks; and they come too upon the hapless treacherous apostle, Judas. Judas is sitting on a rock tormented by possessions he had misused in the past, torments which he nonetheless describes as refreshments compared with the torments he suffers in hell. He explains that he is allowed this qualified refreshment on Sundays and, once more, on the great feasts of the liturgical year, including those of the Purification and Assumption of the Virgin. A further rocky island contains, by contrast, the hermit Paul, served with food by a friendly sea otter, and naked but for his covering of white hair. He tells them they are close to the Promised Land.

One more complete circuit, and they encounter Barrind's fog and then the light. They land on the Island of Paradise. The island is filled with trees and fruit and precious stones as Barrind had said it would be, and they find the same great river which

32. Ibid., 28–31. The measurements of the church are those of Ezechiel 48:16 and Apocalypse 21:16.

33. This story resembles the meeting with Polyphemus in *Aeneid* III, 639 ff. or perhaps the Cyclops of the *Odyssey*; Semmler, *Navigatio*, xxiv

divides the island, and which they may not cross. Once more there appears a messenger, who tells them that:

> After the passage of many times this land will become known to your successors, when persecution of the Christians shall have come.[34]

He also prophesies Brendan's death which, when they have all returned home via the island of delights, comes to pass.

Many efforts have been made to retrace this voyage upon the globe as we know it now, crowned by Tim Severin's fine attempt actually to sail it, and to prove thereby that Brendan and his company could have reached Newfoundland.[35] Identifications along the way include the Faroes as the Island of Sheep, Mykines or perhaps Vagar, in the Faroes, as the Island of Birds, Southern Iceland as the area of the coal-throwing smiths and fiery mountain, and the ice floes off the coast of Labrador as the location of the column of crystal. Much of this reconstruction is most convincing, although, as O'Meara has pointed out, the idea that Brendan had the use of *two* sails is untrue to the text, and, in the final part of his voyage to find the Island of Paradise, Brendan sailed east, not west.[36] Thus, though Severin has proved most admirably that a somewhat similar craft *could* have reached Labrador or Newfoundland, there is no earlier proof that Brendan did. Other less dramatic reconstructions place Brendan in the region of the Fortunate Isles, or Canaries, with Tenerife suggested as the fiery island.[37] And the possibility remains throughout, of course, that the story

---

34. O'Meara, *The Voyage*, 69.

35. Tim Severin, *The Brendan Voyage* (London, 1978).

36. *The Voyage*, xx–xxi.

37. So A. d'Avézac, "Les Iles fantastiques de l'océan occidental au moyen age," *Nouvelles Annales des Voyages et de Science Géographique* N.S.1 (1845), 299.

is, and always has been, one of pure imagination, constructed
as an encouraging allegory of the voyage of the monk through
the monastic life, punctuated as it is by liturgical feasts and the
psalms of the monastic *horarium*, and enlivened by the inclusion
of much-revered abbots and a variety of literary references.

Both types of interpretation, the material and the wholly
literary, remained open, of course, in the late fifteenth century,
but, like Antillia, Brendan's Paradise-island was clearly marked
on many of the maps Columbus could have seen, and in many
different places, from the Canaries to the Azores and Iceland,
and to the far western (eastern) seas. Dulcert (1339) puts it in
the North Atlantic, Pizzigano (1367) puts it far to the west.
Behaim seems to take the story literally, and places the voyage
firmly in time:

> In the year 565 after Christ, St Brandon in his ship came
> to this island, where he witnessed many marvels, and seven
> years afterwards he returned to his country.

He places St. Brendan's island equally firmly in space, deep
in the Atlantic, southwest of Antillia and, significantly as I think,
not far from latitude 5 degrees north.[38] The so-called
"Columbus Map," to which we shall come in Chapter 5 (Plate
13), marks four of the islands mentioned in the legend, together
with the Terrestrial Paradise-island itself, off the eastern coast
of Cathay, close to the Malay Peninsula. Much in the story was
to the taste of Columbus, from the renunciation of home and
kindred (with its attendant rewards) to the Christian prophecies
fulfilled and assured of fulfillment. The *Navigatio* may well
occupy an especially crucial place in Columbus's medieval
cosmology.

The legend of St. Ursula too, in some of its guises, is a story
of monastic virtue; especially about the virtue of virginity.

---

38. Ravenstein, *Martin Behaim*, 77.

Again, like that of St. Brendan, it enjoyed enormous popularity.[39] St. Ursula was reputed to have been a British virgin, perhaps of the mid-fifth century, although her name only surfaces in the ninth. The various versions of the legend (which occupy 230 pages of the *Acta Sanctorum* under her feast day, 21 October) circulated especially widely in the later twelfth century, after the presumed discovery of her relics in Cologne in 1155. The Dominican priory of Sts. Philip and James in Genoa was possessed of relics of St. Ursula, for certain friars had begged them from Cologne when they were at school in that city.[40] Columbus's interest in the saint might, then, first have been awakened in Genoa, and, in that by the end of the fifteenth century there were at least 272 hymns and sequences which included her name, such an interest once aroused was hardly likely to have been allowed to fall asleep again.[41] By the time Columbus appealed to it and named the Virgin Islands after it, the story of St. Ursula had both reached a venerable age and a wide audience of readers, and had assured itself of a place in the Christian liturgy.

It too is a persecution story, though this time the heroines advance across the seas towards the persecution, rather than escaping across them from it. In essence the story is this.[42] Ursula, daughter of a British king, is asked to marry the son of a powerful pagan king (in the *Golden Legend* version, the king

---

39. The legend of St. Ursula is definitively discussed in W. Levison, "Das Werden der Ursula-Legende," *Bonner Jarhbucher* 132 (1927), 1–164. My references will be to this. The study was published separately in Cologne in 1928.

40. Ibid., 138.

41. Ibid., 139.

42. The version most accessible to Columbus and his sailors may have been, once again, that of *The Golden Legend*; G. Ryan and H. Rippenberger, *The Golden Legend*, 627–631. There seem, however, to have been far more versions of the story of St. Ursula in circulation than there were of that of St. Christopher, so it is well to be wary.

of the Angles). Ursula is unwilling, and a dream warns her to collect about her 11,000 companion virgins, and to delay three years. Some versions of the legend describe Ursula and her companions as spending this intervening time in manly sporting exercises, much in the manner of the Amazons; perhaps this inspired the interest of Columbus much as the stories of the Amazons had clearly done. After the three years are up, however, they all take to sea, and sail down the Rhine to Basel, whence they proceed on foot to Rome on pilgrimage. On their return in their triremes to Cologne, Ursula and her 11,000 companions are slaughtered by the Huns, and so martyred. The *Golden Legend* has Ursula shot personally by the prince of the Huns for refusing to marry *him*. The figure of 11,000 may be a simple scribal slip, or it may have developed from the name of Ursula's original single companion, Undecimilla. The versions cannot all be reconciled one with another; sometimes the spiritual Amazons are martyred alone as virgins, sometimes they are joined by men (even a British pope). Sometimes, even, the ladies meet their deaths as respectable married women. We cannot be quite sure which of these many versions Columbus knew best; but all make a truly magnificent tale. St. Ursula was also a favorite subject for artists.[43] Though hardly in the same category as the other sea stories we have examined, the legend of St. Ursula probably played an important and diverting role in the entertainment, and so the encouragement, of crews of men captive both to the physical and the liturgical rigors of Columbus's long sea voyage.

Andreas Bernaldez was sure that Columbus knew Sir John Mandeville's story of his travels, and also that the information

---

43. Morison draws attention to a representation of the legend by the artist Gregorio Lopes, contemporary of Columbus, in which the murderous Huns are represented in Turkish dress; S. E. Morison, *Admiral of the Ocean Sea* ii (Boston, 1942), 87. Morison's preceding account of the legend is, however, a little too fanciful, even for a story so varied as this one.

Sir John provided had, on occasion, actually guided the admiral's judgment, particularly on the second voyage.[44] Ferdinand Columbus was acquainted with the famous book and implies that his father was too,[45] and a copy of the *Book of Sir John Mandeville* is listed in the *Registrum* of Ferdinand's own library. Although we may now doubt whether Columbus thought quite as highly of Mandeville as Bernaldez (and some later historians) would have us believe, it is virtually certain that the *Book* had a place in the great admiral's thoughts and plans.[46]

It told of a (very long) overland journey to the empire of the Great Khan and to the countries east of it, including the Terrestrial Paradise. It told too of sea voyages to the islands off the farthest coasts of Cathay; and it was tremendously popular. I have included the story of Mandeville's travels here among the sea stories, rather than with the *Travels* of Marco Polo upon which Sir John may in part depend (without acknowledgment)[47] for two reasons. Firstly, and most obviously, we have no surviving annotated copy of Mandeville's *Book*. And then, although we now know that the *Travels* of Marco Polo *might* have been devised rather as stories than as a solemn

44. C. Jane, *Select Documents Illustrating the Four Voyages of Columbus* i (London, 1930), 130–131.

45. Keen, *The Life*, 42–44.

46. Despite Rumeu de Armas's categorical denial that Columbus knew Mandeville's work, the admiral does, in fact, seem to rely upon Mandeville in the version of the letter on the third voyage given in the *Libro Copiador*; A. Rumeu de Armas, *Libro Copiador de Cristóbal Colón* (Madrid, 1989), i, 195–196, ii, 360. The relevant passage concerns the Terrestrial Paradise, and will be discussed more fully in Chapter 5 below.

47. In a recent study of Mandeville's *Book* Christiane Deluz casts doubt upon this dependence, and suggests that Mandeville knew Marco Polo primarily through Odoric of Pordenone; C. Deluz, *Le Livre de Jehan de Mandeville, une "Géographie" au XIVe Siècle* (Louvain-la Neuve, 1988), 51–52. This seems to me the only slightly questionable section of an otherwise excellent discussion.

treatise of instruction,[48] the *Book of Sir John Mandeville* was quite obviously so designed. It was a sophisticated piece of literary construction, as are all good storybooks, and one compounded of an exceedingly impressive range of sources, but still it was a storybook supreme, and seen, and employed, as such.

Certain features of Mandeville's reputed personal career add zest to the reading of his book, and were possibly meant to do so. One plausible account of it tells of a deathbed scene, wherein Sir John confesses to one John of Outremeuse that he, Mandeville, had murdered a fellow-countryman in England, a count, no less.[49] This event both precipitated the author's departure from the land of his birth, and prolonged his wanderings. He may have lived in Alexandria for seven years, collecting tales in the great port (including perhaps those of Sinbad to be discussed below), but we cannot be certain that he himself traveled any further. At some point (perhaps in England or Paris or even in Alexandria) he seems to have become qualified as a physician, practising as one "Jean de La Barbe" or "Jean de Bourgogne." He settled in Liège, perhaps in about 1343, and died there it seems in 1372. He wrote his book, in French in the first instance, shortly after the middle of the fourteenth century.[50] He may have written it in Liège.

---

48. J. Heers, "De Marco Polo a Christophe Colomb: comment lire le *Dévisement du Monde?*," *Journal of Medieval History* 10 (1984), 125–143.

49. *Edit.* M. Letts, *Mandeville's Travels, Texts and Translations* i (London, 1953), xix. There are many translations into English of the various versions of Mandeville's *Book* but this is the one most attentive to the manuscript tradition. For this reason my references will be to it, but the English used is, at times, tortuous in the extreme. Deluz, *Le Livre*, 3–24, surveys all previous discussions of Mandeville's career, including that by Letts. The problem of the true identity of the author of the book remains ultimately unresolved, but I shall call him Sir John Mandeville pending a better solution.

50. Letts, *Mandeville's*, xviii–xxiv; Deluz, *Le Livre*, 15–24. Letts (xxvii–xxviii) would place the completion of the *Book* in the 1360s, but this date must now be viewed with reserve.

Sir John, whoever he was, was clearly a Christian of a sort. The first ten chapters of the *Travels* purport, indeed, to be a guide for the would-be pilgrim to the Holy Land, though pity help the hapless pilgrim who actually turned for practical assistance to these chapters.[51] Mandeville's brand of Christianity was rather attuned to aspiration than to achievement. In this way, and also by reason of its hatred of the Jews,[52] its firm assertions that beyond the lands of the hated infidel there lay both the Christian realms of Prester John and a Great Khan at least tolerant of Christianity (perhaps even susceptible to it), and its frank entertainment value, his book was much to the taste of the late fifteenth century. Translations of the *Travels* into Latin, Italian, German and English were quickly printed, proliferating in the 1480s.[53]

Chapters XVIII to XXXIV of the *Travels* are those which concern us here. These tell of Mandeville's supposed journey eastwards from India, via the lands of the Great Khan, to the islands of the Indian Ocean and the edge of the Terrestrial Paradise itself. All the familiar hopes of immense wealth in gold and silver, diamonds, precious jewels and spices, and of strange customs and monsters and marvels are once again abundantly supported, sometimes with the help of Pliny, and Solinus and the *Imagines Mundi*, sometimes with that of Marco Polo or Odoric of Pordenone or Vincent of Beauvais.[54] In addition to its tremendous supplies of pepper, black and white, and of precious stones, India (XVIII) has a healing well (perhaps

51. "Never, surely, was a pilgrim to the Holy Land so long delayed", Letts, *Mandeville's*, xxvi.

52. In Chapter XXI, for instance, we are told a peculiarly unsavory tale of Jewish attempts to poison Christendom with tree-venom, for which there is no known antidote; ibid., 134.

53. Letts, *Mandeville's*, xxvii–xxxviii.

54. A list of Mandeville's possible sources is given in Deluz, *Le Livre*, 57–58.

drawing on the waters of Paradise), and ginger and other spices. The inhabitants of Lamory (Sumatra) go naked, and women are held in common and so is the land. Java (XXI) boasts all manner of spices, and palaces with alternate gold and silver steps, and rooms with walls and floors of great plates of gold and silver, the wall-plates engraved with heroic deeds, and studded with gems. The Great Khan's court is filled with golden tables, with great golden peacocks placed upon them, able to strut and flap their wings, and golden vines hung with grapes made of priceless gemstones.[55] Every form of monstrous behavior and creature is to be expected, from those who (as in Marco Polo) kill and eat their ailing loved ones (XXII), through *Cyclopes*, dog-heads, headless persons, persons who join both sexes in one, and one-footed persons, to mere ordinary cannibals and giants. The eastern islands grow reeds at whose roots lie magical protecting-stones which warriors carry with them. These stones ensure that iron cannot wound them. For that reason wars are waged with weapons untipped by iron.[56] In "Silha" (perhaps Ceylon) there is a lake filled with the tears of Adam and Eve, when, banished from Paradise, they wept upon a nearby hill.[57] The Great Khan has, John tells us, a whole room lined with the scented wood of lignum-aloe, wood periodically swept down to him by the rivers of Paradise, when they are in flood.[58]

Sir John is immensely interested in the Terrestrial Paradise, which he places at the uttermost ends of the east "at the beginning of the earth." He admits, with a rare modesty, that

---

55. XXIII; Letts, *Mandeville's*, 151–152.

56. XXI; ibid., 135.

57. Ibid., 139.

58. XXV; ibid., 167.

he has not actually visited it; but he has heard a very great deal about it:

> Paradise terrestrial, as men say, is the highest land of the world; and it is so high that it touches near to the circle of the moon. For it is so high that Noah's flood might not come thereto. . . . There is also so great noise of waters that a man may not hear another, cry he never so high. Many great lords have assayed divers times to pass by those rivers to Paradise, but they might not speed of their journey; for some of them died for weariness of rowing and over travailing, some waxed blind and some deaf for the noise of the waters, and some were drowned by the violence of the waves of the water.[59]

The full passage must await Chapter 5. I have included a part of it here, however, because it conveys so well the general flavor of the work. I have done so also because I hope to argue that some of the works upon which this description depended, and with which it was associated, exercised a particularly powerful influence upon Columbus. Indeed, this description itself may well have done so.

Together with the *Book* of Sir John Mandeville, some mention must now be made of the writings of one John of Marignolli, scion of the aristocratic house of Marignolli of San Lorenzo in Florence, and a Franciscan Friar at Santa Croce in the same city. Chief of these writings is a *Chronicle* written by John in the Bohemia of Charles IV, when he was domestic chaplain to the emperor.[60] John of Marignolli joined the service of the Emperor Charles IV at some point in 1355 (after a seemingly

---

59. XXXIII; ibid., 215–217.

60. The *Chronicle* is edited by J. Emler, *Kronika Marignolova*, in *Fontes Rerum Bohemicarum* iii (Prague, 1878), 492–604.

unhappy spell as Bishop of Bisignano in Calabria). He died in
1358/59,[61] and his *Chronicle* was therefore produced at a period
close in time to the *Book* of Sir John Mandeville. It shows itself
close to this *Book* in certain of its contents too, especially in its
discussion of the matter of the monsters of the east, and in its
description of Paradise.[62]

Marignolli's *Chronicle* is a world chronicle of a kind familiar
among proud nations, conscious, perhaps recently conscious,
of their history. This one was produced primarily with Bohemia
in mind. Its particular interest for us (and for Columbus) lies,
however, not in its nationalist concerns, but in the fact that,
within the first chapters standard to such chronicles (a discussion
of the earlier books of Genesis and of the race of Adam, that
is, from which all good Christian kingdoms sprang), Marignolli
incorporates firsthand tales about the riches of the Great Khan,
about the east and about the Terrestrial Paradise. For he had,
he says, been there. He had certainly been to the Khan and
to the east, for he was sent as papal legate to the court of the
Great Khan in 1338, reaching Cambaluc (Peking) in 1342.
Marignolli remained in the east until his return in 1353. On
his way home he traveled from Peking to Zayton, through
Mangi, and he, like Mandeville, dilates upon its great cities and
riches. He sailed then from the Malabar to the shrine of St
Thomas and the Madras country, to "Saba" and to the island
of Ceylon. And, when in Ceylon, he at least thought himself
in the neighborhood of the Terrestrial Paradise. He tells of
the life of Adam and of his fall, of his sorrows and of those

---

61. The essential facts about the career of John of Marignolli are given by L.
Oliger, "De anno ultimo vitae Fr. Iohannis de Marignollis missionarii inter
Tartaros atque episcopi Bisinianensis," *Antonianum* 18 (1943), 29–34.

62. The problems of the exact chronological and literary relationship between
the *Chronicle* of John of Marignolli and the *Book* of Sir John Mandeville have
not been adequately resolved and would repay further attention. The matter
of the monsters of the east will be further discussed in Chapter 4, and that of
Paradise in Chapter 5.

of Eve, of a great surviving statue of Adam (probably a Buddha), of Adam's marble house (made like a sepulchre), and of the huge footprint Adam made on a nearby mountain when he left Paradise.[63] He speaks as does Mandeville of the height of Paradise, of its nearness to the moon, of its marvellous serenity, and of its temperate climate. Like Mandeville, Marignolli conjures up, and makes us hear, the sound of its rushing waters.[64] He had learnt much, he says, from an astronomer, Lemon of Genoa ("Dominus Lemon de Ianua, nobilis astrologus").[65] This connection alone might have aroused Columbus's sympathy; but there is a very great deal more in the *Chronicle* tempting to such as the admiral. As John of Marignolli sails about the Indies he is full of wonders about their islands, wonders deeply to the taste of a Christian adventurer, and especially to one both partial to the Friars and with access to their libraries. It is more than probable on these counts alone, then, that Columbus knew of Marignolli's tales; and it may be that we can prove that he did.[66]

For all of the sea stories touched upon so far, there is at least some evidence that Columbus knew of them. The same cannot quite be said of the one to which we now turn; but, surely, he *must* have known it. No great sailor of the late fifteenth century could have managed without the story of Sinbad the Sailor, and especially not Columbus; for Sinbad too is filled with tales of the marvels of the east, and with some of the most wondrous of all. Distinguished geographers place Sinbad firmly on the same

---

63. *Edit.* Emler, *Kronika*, 499–500.

64. Ibid., 497–499.

65. Ibid., 509.

66. See below, Chapter 5.

shelf as Mandeville,[67] and Marco Polo seems to have been acquainted with at least some of Sinbad's adventures. So does the maker of the Catalan Atlas.[68] I have already tried to suggest that Columbus's own comments on the amber he found on Hispaniola may have been brought in part to his mind by his memories of Sinbad.[69] All of these indications make it probable that Sinbad was of the same company as the other storytellers we have mentioned here, and that Columbus kept is company as willingly as he did that of the others.

The story of Sinbad the Sailor or, to put the matter more precisely, Sinbad the Landsman and Sinbad the Seaman, is one

---

67. For example E. G. R. Taylor "The Cosmographical Ideas of Mandeville's Day," *in* Letts, *Mandeville's*, i, lix.

68. In Chapter 1 I pointed to the similarity between Sinbad and the Catalan Atlas in the matter of the great black cannibal giants. Marco Polo, like Sinbad, uses the name "Sarandib" for an island off the coast of India (possibly Ceylon); R. F. Burton, *The Book of the Thousand Nights and One Night* iv (London, 1894), 398, 403. All of my references will be to this distinguished translation of the Sinbad story into English, though it must be remembered that it is not wholly true to the original state of the texts; M. I. Gerhardt, "Les Voyages de Sinbad le Marin," *Studia Litteraria Rheno-Traiectina* 3 (Utrecht, 1957), 24–25. In his story of his second voyage, Sinbad tells how he came upon a group of diamond merchants. In a passage splendid even by Sinbad's standards, he describes how the merchants collect diamonds from valleys inaccessible to man. They throw pieces of fresh and bloody meat down into the valleys, to which the diamonds stick. The meat attracts eagles, which fly down into the valleys after it, then bring it up to eat it safely at the tops of the mountains. The merchants lie in wait at the tops of the mountains, scare off the eagles and gather up the diamonds; ibid., 360. Sinbad himself escapes from a valley by the simple expedient of clinging to a large piece of meat and being scooped up by an eagle. An identical account of this method of gathering diamonds appears in Marco Polo's *Travels*, III, xix; H. Yule, *The Book of Ser Marco Polo* ii (London, 1903), 360–361. Columbus comments upon this description (which is included in Pipino's translation); L. Giovannini, *Il Milione con le Postille di Cristofero Colombo* (Rome, 1985), 262. The Catalan Atlas includes the same account; H. Freiesleben, *Der katalanische Weltatlas vom Jahre 1375* (Stuttgart, 1977), 23, 32. Freiesleben marks its similarity to the account in *The Thousand and One Nights* but does not note the passage in Marco Polo. Heers, of course, had made out a convincing case that Marco Polo was in part a storyteller himself; Heers, "De Marco Polo a Christophe Colomb", 127–128.

69. See above, Chapter 2.

of the tales of *The Thousand and One Nights*. *The Thousand and One Nights* (or *The Arabian Nights*) was among the most popular of the collections of tales to circulate in the late medieval west, rivalling even the *Decameron*, and owing its popularity in part perhaps to certain characteristics it had in common with the latter; a combination, that is, of rousing story with (to put the matter at its mildest) a certain detachment from the more demanding of the dictates of the medieval Christian Church. Many of the stories in *The Thousand and One Nights* go back to the ninth century, perhaps even to the reign (786–809) of their sometime hero, Caliph Harun-al-Rashid himself. Sinbad appears on the 517th night, and tells the landsman, his namesake, of his seven fabulous voyages. Each of these voyages rivals the others in improbability, but each contains valued evidence, too, of the experiences of early Abbassid navigators to the east, and, more importantly for Columbus and for us, of the peoples and types of merchandise they found.

Some of Sinbad's adventures have been associated with those of the *Odyssey* and St. Brendan; his encounter with the whale, for example, on the first voyage,[70] the pelting of his ships with rocks by the blinded giant and ogres of the third voyage (ogres "with eyes like red-hot coals"), and the drugged food and drink of the fourth, to which several of his companions succumbed (but not, of course, our hero).[71] Many of these stories were doubtless common stock; but they were in fact so good, so inspiriting, and so widespread as to render the question of which was the borrower and which the source seem now a little arid. The important point to remember is that they seem to have done their job. They caught attention, and they imparted instruction. They told of adventures of a kind about which persons of spirit

---

70. The whale here also reveals himself by reacting to the cooking fire lit upon his back; Burton, *The Book*, 347–348.

71. Ibid., 368, 377.

loved to hear, and, as they did so, they informed them (or they persuaded them that they informed them) of real things along the way.

Sinbad certainly conjures up a world made alive and, above all, rich, upon trade with the islands of the east. Every story begins with his passing "from isle to isle and sea to sea" with a great cargo of merchandise, and every one ends with Sinbad's safe and prosperous return. Great birds ("Rukhs," again in Marco Polo) carry Sinbad up by his turban into mountains,[72] and drop stones and sink his ship.[73] His craft is dashed upon rocks, and whirled about amid stormy straits, and huge hairy apes swarm all over it.[74] When the ship's crews struggle at last to shore, giants and cannibals consume the fatter among them, and serpents gobble up the rest. Sinbad is buried alive with dead loved ones in an underground cavern, and (in a remarkable reversal, almost a parody, of the St. Christopher story) bound in seemingly perpetual slavery to a dreadful old man he had carried across a stream. This horrid figure resolutely refuses, once over, to climb down from Sinbad's neck, and belabors and defecates upon his unfortunate victim at will.[75] It is no accident that the Sinbad stories, sometimes a little expurgated, still find a place in children's storybooks. Again and again Sinbad escapes and, more importantly perhaps, returns from his adventures both with his original investments still intact, and with added cargoes of diamonds, precious stones and pearls. He finds sandalwood, and aloes (of two kinds), and cloves, and amber "crude and pure," and cinnamon, and camphor, and ginger,

---

72. Second voyage; ibid., 358.

73. Fifth voyage; ibid., 388. On his annotations to his copy of Plutarch's *Lives* Columbus makes a special note against the account of the falling of the great stone at Aegospotami as Lysander sailed out to victory; de Lollis, *Scritti* 489.

74. Fourth, sixth and third voyages; ibid., 375, 397, 363.

75. Fifth voyage; ibid., 390–392.

and pepper, and "India nuts," and amazing fish, and colossal turtles. He also comes upon an island "as it were one of the garths and gardens of Paradise."[76]

The accounts of the invariable honesty of the merchants Sinbad met, the generosity of all of the sea captains who rescued him, and the good humor with which Sinbad's goods were always safely returned to him once his true identity became known, may have aroused as much incredulous amusement as did the more outrageous renderings of his adventures; but, beneath all the wild imaginings, there lay a deeply serious message. There *was* rich merchandise to be had in the east; there *were* fortunes to be made by trading there, and it was and is legitimate to claim a part in them. It may even be a virtue. The Sinbad stories are as notable as the Brendan and related ones, both for their high moral tone, and for the resounding message they drive home. This is, that merit, even trading merit, is certain to be rewarded. Sufferings and temptations there are and always will be in abundance; but courage and honesty will always prevail, sometimes by means of the most shining of examples of human probity. The sea captain who befriends Sinbad after the latter's dreadful experiences in the cavern of the dead, for instance, sets out for him, and for everyone, the principles of good sailorly behavior. He refuses Sinbad's grateful proffer of a gift of pearls in thanks, saying:

> When we find a ship-wrecked man on the sea-shore or on an island, we take him up and give him meat and drink, and if he be naked we clothe him; nor take we ought from him; nay, when we reach a port of safety, we set him ashore with a present of our own money and entreat him kindly and charitably, for the love of Allah the Most High.[77]

---

76. Fifth voyage; ibid., 389.

77. Ibid., 386.

If such words brought a few cynical grins to the faces of some of their hearers, they were there nonetheless as a standard, and also, more importantly, as a justification of a most important kind for profitable seafaring. A profession productive of such paragons of virtue must surely be, at root, a noble one. It may not be wise, furthermore, any longer to entrust such opportunities for material and spiritual reward to the infidel Arabs. Such sentiments would find many willing ears in the Christian west, and, among them, Columbus.

Book- and map-reading are, to many of the inhabitants of the "developed" world of the twentieth century, activities distinct from, and infinitely more serious than, the activity of storytelling; but this distinction was by no means so clear when Columbus undertook his own great enterprises. Then, the more significant of the dividing lines were those which lay between the written method of conveying information, and the spoken or dramatic one. The vehicles differed, but they differed in form, not in capacity; and the information they conveyed might be, in each case, of the most serious possible kind. It is deceptive in this period, therefore (as also, of course, in many others in which a high percentage of the population cannot or will not read), to associate stories purely with the unreal or escapist world of dreams, or with a somehow inferior world of entertainment.[78] On occasion, of course, such an association might validly be made; but so might a wholly opposing one, for stories and dramatic entertainments could be, to persons of the fifteenth century, as vital a means of constructing reality, and of urging human beings to face up to it, as they had been to their revered forebears, the Greeks. It is arguable, moreover, that when dealing with a mixture of illiterate sailors, and (to speak gently) passengers perhaps rather of an adventurous than

---

78. Here I part company with Heers, "De Marco Polo," 142, in which he suggests that Columbus turned to a Marco Polo who was solely a "purveyor of dreams."

a scholarly turn of mind, this second method of conveying information and encouraging participation was the most effective one there was.

Through the stories we have just explored, we have entered into a third region of the great admiral's medieval universe. Columbus could spend time here perhaps in less solemnity of spirit than he could in the first two places, and some of these sea stories are the purest play. Together with the refreshment such playfulness brought with it, however (and probably all the more effectively because of it), these stories filled their hearers with precious material about their perils, their duties and, at the end, their prospects. The sea stories, enlivening, instructive, and, above all, amusing, were essential to the voyages westwards to the Indies. Like the mappae mundi and the contents of the annotated books, they printed their vivid images deeply into the admiral's mind, as we shall shortly see. They may also have been crucial to Columbus's surviving some of the most testing moments of his career.

PART II

The Imprint on Columbus

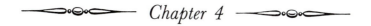

Chapter 4

Marvels of the East

To the end of his life Columbus maintained that he had reached the "Indies" he set out to find. He had landed on islands close to Cipangu, and on the mainland of Cathay. He had skirted the coasts of Marco Polo's Mangi, and been only leagues away from the domains of the Great Khan himself. He had constantly heard tell of the accessibility of what he took to be the "Aurea Chersonese" or "Patalis regio," (the modern Malay Peninsula), with all its fabled gold. He had traveled along the pearl coasts bordering the Indies, and had come within an hair's breadth of the strait leading from Cathay to India itself. He had visited many of those islands of which earlier travelers had told. He had gazed upon lands close to the Terrestrial Paradise, as some of the travelers had too, and he had discovered a great southern continent, previously unknown. He had brought back for his sovereigns all manner of treasures; gold and silver, precious jewels, medicines, spices, strange creatures and fishes salted down, and wholly remarkable peoples. He was assured of infinitely more. It was no wonder, then, that, again to the end of his life, he felt himself to be but miserably rewarded.

Of course, there really was a resemblance between the islands Columbus progressively discovered, and the islands of the Indies in which his mappae mundi had led him to believe. A striking similarity really did exist between the shoreline of that which we now call the Gulf of Mexico, and the coast of the China described by Marco Polo, and depicted upon Columbus's maps. It was as though the mainland and islands of the New World had conspired to play a giant geological trick upon the admiral before historical time began. But there was much more to the matter than this. Columbus's picture of the east was built of layer upon layer of medieval mental geology. Trick or no trick, he was overwhelmingly likely to believe that he had in fact reached the Indies. The part played by the coastlines he actually explored in the texturing of his expressed convictions was a very small one; and that played by the richly colored realms of his imagination was a very large one indeed.

In the first section, we brought up into the light some of the medieval materials from which these imaginative strata were compounded. Now, in the chapters of this second section, we shall explore the impact they made upon the great admiral's understanding and, especially, upon the manner in which he spoke of his discoveries. This first chapter will concern itself with the first two voyages. The success Columbus had, throughout these two voyages, in maintaining his original cosmology substantially intact, led directly, I shall suggest, to his recognition of the Terrestrial Paradise and the unknown southern continent in the Central and South American lands he later found. His medieval cosmology was, in other words, seemingly so well substantiated by the events of these first two voyages, that Columbus had no need to think about it too hard again, still less to question it in any way. The incentives were all to the contrary. There was every reason for him to deepen his trust in it. And, as his voyages continued, that is what he did.

I shall investigate the powerful initial impact of this cosmology in two main ways. First will come an attempt to trace Columbus's two first journeys through the Indies in outline on his own mental map. I shall give priority, therefore, in this attempt, to the type of map *he* might have had, rather than to those we have. In that I have already suggested that Behaim's globe was spectacularly close to those medieval mappae mundi of which Columbus speaks in his early journal, I shall draw especially heavily upon this. A hypothetical sketched reconstruction of these imagined voyages, placed upon a projection from Behaim, is given at the end of this section (Fig. 1).[1] I have added, to the reconstruction of the first voyage, the dates of some of the more illuminating of the references in Columbus's journal of that voyage. A sketch map of the journeys he actually made is appended for comparison (Fig. 2).

In second place, I shall compare those descriptions of the east which were available to Columbus in his medieval sources with the descriptions he, and some of those with him, offered of the products and peoples of the lands they thought they had visited. None of them knew, of course, where they had *really* been; but some of them had pictures of Cipangu, Cathay, and the islands of the east very ready for use in their minds, and Columbus had them, I think, particularly well to hand. Speculative as much of this second effort also is, it may, I hope, nonetheless make a contribution towards our greater appreciation of Columbus's achievement, and this in two main respects. Firstly, it may render the discrepancies between Columbus's perceptions and our own hindsight a little more comprehensible than it can sometimes be; and secondly, and most importantly, it may help to show how very well founded in medieval ''fact'' were many of the most apparently fantastic of the admiral's tenacious beliefs. In this way, some of the great admiral's decisions and declarations might be met with a little more admiration and sympathy than has always been the case in the past.

---

1. The projection is based upon that made by E. G. Ravenstein, *Martin Behaim, his Life and his Globe* (London, 1908), map 2. I have reversed the order in which Ravenstein sets out his projection, in order to concentrate upon the Atlantic crossing to the ''Indies,'' and have modernized and added certain names for clarification. I have not, however, departed in substance here from the information afforded by Behaim. Thus some of the directions I sketch in necessarily do violence to the directions given in the Journal.

Toscanelli, in his letter to Martins and in his lost chart, gave a most encouraging and tantalizing distance by sea to Marco Polo's Quinsay (the modern Hang Chow):

> From the city of Lisbon westward in a straight line to the very noble and splendid city of Quinsay twenty six spaces are indicated on the chart, each of which covers two hundred and fifty miles. [The city] is one hundred miles in circumference and has ten bridges. Its name means City of Heaven; and many marvellous tales are told of it and of the multitude of its handicrafts and treasures.

He spoke also of the great port of Zaiton (the modern Ch'uan Chow) and the yearly pepper fleet which sailed there, and measured, equally optimistically, the voyage from Antillia to "Cippangu," or Japan:

> But from the island of Antilia, known to you, to the far-famed island of Cippangu there are ten spaces. That island is very rich in gold, pearls and gems; they roof the temples and royal houses with solid gold.[2]

Toscanelli thus encouraged that now famous underestimate of the circumference of the earth which captured Columbus, and Behaim set it out upon his globe. We have seen too how both d'Ailly and Pope Pius allowed for a tremendous extension of the inhabited landmass eastwards, and how the admiral seized upon these possibilities in his notes. He stressed again and again how long was the journey by land to the Indies, and how short by comparison, therefore, must be the one by sea.[3] The

---

2. S. E. Morison, *Journals and Other Documentations on the Life and Voyages of Christopher Columbus* (New York, 1963), 14. A copy of this letter, perhaps in Columbus's own hand, is to be found at the back of the latter's copy of Pope Pius II's *Historia Rerum*.

3. *Imago Mundi* VIII, X, XI, XV: E. Buron, *Ymago Mundi de Pierre d'Ailly* i (1930), 206–215, 224–227 , 232–233, 262–263. *Historia* I,ix; C. de Lollis, *Scritti di Cristoforo Colombo*, in *Raccolta di Documenti e Studi Pubblicati dalla R. Commissione Colombiana pel Quarto Centenario dalla Scoperta dell'America* I (ii) (Rome, 1894), 297.

admiral's note to Chapter VIII of the *Imago Mundi*, and the quotation from Augustine's *City of God* (Book XVII, xxiv), which Columbus appends to his copy of Pius's *Historia* (the passages in defense of the prophet Ezra, that is, and Ezra's estimate that the earth's landmass occupied six-sevenths of the surface of the globe), are vital parts of this whole argument.[4] The admiral set out, then, from the first, with high and hopeful expectations of marvels quite close at hand, but expectations perfectly in accordance with medieval sources of the most respectable kind.

Eight days out from Gomera, in the Canaries, the sailors were quite sure they were near land, for they saw what they took to be a tern.[5] Toscanelli's letter and, especially, Behaim's globe would indeed have led them to expect Antillia at about these latitudes, a group Behaim depicts as two islands and which Columbus was later prepared to extend, as the lesser Antilles, to many more.[6] The legend of Antillia lay ready to strengthen such expectations, and to help Columbus to reassure his men with the prospect of a possible landfall on their return. Five days later the admiral thought they were still passing between islands and manifested great strength of character by wishing to press on to the Indies (though hoping openly for further enlightenment on the way back). This decision and the one recorded in the Journal under 6 October, whereby Pinzon's wish to steer southwest by west for more islands is rejected by the admiral, are again perfectly in accordance with the directions given on the globe, and with Columbus's wish above all to reach the richest areas of the east.

---

4. De Lollis, *Scritti*, 366. Buron, *Ymago*, 210–211. The whole chapter from Augustine, copied out by Columbus in Latin, may be read in English in *edit.* E. M. Sanford and W. M. Green, *Saint Augustine the City of God Against the Pagans* v (Loeb, London, and Harvard, 1965), 356–359.

5. Entry for Friday 14 September in the journal of the first voyage; C. Jane, *The Journal of Christopher Columbus* (London, 1960), 10.

6. Morison, *Journals*, 53 suggests that they might have expected the islands of St. Brendan, but this is less likely, for reasons to be explored in the next chapter.

The landfall at San Salvador on 12 October, and the successive discovery of many small islands, were, of course, readily conformable with the mappae mundi, as, it seems, was the chart Columbus carried with him,[7] but Cipangu caused endless confusion. At first, Columbus believed Cuba to be Cipangu, and, when he wrote his entry in his journal for Wednesday 24 October, presumably thought himself to be heading for Cipangu's northern shore.[8] He subsequently decided he was skirting the coast of Cathay. This initial mistake, and the substitution of what, with hindsight, we now know to have been another one, are both of them immediately understandable when one looks at Behaim. Behaim's Cipangu was an enormous island north to south.[9] It was, however, comparitively narrow east to west. Thus, as Columbus in fact proceeded along a seemingly very long shore northwestwards, he decided with very good reason that it was not Cipangu after all, but must instead be the mainland. Pinzon, captain of the Pinta, had in any case understood from the Indians he consulted:

> that this Cuba was a city, and that land was a very extensive mainland which stretched far to the north, and that the king of that land was at war with the Grand Khan, whom they called "cami", and his land or city they called "Saba" and by many other names. The admiral [Las Casas is reporting] resolved to . . . send a present to the king of the land, and send him the letter of the Sovereigns . . . and he says that he must attempt to go to the Grand Khan, for he thought he was in that

---

7. Jane, *The Journal*, 14.

8. This passage is quoted at the beginning of Chapter 1.

9. "about the same distance as from Londonderry to Gibraltar, and crossing the Tropic of Cancer, which also runs through the Canaries"; Morison, *Journals*, 81.

neighbourhood, or to the city of Catay, which belongs to the Grand Khan, which, as he says, is very large, as he was told before he set out from Spain.[10]

By 1 November Columbus was absolutely convinced that he was coasting mainland China;

"It is certain," says the admiral, "that this is the mainland, and that I am," he says, "before Zayto and Quisay, a hundred leagues, a little more or less, distant from one and the other, and this appears clearly from the sea, which is of a different character from what it has been to the present, and yesterday, going to the northwest, I found that it was becoming cold."[11]

Thus, he made his famous decision to turn back, missing the shores of Florida and failing to see Cuba ever as an island. We are equipped now to see, however, how very wise, in fact, this decision was, and how well attuned to the best of the advice Columbus had at his disposal. It was on their journeys *southwards* from Quinsay to Zayton, after all, that Marco Polo and John of Marignolli, for example, had come upon the true riches of Cathay. The northern areas mentioned in Pipino's version of his *Travels* were distinctly uninviting, full of snow and ice and wildernesses. Sail a little too far northwest and one might come upon the Tartars or the terrifying Rukh mentioned by both Marco Polo and Sinbad.[12] Also, some of the mappae mundi we have discussed placed the dreadful Gog and Magog and their followers in these regions. Pius II had allowed in his *Historia Rerum* (I,ii) that one might possibly sail this far, and Columbus

---

10. Jane, *The Journal*, 49. Las Casas suggests that the Indians here had been talking of Cubanacan, a district in the interior of Cuba, and that this had led the Spaniards to take the word for "El Gran Can"; Morison, *Journals*, 85.

11. *Ibid.*, 51.

12. *De Consuetudinibus* III, xl,xlv-1.

had noted as much with some vigor in his postille,[13] but it would hardly serve to do so on this voyage. The decision to turn back, then, made absolute sense, and was readily reconcilable with all of the information we can suppose Columbus had before him. He might, furthermore, still come upon Cipangu as he returned.

If Cuba was not Cipangu but the mainland, then the island he did in fact come upon in his retreat southeastwards from Cathay/Cuba, the island he later named Hispaniola and is now Haiti, must be Cipangu instead. And so, he declared at first, it was. This perception, true in some part to his map and his authorities, especially Marco Polo and Toscanelli, seemed once more to be confirmed by the Indians he interrogated:

> among the other places which they named where gold was found, they spoke of Cipangu, which they call "Cibao", and they declared that there was a great quantity of gold there, and that the cacique carries banners of beaten gold. He concludes that Cipangu is on that island, and that there is much gold and spice and mastic and rhubarb.[14]

This, again, was in absolute accord with the information given in Behaim. In this second entry to the journal of the first voyage (under Friday 5 January), Columbus had earlier observed a land formation looking, as he said, like "a very lovely pavilion" (*alfaneque*, or Moorish tent). Behaim, interestingly, depicts a Moorish pavilion at about this point on his Cipangu, and it is possible, then, that Columbus had a markedly similar map before him, from which he looked hopefully across as he approached the island of Haiti. Behaim places tent-like dwellings

---

13. De Lollis, *Scritti*, 292.

14. Jane, *The Journal*, 118, 137. This "Cibao" was indeed in Haiti. Morison suggests, convincingly, that that confusion came about because the Spaniards pronounced "Cipangu" also with an "S"; *Journals*, 133.

all over the east and the Indies on his map, and this picturing may perhaps be related, too, to the frequency with which Columbus mentions tent-like dwellings in his journal of the first voyage.[15]

The island of Cipangu, however, on the basis of Marco Polo, Toscanelli, and all maps similar to Behaim, should have been both far further from the mainland of Cathay than was this island, and far more evidently filled with cities. Thus, when Hispaniola was inspected more closely, and charted, and the central districts further explored on the second voyage, Columbus began to abandon the idea that it could be their Cipangu/Japan. The letter he wrote home to his sovereigns giving an account of the first voyage shows no sign of this earlier association. Perhaps he had begun to change his mind then. There were, after all, many other possibilities. The Bible offered excellent ones. 1 Kings 10:11 speaks for instance, as we have now often noted, of the fleet which plied the seas from Ophir to King Solomon, bringing gold and gems and spices to him, as the Queen of Sheba did. According to the same chapter (1 Kings 10:22) the fleet of Tarshish sailed with the fleet from Ophir, and, every three years, brought Solomon gold, silver, ivory, apes and peacocks, just like the quinquereme in John Masefield's *Cargoes*.[16] 2 Chronicles 9:22 speaks of Hiram's fleet from Ophir once again. Tarshish, through Psalm 71:10–11, and its kings of Tarshish and the isles and kings of Sheba and Seba (Saba in the Latin) was also associated in the Middle Ages with the three magi/kings of Matthew 2:1–12, and their gifts of gold, frankincense and myrrh.

---

15. Marignolli also, we might remark, had drawn attention to the fragile palm-fronded cabins of the inhabitants of these regions; *edit.* J. Emler, *Kronika Marignolova*, in *Fontes Rerum Bohemicarum* iii (Prague, 1878), 500.

16. Quinquireme of Nineveh from distant Ophir
Rowing home to haven in sunny Palestine,
With a cargo of ivory,
And apes and peacocks,
Sandalwood, cedarwood, and sweet white wine.

Columbus's medieval reading also offered him manifold opportunities to ponder upon such associations and, as we have seen, he seized upon these opportunities. D'Ailly's *Imago Mundi* (XXIV) speaks of Tarshish in connection with Cathay. Columbus added a tremendous postillum to this chapter, a postillum filled with (accurate) biblical chapters and verses, and learned references to such as St. Jerome and Nicholas of Lyra and someone he calls a great Carthusian:[17]

> Note that the kingdom of Tarshish is at the end of the Orient, in the end of Katay. It was in this country, at the place called Ophir, that Solomon and Jehoshaphat sent ships which brought back gold, silver and ivory. . . . Note that the king of Tarshish came to the Lord at Jerusalem, and spent a year and thirteen days en route, as the blessed Jerome has it[18]

He adds to his copy of the *Historia* of Pope Pius both 2 Chronicles 9:22 and a redoubtable passage from the *Antiquities* of Josephus in which the latter comments again on these crucial sections of the Bible, and stresses especially the rich merchandise of this fleet.[19] The later sections of Columbus's *Book of Prophecies* are filled with references to Tarshish.[20] Finally, there is the

---

17. Buron, *Ymago*, i, 306–307, could not identify this figure, but Columbus must here be referring to the *Expositio Psalterii Davidis* of the Carthusian Ludolf of Saxony (d, 1377), and, in particular, to the latter's exposition of Psalm 71:10. Ludolf was well known in Spain as "El Cartujano." His *Expositio* was printed in 1491 and, in default of a modern edition, I have verified the reference in a copy of the 1491 printing, held in the Wing collection of the Newberry Library, Chicago.

18. Translated in Morison, *Journals*, 22.

19. De Lollis, *Scritti*, 365, 366–367. The passage, made up of two extracts from Josephus's *Antiquities* run together, VIII, 163–164 and 176–183, may be read in English in *edit*. H. St. J. Thackeray and R. Marcus, *Josephus* v (Loeb, London, and Harvard, 1966), 658–661, 664–671.

20. De Lollis, *Scritti*, 148–153.

evidence of the *Chronicle* of John of Marignolli. John had sailed from the Malabar to an island he called Saba (probably Java or Sumatra). It was connected with the realm of the Queen of Sheba, Solomon's friend (it was still, in fact, much under the dominion of women), and it was close to the region whence the three kings had come.[21]

Ophir, Sheba/Saba, the three kings and Tarshish and the isles, then, on the authority of the Bible, medieval exegesis of these passages offered under highly respectable names, and at least one highly accredited observer, were readily available as possible solutions to the problem of identifying the more important of the Indies, and as sources of those great riches for which Columbus continued to hope. An obvious alternative to Cipangu lay to hand. We cannot be sure quite when Columbus made his additions to d'Ailly; whether before or after he had solved the problem to his own satisfaction. We cannot be certain yet that he even knew of the *Chronicle* of John of Marignolli, though the next chapter will make clear, I hope, that this is very likely. When he made his annotation to Pliny on the matter of amber, the admiral was still juggling with three possible names for Haiti.[22] But Michael de Cuneo, gentleman volunteer on the second voyage, tells us that Columbus, by this voyage, had absolutely identified Hispaniola/Haiti with Saba:

> "Gentlemen" [Michael here purports to give Columbus's own words], "I wish to bring us to a place whence departed the three Magi who came to adore Christ, the which place is called Saba." When once we made that place and asked the name of the place it was answered

---

21. *Edit.* Emler, *Kronika*, 497, 502, 512, 583.

22. "la isola de Feyti [Haiti] vel de Ofir vel de Cipango, a la quale habio posto nome Spagnola"; de Lollis, *Scritti*, 472. For the whole passage, see Chapter 2 above.

Sobo. Then the Lord Admiral said that it was the same word, but that they could not pronounce it correctly.[23]

The letter Syllacio wrote to the Duke of Milan in December 1494, another important source for the second voyage, confirms Cuneo's information admirably when it tells of Columbus's orders for the exploration of the district of Cibao, on Hispaniola;

> The Admiral sent (Hojeda and Gorbalon) with a company of light-armed troops to the interior of the land of the Sabaeans to make their way to King Saba, a monarch of great wealth who, as he had learned from the Indians, resided at no great distance. It is believed that these are the Sabaeans from whom frankincense is obtained and who are mentioned by our histories and foreign chronicles. For according to the well-known text, kings shall come forth from Saba bearing gold and incense, and the island produces these in great abundance.[24]

Again, this solution found support in, was perhaps indeed initially prompted by, his medieval maps. Ophir is marked on the Hereford Map as one of the islands off the coast of India, near "Taprobane" (then possibly equated with Ceylon), and also close to Pliny's islands of Crise and Argire.[25] Behaim

---

23. Michael de Cuneo of Savona's merry account of this second voyage is a valuable source in default of a surviving journal. He had been in all probability a childhood friend of Columbus, and wrote his account, in Italian, in a letter to his own friend, Hieronymo Annari, when he got back to Savona in 1495. Both Michael de Cuneo, and Syllacio, in his letter to the Duke of Milan, telling of the second voyage, refer to this association. Morison, *Journals*, 227–228, 244.

24. Ibid., 244. The reference here is to the psalm, and to its association with Matthew's three magi, not to the passage from Kings suggested by Morison. The Syllacio letter, or tract, was a distillation into Latin by the Sicilian Professor of Pavia, Syllacio, of letters written to him in Spanish by a friend who had actually been on the second voyage.

25. *Natural History* VI,xxiii,80; *edit.* H. Rackham, *Pliny Natural History* ii (Loeb, Cambridge, Mass, and London, 1961), 389–399.

places "Crisis" quite close to his Cipangu, and Argire somewhat further south, a placing which readily admits of the intrusion of Hispaniola or Saba among the many unnamed islands there. The divorce, therefore, of Hispaniola from Cipangu, rendered a marriage between Hispaniola and one of the rich islands of the realm of Tarshish, close to Ophir, wholly plausible. The crucial aspect of the identification of Hispaniola/Haiti with Saba, and the one for us to note here, is that the solution Columbus in the end advanced, was a totally logical one, and wholly in accord with his medieval authorities once more.

Other aspects of Behaim's settings and descriptions are, at first sight, somewhat less encouraging, for he places Saba and one set of three kings in Africa, and Tarshish, Ophir and another set of kings on the mainland of India—a duplication in the matter of kings and a muddle in the matter of Saba which show how puzzling the whole matter was to traditional mapmakers, and how wide were the choices they offered; especially when they drew, as Behaim did, upon Ptolemy's mistaken extension of the mainland and coasts of India. It is well to keep constantly in mind how appallingly varied and confusing were the possibilities with which his maps confronted Columbus, for only by so doing can we appreciate a most important fact; namely, that some of his errors of identification were, in reality, deductions of a deeply impressive order from the most complex of evidence. Behaim does help us a little to understand this particular deduction, for his second set of kings is placed in Marco Polo's "Loach," not far from Cathay, and one of the three, furthermore, is marked as ruling on the mainland of India opposite "Taprobana."[26] This would put this king, and Tarshish and the isles, very close to the Hereford Map's Ophir, and so well within range of John of Marignolli's and of Columbus's Saba. No one knew for certain how big was the "Aurea Chersonese" nor how far distant it was in fact

26. Ravenstein, *Martin Behaim*, 86, 95–96.

from India and Cathay, respectively. Behaim founds his representation of India and the far east upon Ptolemy's mistaken one; yet he rejects Ptolemy's idea of an Indian Ocean enclosed by land. Columbus had seen Ptolemy's distances and Ptolemy's view of the Indian Ocean rejected at the start of his adventures. Perhaps the great Alexandrian geographer might have to be overriden once again. We may here be dealing with a source intermediate between the Hereford Map and Behaim, and with a speculative correction of this kind. But these possibilities still rendered an equation between Hispaniola and Saba a perfectly credible one. And Cipangu/Japan, Ophir with its rich merchandise, and the gold-and-silver-bearing islands of Chrise and Argire remained, of course, to be discovered (with the help of Columbus's sovereigns) on some glorious future journey.

Columbus betrayed no such flexibility in the matter of Cuba/Cathay. Clearly there were doubts in the minds of his sailors about the idea that Cuba was mainland and not island, or the admiral would never have had to demand of them a sworn declaration that Cuba/Juana was the mainland of Cathay, as he did, on 12 June 1494, during the second voyage. Cuneo (one of the few who refused to sign the declaration) tells how his brother was further assured by the admiral that, if he sailed north from Hispaniola/Saba he would certainly find Cathay.[27] All of the descriptions advanced on the first and second voyages of that which we now know to have been Cuba, and which we shall further explore below, were, then, to Columbus, descriptions of the further exploration of Cathay (or, more precisely, of the Mangi of the great Khan's empire).

Again, all is readily explicable when we look at Columbus's supposed maps. By the second voyage, of course, Behaim's dimensions and approximate distances had been shown clearly to be fallible, but still some general outlines might be trusted.

---

27. Morison, *Journals*, 277

Thus, as the admiral in fact traveled the southern coast of Cuba on this second voyage, he saw himself, and with good reason, to be traveling the coast of Mangi. It was understandable, then, that the moment he heard of Jamaica, he should have wished, as he did, to inspect it closely, for this was presumably yet another of the rich isles of Tarshish. It might even have been the gold-bearing island of Chrise, mentioned by both Pliny and Ptolemy, for, as Cuneo tells us, the Indians had told him it was full of gold. There was no gold, of course; but Bernaldez speaks of the hopeful signs which may have fulfilled at least some of their expectations. The "mainland" close to Jamaica had two crop-bearing seasons a year; a well-known characteristic of India and perhaps of the islands of the Indian Ocean.[28] There were plenty of large and well-armed canoes, as one version of the adventures of Sinbad the Sailor would lead them to suppose there would be. This version of Sinbad, with its mention of ivory (if not apes and peacocks) might lead them also to think themselves near to Ophir, and so to confirm the identification of Saba.[29]

When, on the second voyage, the three caravels turned back to Cuba from Jamaica in mid-May 1494, they *should* then, upon

---

28. Bernaldez on the second voyage, in C. Jane, *Select Documents Illustrating the Four Voyages of Columbus* i (London, 1930), 120–121. The capacity to produce two crops a year was, in a passage deriving ultimately from Pliny, attributed to India by Pierre d'Ailly in Chapter XV of his *Imago Mundi*; Buron, *Ymago*, i, 260–261.

29. "They [that is, the islanders of Jamaica] have more canoes than in any other part of those regions, and the largest that have yet been seen. . . . As soon as the admiral arrived off the coast of Jamaica, there immediately came out against him quite seventy canoes, all full of people with darts as weapons. They advanced out to sea with warlike shouts and in battle array", Bernaldez, in Jane, *Select Documents*, i, 124–125. The Calcutta version of Sinbad's seventh voyage tells of a "number of canoes, wherein were men like devils armed with bows and arrows, swords and daggers; habited in mail-coats and other armoury." Sinbad was obviously among ivory-yielding islands, like Ophir, on this voyage for, after a bruising encounter with an elephant, he is rewarded with a huge find of tusks; R. F. Burton, *The Book of the Thousand Nights and One Night* iv (London, 1894), 418–419

their return to the supposed mainland, have come quickly upon Zaiton and the Golden Chersonese. The *Book* of Sir John Mandeville, of course, gave some comfort to them in the matter of the great numbers of islands through which they had to thread their way,[30] and the crews all saw some indicative methods of fishing, great numbers of cormorants and some enormous turtles, which was hopeful.[31] The successive disappointments, the shoals, the curious colors of the waters and the impenetrable vegetation must, however, have been very distressing, and may perhaps have accounted in part for the admiral's poor health upon the later part of this second voyage.

Cuba was first Cipangu, then mainland Cathay. Hispaniola/ Haiti was first Cipangu, then one of the isles of Tarshish near to Ophir, most likely Saba or Sheba. Jamaica was yet another of the isles of Tarshish, and should have been full of riches worthy of Solomon. Though some of his sailors wavered before these definitive identifications, Columbus, if we are to believe his own words and actions, refused to do so. I have tried to demonstrate that Columbus could have found, for each of these identifications, good evidence in his medieval maps. We have begun, in addition, to see how biblical texts and the geographical observations of certain of his authorities, could, in association with these maps, provide alternative identifications at need. All might then justify those changes of assumption made necessary by physical progress. Even as difficulties mounted, in short, Columbus had no need to step outside his rich and complex medieval world. His final

---

30. Bernaldez, in Jane, *Select Documents*, i, 130–131.

31. Bernaldez, in Jane, *Select Documents*, i, 150–151. These are also described in Ferdinand's life of his father, in the passages on the second voyage. See *transl.* J. M. Cohen, *The Four Voyages of Christopher Columbus* (Harmondsworth, 1969), 174. The notice taken of them will be more fully discussed below.

inflexibility sprang, paradoxically, from the very flexibility, scope and latitude his medieval sources allowed him. Columbus was not required, then, to leave or to doubt them. And so, or so I would argue here, for the very *best* of reasons, he rarely did.

In order to explore the riches of this world a little further, and so to deepen our understanding, and indeed appreciation, of its hold upon the great admiral, we shall now change the perspective just a little. We shall turn our attention directly to those of his medieval sources we have in writing, and then to the accounts Columbus himself provided of the things he saw on the voyages. Many of the written sources underlay, and were indeed inscribed upon, his maps, and notably so upon Behaim's globe. Others were, as we have seen, consulted independently, and perhaps by oral means.

I shall argue here that the continued correspondences between these sources and the actual physical experiences of the admiral as his exploration progressed, continued to affect Columbus's understanding, both powerfully and progressively, of all the products and creatures, animal and human, whose discovery he claimed. And they affected his descriptions of them. The many similarities upon which we shall come do not reduce the value of his journals and letters. The admiral's descriptions were not wholly dependent upon preconditioned ideas. Any venturer into the unknown needs texts and stories to guide him, and can use them as such without necessarily becoming their slave. To assert that Columbus was governed by an inner eye would be too much. When all this is said, however, there are, in his case, some echoes which are very notable. There are similarities between certain of the medieval authorities we know he used, and some of the accounts of a given people, custom or product, which he gave to his sovereigns, which are exceedingly striking; and some of these can seem, in addition, to be more than a little forced. This combination does indicate that, on occasion, Columbus's sources came close to exercising at least a measure of control over him. I shall try to show here that they in fact formed the great admiral's expectations, and directed his gaze, far more often than we have been inclined to recognize. They led him to emphasize certain aspects of his discoveries to the exclusion of others, tinted what he saw, and dictated at least a part of what he said.

Both Marco Polo and Behaim describe the features of Cipangu. To Marco Polo its principal feature is that it is full of gold, bursting at the seams with it indeed, and that in part because Cipangu is too far from the mainland for the merchants of Cathay to go there. The lord of Cipangu has a palace roofed and paved with gold, and a great treasury full of pearls and precious stones. He and his subjects are "white, civilized and well-favoured," even though they worship idols.[32] Columbus marks in his copy of the *De Consuetudinibus* the description of the amounts of gold, "aurum in copia maxima," and the red pearls of which Cipangu boasts, and also the idols.[33] Behaim confirms the account of riches in gold and jewels (referring, indeed, to Marco Polo), stresses, as Marco Polo did, the idolatry of its inhabitants, and speaks too of spices, nutmeg and pepper.[34] Columbus, rather hopefully, found aloes on the outer islands as he approached, as he thought, Cipangu,[35] and mussel shells which he took to be indicators of pearl fisheries on Cuba/Cipangu itself.[36] He also found splendid houses and, apparently, evidence of idolatry—"many images made like

32. *De Consuetudinibus* III,ii, vii. *Travels*, III,ii, iv; *transl.* H. Yule, *The Book of Ser Marco Polo* ii (London, 1903), 253–255, 264. I cite the translation into English of the *Travels* here for convenience of reference.

33. L. Giovannini, *Il Milione con le Postille de Cristofero Colombo* (Rome, 1985), 237,241.

34. Ravenstein, *Martin Behaim*, 89. Behaim's texts are in German, but Ravenstein translates them into English.

35. 21 October; Jane, *The Journal*, 40.

36. 28 October; ibid., 46.

women and many heads like masks, very well worked."[37]
So far the imprint of Columbus's sources could be made
to correspond with what he found.

When the identification of Cipangu with Cuba had been
abandoned and that of Cathay substituted for Cipangu,
Columbus's men reported villages of 1,000 houses, and gold
and spices and pepper and rhubarb on the next candidate for
the position of Cipangu, Hispaniola. Still all was as the sources
led them to expect it to be.[38] When Hispaniola had to be
identified instead with Saba, this change again takes place first
of all against the background of Marco Polo's description of
Cipangu.[39] The biblical imagery, and perhaps the passages
from Marignolli, which then displace Marco Polo, however,
extends its sway well through the second voyage. Syllacio's
description of Hispaniola is rhapsodic, and he claims not merely
the usual spices and rhubarb for Hispaniola/Saba, but silk and
frankincense as well.

> I should be justified in calling this island fertile whether
> it be an Arabian or an Indian isle. In addition to all kinds
> of vegetables it yields large quantities of cinnamon, which
> men of ancient times were not permitted to harvest except
> with a god's permission. Ginger grows there as well as
> Indian spice with branches three cubits long and white bark.
> It abound in silk, is redolent with castor (which we call
> musk), and offers favourable conditions for the growing
> of frankincense. . . . The place abounds in rhubarb, a useful
> remedy in all maladies. Pliny calls it raconia. . . . Wax-
> bearing trees flourish there; and wool-bearing trees, very
> useful for bedding and cushions, also bloom. There is a

---

37. 29 October; ibid., 48.

38. 13 and 30 December, 1–4 January; ibid., 95, 130, 132–137.

39. Cipangu is far further from Cathay than Hispaniola is from Cuba. *De
Consuetudinibus* III, ii. *Travels* III, ii; Yule, *The Book*, 253.

wide production of flax-like thread, thin as a hair, which
the natives use for thread, and out of this they manufacture
ropes stronger and more durable than those made of hemp.
There is a great variety of odiferous trees[40]

As we know, some of these "finds" were hopeful ones only.
But many were encouraged by the sources. The "wool-bearing
trees," for instance, were both really there in Haiti, and well
described by, for example, Mandeville, as a characteristic of
the islands beyond Cathay.[41] The deceptions were most
convincingly compounded.

I have mentioned how Behaim's map of Cipangu, with its
Moorish tent, corresponded at first with Columbus's
Cipangu/Cuba and the tented appearance of Monte Christi.
When Cuba became mainland Cathay, or Mangi, many more
written preconditions of the admiral's expressed convictions are
to be found. The anxiety and forcedness with which, at times,
Columbus appears to seize upon his written sources and
interpret, through them, his findings for his sovereigns, adds
great poignancy here to the story of his real discoveries. Marco
Polo, for instance, had described the coastal regions of Mangi
from Peking through Quinsay to Zaiton, and he had recorded
carefully the wealth and customs of the region. There were all
manner of spices and medicinal plants; aloes, camphor,
cinnamon, cloves, ginger, galingale, nutmeg, pepper, rhubarb.
There was salt and sandalwood and silk and sugar and cotton
and "India nut" (the coconut). We have seen in Chapter 2 how
carefully Columbus made notes upon all these descriptions, and
how he had marked too, in his notes on the _Imago Mundi_ and
on Pope Pius's _Historia_, numbers of these products. There were
also great rivers and harbors for the ships of the Khan.

40. Morison, _Journals_, 242.

41. XXIX; _transl._ M. Letts, _Mandeville's Travels, Texts and Translations_ i (London, 1953), 186.

Accordingly, on the first voyage Columbus finds rivers and
harbors in Cuba for such ships, and cotton and aromatic plants
and "lignaloe" as Marco Polo had. Pinzon purports to find
nutmeg and cinnamon (though Columbus corrects him).[42]
Columbus, this time in error himself, finds India nuts (Sinbad
had also found these). Ciamba, near Mangi, also produces
musk, says Behaim. Columbus marks a strong smell of musk
when sailing, as he thought, off the coast of Cathay on 17
November.[43] Off Hispaniola his sailors identify (wrongly)
Chinese rhubarb, and in Hispaniola Columbus finds (also
wrongly) a spice "more valuable than pepper or allspice."[44]

A notable passage in Marco Polo tells of the peacefulness of
the inhabitants of Quinsay:

> They know nothing of handling arms, and keep none in
> their houses. You hear of no feuds or noisy quarrels or
> dissensions of any kind among them. . . . And this familiar
> intimacy is free of all jealousy or suspicion of the conduct
> of their women.[45]

This passage about the peace-loving nature of the Chinese is picked
up in Pope Pius's *Historia*, (I,ix) and is noted by Columbus.
Marignolli too comments upon the peace-loving natures of the
naked peoples thereabouts and in the region of Paradise.[46] This

42. 1–5 November; ibid., 50–54. Aloe wood was one of the products of Ciamba,
adjoining Mangi, according to Marco Polo (III, v). Behaim specifically mentions
aloe wood, in his notes upon Ciamba, and speaks of nutmeg there too;
Ravenstein, *Martin Behaim*, 85.

43. Jane, *The Journal*, 65. Morison, *Journals*, 97, says the Indian nuts were not
coconuts but the "Crysobolanus icaco."

44. Morison, *Journals*, 141.

45. *Travels* II, lxxvii; Yule, *The Book*, ii, 204.

46. *Edit.* Emler, *Kronica*, 500.

may throw a little more light upon the care with which Columbus reports upon the peacefulness of the inhabitants of Cuba, and, indeed, of all the peaceable peoples he could find as he traversed, as he thought, the areas of which Marco Polo, Pius and Marignolli spoke:

> The People are very gentle
>
> these people are very unskilled in arms
>
> These people are very mild and very timorous, naked, as I have said, without arms and without law
>
> "They are," says the admiral, "a people very free from wickedness and unwarlike; they are all naked, men and women, as their mothers bore them. It is true that the women wear only a piece of cotton, large enough to cover their privy parts and no more, and they are of very good appearance, and are not very black, less so than those of the Canaries."[47]

Not every part of such a description would hold good of the respectable citizens of Quinsay, of course, but Marco Polo had spoken in similar terms of near-nakedness in the nearby eastern parts of India, again mentioning the merest scrap of cloth.[48] Columbus's observations, then, are precisely those we might expect of a man who read the *De Consuetudinibus* of Friar Pipino, the *Historia* of Pope Pius, and perhaps the *Chronicle* of John of Marignolli, who had a map or maps similar to those which informed Behaim, and who thought himself to be traveling the coasts of Cathay. There were things he did find, and others, great cities and gold and iron especially, that he as yet did not, but all encouraged him to believe ever more strongly in his medieval world. Pliny speaks of the iron in China as being of

---

47. 13 and 14 October, 4 and 6 November; Jane, *The Journal*, 26,28,52,57.

48. *De Consuetudinibus* III, xxiii. *Travels* III, xvii; Yule, *The Book*, ii, 338.

the highest quality.[49] In a passage of great interest, and one to which I have already drawn attention, Sir John Mandeville spoke of the protective stones which were carried by men of the Indies; stones which rendered iron weapons useless, and so superfluous.[50] These references might in part explain the numerous mentions Columbus makes in his journal of the lack of iron in these regions. The admiral's descriptions, both of that which appeared before him and of that which obstinately refused to do so echo and reecho his medieval sources, and were deeply influenced by them; far more deeply so than has been in general allowed.

Cuba/Mangi should also, according to Behaim, and according to Marco Polo, on whom Behaim here relies, have yielded cane of an extraordinary size, and pearls and remarkable snakes and worms, as well as, eventually, the Great Khan himself:

> In this region are fished many pearls; various snakes and worms are likewise caught.

Columbus comments on the canes to be found in Mangi (*hyrundines grossi*) in his annotations to the *De Consuetudinibus*.[51] On the first voyage Columbus is much preoccupied with cane, and with pearl fishing and large snakes. He records the cane weapons of the Indians, observes when he finds cane on the

---

49. *Natural History* XXIV, xli, *transl.* H. Rackham, *Pliny Natural History* ix (Loeb, London, and Cambridge, Mass, 1968), 232–233. Odoric of Pordenone also speaks of Seric iron, and (in Chapter 22 of his story of his own travels) draws special attention to peoples who had weapons tipped with iron and peoples who had not; H. Yule, *Cathay and the Way Thither* i (London, 1866), 91, 94.

50. XXI; Letts, *Mandeville's*, 135.

51. Ravenstein, *Martin Behaim*, 92–92. *De Consuetudinibus* III, lxvi. *Travels* II, lxxix; Yule, *The Book*, ii, 219. Giovannini, *Il Milione*, 223.

shores, and orders searches to be made for pearls.[52] He also records encounters with large sea snakes in a way which suggests he found these particularly important:

> As I was going round one of these lagoons, I saw a snake, which we killed, and I am bringing its skin to Your Highnesses. When it saw us, it threw itself into the lagoon and we went in after it, for the water is not very deep, until we killed it with our spears. It is seven palms in length; I believe there are many similar snakes here in these lagoons.[53]

Many of the most striking of the resemblances between supposed eyewitness description and medieval source, however, become evident when Columbus and his reporters deal with what seem to them amazing customs, and with monsters. In his letter to his sovereigns after the first voyage, the great admiral tells of the province of Avan in Cuba/Cathay, where there are men with tails. This echoes an entry in Marco Polo's *Travels* in which he speaks of tailed men in the kingdom of Lambri (perhaps Sumatra).[54] Columbus speaks also, on that voyage, of the fears the Indians he had on board expressed of the people on Bohio/Hispaniola, who:

> had only one eye and the face of a dog. The admiral believed they were lying, and he thought that they must be under the dominion of the Grand Khan who captured them.[55]

---

52. As, for example, on 16 November; Jane, *The Journal*, 64. When his search for pearls is unsuccessful, he concludes that the time of year is wrong, and that May or June would yield better results. This is a direct reference to Marco Polo III, xvi where he remarks that pearl fishing is over in May; Yule, *The Book*, 332.

53. 21 October; ibid., 40.

54. *De Consuetudinibus* III, xviii. Columbus notes "homines cum cauda"; Giovannini, *Il Milione*, 250. *Travels* III, xi; Yule, *The Book*, ii, 299. It echoes Mandeville too.

55. 23 and 26 November; Jane, *The Journal*, 68, 74.

The Grand Khan might well have told them such stories, for, if Marco Polo was to be believed, monsters of this order did indeed live within his reach.[56] Marco Polo and Pope Pius too seem to have rendered Columbus peculiarly alert to the existence of male and female islands during this first voyage (if we may number these among the monstrous); islands, that is, inhabited solely by males and females, respectively, apart from certain restricted times of the year when the necessary task of procreation is attempted.[57] Pius II's Amazons (I, xx) behaved in a similar manner, and Columbus noted that they had many settlements in Asia.[58] Thus, when Columbus hears of the female island of "Matinino" (later Martinique) he reports the event carefully, for it reinforces his conviction that he is in Asia and among the island of the Indies.[59] The same holds true of the supposed Sirens. Columbus claimed he had seen Sirens off the coast of Hispaniola on 9 January (though their appearance disappointed him somewhat).[60] Behaim has an entry about Sirens, near Cipangu:

> Here are found sea monsters such as Sirens and other fish. And if anyone desire to know more of these curious people, and peculiar fish in the sea or animals on the land, let him read the books of Pliny, Isidore, Aristotle, Strabo, the "Specula" of Vincent and many others.[61]

---

56. *De Consuetudinibus* III, xxi. "People have heads of dogs and eyes likewise"; *Travels* III,xiii; Yule, *The Book*, ii, 309.

57. *De Consuetudinibus* III, xxxvii. Columbus notes it; Giovannini, *Il Milione*, 271. *Travels* III,xxxi; Yule, *The Book*, 404. Male and female islands are marked in the Indian Ocean on Behaim's globe, and Behaim shares Marco Polo's view that such practices are Christian; Ravenstein, *Martin Behaim*, 77.

58. de Lollis, *Scritti*, 311–312.

59. "The admiral also says that he learned that towards the east, there was an island where there were none save women only." 6 January; Jane, *The Journal*, 140.

60. Jane, *The Journal*, 143.

61. Ravenstein, *Martin Behaim*, 86.

They are depicted clearly on the Catalan Atlas in the Indian Ocean. Columbus, I have argued, had indeed read such writings, and seen such maps.[62]

In his record of the second voyage, a record which seems to derive directly from Columbus, Andres Bernaldez speaks of the tracks of animals the voyagers found as they pressed westwards towards India, along that which they took to be the southern mainland of Cathay. They judged the tracks to be those of lions and griffons. Bernaldez tells also of cranes "twice as large as those of Castile."[63] The first two of these creatures are, with the best will in the world, hard definitively to associate with Cuba; but Pliny and d'Ailly had spoken of the lions of India. In his chapter (XVI) on the marvels of India, moreover, d'Ailly had included ancient passages from Solinus (most probably via Honorius) which told of the Macrobians of India who fought with griffons, and the pygmies, two cubits high, who fought with cranes. Columbus had made notes on all these passages.[64] Nothing was more probable, therefore, than that the three should be found together so close to the Indian mainland.

The word "cannibal" has come down to us, of course, because of the profound fears Columbus's peaceful "Indians" undoubtedly had of the man-eaters, or Caribs, they believed lived nearby. But, equally, Marco Polo and his other sources had led Columbus to expect them in the east, close to the

---

62. Many entries in Columbus's journals concern common or uncommon fish in addition to the one he makes under 16 November, in which he says that he has had a peculiarly strange specimen salted down for presentation to the sovereigns; Jane, *The Journal*, 64–65. On the Genoese Pitti Palace map (1457) there is recorded the fact that a monster fish, taken in the Indian Ocean, had been brought to Venice; Ravenstein, *Martin Behaim*, 88.

63. Jane, *Select Documents*, i, 144–145.

64. Buron, *Ymago*, i, 264–269.

dog-headed people, and on other islands as well.[65] Pius II
(I,ix) had spoken of cannabalism among the peoples of Cathay
and Columbus had marked the passage.[66] Syllacio, in his
report upon the second voyage, sees cannibals everywhere,
together with evidence that they eat their spoils of war, as
Marco Polo says.[67] Cannibalism necessarily attracts attention,
and we may of course be dealing here with customs that
were in fact shared both by Marco Polo's peoples of the
Indies and Cathay, and the native Americans with whom
Columbus all unknowingly came into contact. But just sometimes the flavor of the source is so pervasive as to lead one
to conclude that it has dictated the recording of the findings.
Take this passage from Cuneo on the second voyage, about the
customs of the carib-cannibals:

> We went to the temple of those Caribs, in which we found
> two wooden statues, arranged so that they look like a Pieta.
> We were told that whenever someone's father is sick, the
> son goes to the temple and tells the idol that his father is
> ill and that the idol says whether he should live or not; and
> he stays there until the idol answers yes or no. If he says
> no, the son goes home, cuts his father's head and then cooks
> it; I don't believe they eat it but truly when it is white they
> place it in the above mentioned temple.[68]

This bears a very singular resemblance to a passage in Marco
Polo about the customs of the people of Dagroian (possibly on
Sumatra), and also to one in Mandeville:

---

65. *De Consuetudinibus* II,lxvii, III,vii,xxi *Travels* II,lxxx, III,iv,xiii; Yule, *The
Book*, ii, 225, 264, 309. Columbus comments on the first passage.

66. De Lollis, *Scritti*, 297.

67. Morison, *Journals*, 233–236.

68. Ibid., 220.

> When one of them is ill they send for their sorcerers, and
> put the question to them, whether the sick man shall recover
> of his sickness or no. If they say that he will recover, then
> they let him alone till he gets better. But if the sorcerers
> foretell that the sick man is to die, the friends send for
> certain judges of theirs to put to death him who has thus
> been condemned by the sorcerers to die. These men come,
> and lay so many clothes upon the sick man's mouth that
> they suffocate him. And when he is dead they have him
> cooked, and gather together all the dead man's kin and eat
> him.[69]

The last sentence especially suggests that Cuneo may have had
such a passage in mind. Again, the two customs may have been
quite independently similar. The two peoples may even, just
conceivably, have learned the customs one from another. But
the medieval sources, or so it seems to me, were more than
helpful in alerting the discoverers to the possibility of such
practices, and in their recognition and description. They may
also stand behind the entry in Columbus's Journal of the first
voyage under 29 November (supposedly made off the coast of
Cathay):

> The sailors also found in one house a man's head in a small
> basket, covered with another basket, and hanging to the
> post of a house. They found another of the same kind in
> another village. The admiral believed that they must be
> the heads of some principal ancestors[70]

Whilst speaking of customs, one more similarity between report
and source, though one this time at a little distance from

---

69. *De Consuetudinibus* III,xvii. *Travels* III,x; Yule, *The Book*, 293. Columbus
notes "homines comedunt"; Giovannini, *Il Milione*, 249. Letts, *Mandeville's*,
140–141.

70. Jane, *The Journal*, 79.

Columbus's own writing, may perhaps claim our attention for a moment. In his *Life of the Admiral,* and when writing of the second voyage, Ferdinand Columbus tells of a remarkable fishing practice the sailors and Columbus observed when they were sailing (as they then thought) among the isles of the Indies:

> Their method is this: they tie thin cord to the tails of certain fishes which we call "remora" and send these after the other fish. These remora have a rough patch on their heads which extends down the spine and attaches itself to any other fish that comes near. When the Indian feels that the other fish has stuck he pulls on the cord and brings the two fish out together; and our men saw these fishermen bring out a turtle to whose neck this fish had attached itself. . . . I have seen them cling in this way to big sharks.[71]

This account gives every appearance of being based upon direct observation; but it remains true that Odoric of Pordenone advances a strangely similar description of fishing in Cathay with captive creatures (this time cormorants). A shorter Italian version in Ramusio's printed edition is even closer:

> we found many boats, and there was one of them employed in fishing by the aid of a certain fish called *Marigione.* The host had another such, and this he took and kept it by a cord attached to a fine collar. And this indeed is a creature that we have seen in our own seas where many call it the sea calf. . . . Mine host made him go in the water, and he began to catch quantities of fish with his mouth, always depositing them in the boat.[72]

---

71. *Transl.* J. M. Cohen, *The Four Voyages,* 175.

72. Both are quoted in Yule, *Cathay,* i, 112, and the translations are his. The shorter version of Odoric was not printed by Ramusio until 1574, but two Italian manuscript copies of it survive, both possibly of the fourteenth century. It is possible that Columbus himself had access to such a version.

With Ferdinand Columbus and Odoric of Pordenone we approach territories even more speculative than those upon which we began. Yet Ferdinand does seem to be reporting here information he had had from his father, either directly or through a lost journal of the second voyage. There are one or two seeming echoes of Odoric in the surviving sections of the journal of the first voyage.[73] Such echoes, although so distant, are still suggestive.

A final word needs to be said about Columbus and the medieval monsters. We have seen that the admiral was prepared to accept the existence, in his Indies, of tailed and one-eyed and dog-headed men, as well as that of cannibals; this all on the best of medieval authority. He is also, it seems, most receptive to human physical beauty. He remarks, for example, upon the comparitive whiteness of the native peoples he meets, upon their fine stature and straight limbs:

> In these islands I have so far found no human monstrosities, as many expected, but on the contrary the whole population is very well formed, nor are they negroes as in Guinea, but their hair is flowing and they are not born where there is intense force in the rays of the sun. . . . Thus I have found no monsters, nor had any report of any, except in an island "Carib" . . . which is inhabited by people who are regarded in all the islands as very fierce and who eat human flesh. . . . They are no more malformed than are the others, except that they have the custom of wearing their hair long like women. . . . They are ferocious among these other people who are cowardly to an excessive degree, but I make no more account of them than of the rest.[74]

---

73. This journal, for instance, frequently draws attention to the size of the turtles the sailors found; for example under 9 January, Jane, *The Journal*, 142–143. This is similar to a report by Odoric of massive turtles; Yule, *Cathay*, 96.

74. Jane, *The Journal*, 57, 200.

This passage prompted Jane to suggest that Columbus had the outrageous monsters of Mandeville XXII in mind when he dilated on this human excellence; and perhaps to some extent he had, but not quite in that spirit of trust Jane seems here to visit upon him. For Mandeville's picture of the monsters of the east was not without its challengers, even within the later Middle Ages. The matter of their very existence was still a most contentious one, and John of Marignolli, for instance, had taken up a firm position on it. The human monsters of which Pliny and Solinus spoke did not, he says, exist. There are no such monstrous men.[75] It looks from this passage, and within this context, as though Columbus may here be taking sides. His medievalism was not, then, of a wholly credulous kind; but still his medieval sources guided his eyes. They may not here distort his actual descriptions, but they seem once again, to have determined his selection of items upon which to report.

If we accept that there is indeed evidence, on the first two voyages, that Columbus's medieval sources affected both his vision and his reporting, then a further question still remains to be answered, perhaps the most interesting one of all. Was this correspondence between source and report largely an unconscious one, compounded of a tenacious memory and self-delusion brought on be disappointment? Was Columbus so saturated by his particular cosmology that it soaked through him, as it were, and seeped into his accounts? Or was the whole matter a little more intricate than that, and better within the admiral's control? Could Columbus *deliberately* have compounded this effect, perhaps to convince others who knew these same medieval sources, and who also respected them greatly? The two mental activites are, of course, by no means incompatible, though the second is a good deal more shrewd and more manipulative and

75. *Edit.* Emler, *Kronika*, 508–509.

exploitative than the first. Columbus might have been engaged in each of them—but if this was indeed the case, then which of them was uppermost? It may never be possible to answer such a question to our own absolute satisfaction; but we might perhaps bear it in mind as we press on through the admiral's two final expeditions.

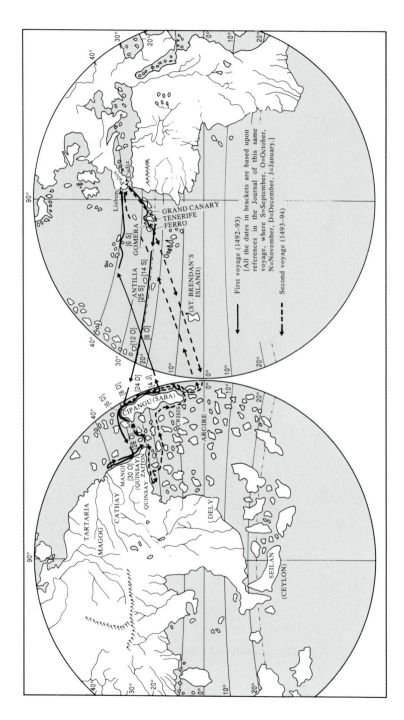

Figure 1. The first two voyages of Columbus (superimposed on a reconstruction of Ravenstein's projection from Behaim's Globe).

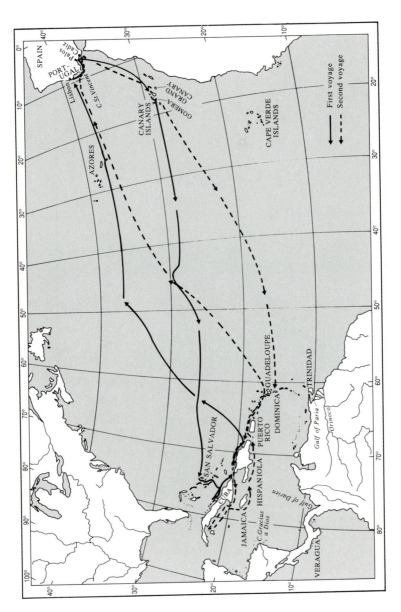

Figure 2. The voyages in reality (map adapted from C. Jane, Select Documents Illustrating the Four Voyages of Columbus).

Chapter 5

The Terrestrial Paradise

The third voyage of discovery was in many ways the most spectacular of them all. This was the voyage in which Columbus recognized that he had come upon a great and previously unknown land. This was the voyage, too, from which he returned in as deep a disgrace as he had begun in elation; and this was the voyage during which Columbus touched upon, as he proclaimed to his sovereigns, the edge of the Terrestrial Paradise.

There is a hint towards the end of the journal of the first voyage that Columbus was thinking of the Terrestrial Paradise then. The image of it was perhaps brought wistfully to the surface of his mind by the unfriendliness both of the weather and of the captain of the Azores:

> He says that he was amazed at the very bad weather which he experienced in those islands and in that neighbourhood, because in the Indies he navigated all that winter without dropping anchor, and had always good weather. . . . In conclusion, the admiral says that the sacred theologians and learned philosophers were right in saying that the earthly paradise is at the end of the east, because it is a very temperate place, so these lands which he had now discovered are, he says, "the end of the east."[1]

---

1. 21 February; C. Jane, *The Journal of Christopher Columbus* (London, 1960), 176.

He came back to the matter in his "Lettera Rarissima," written to Ferdinand and Isabella during the deprivations of the fourth voyage, and dated 7 July 1503:

> The world is small and six parts of it are land, the seventh part being entirely covered by water. Experience had already shewn this and I have already written other letters with illustrations drawn from Holy Scripture concerning the site of the earthly paradise accepted by Holy Church.[2]

The crucial passages telling of Columbus's purported discovery of this paradise, however, are to be found in the letter he wrote home to his sovereigns as he returned to them from the third voyage.[3] Columbus's idea that he might, on this third voyage, actually be skirting the shores of the Terrestrial Paradise was clearly taking firm shape as he ventured on westwards along the Caribbean Coast of the Paria Peninsula, for, in his abstract of the Journal, Las Casas mentions how puzzled Columbus had been, and still was, by the magnitude of the flow of fresh water into the Gulf of Paria. He doubted, reports Las Casas, that the Ganges, Nile or Euphrates (three of the postulated four rivers of Paradise, we may remember, one of which, the Ganges or "Phison," was known to flow into the ocean near the islands of the Indies) could possibly have provided it. He therefore suspected (quite rightly, as we now know) that he may be close to a great continent, unknown so far to Europeans,[4] but marked with confidence upon some of the mappae mundi he may have seen. Paradise and this continent clearly wrestled

---

2. J. M. Cohen, *The Four Voyages of Christopher Columbus* (Harmondsworth, 1969), 289.

3. The letter to Santangel is dated 18 October 1498, the copy to the sovereigns in the *Libro Copiador* to the previous September.

4. S. E. Morison, *Journals and Other Documents on the Life and Voyages of Christopher Columbus* (New York, 1963), 277–279.

together in his mind for priority; but, by the time he came to write his report to his sovereigns, Paradise seems, on this voyage, to have taken precedence.

I shall quote from this letter here extensively. It is, in itself, a remarkable document; but it is peculiarly relevant to the present study, for it is bursting with information about that medieval inner world within which Columbus so enthusiastically traveled, which he had fortified with such success on his first two voyages, and from which he continued to look out upon his adventures. The version of the letter found in the *Libro Copiador*, moreover, includes variants and additions on the Terrestrial Paradise which are of surpassing interest. These variants both add to our previous knowledge of Columbus's sources, and help to show that the admiral was, when he wrote this letter, very far removed from that twilight land of mystical fancies to which many have chosen to consign him.

The relevant passages in the 1498 letter read, in the most accessible full translation into English, as follows:

> Each time I sailed from Spain to the Indies I found that when I reached a point a hundred leagues west of the Azores, the heavens, the stars, the temperature of the air and the waters of the sea abruptly changed. I very carefully verified these observations, and found that, on passing this line from north to south, the compass needle, which had previously pointed north-east, turned a whole quarter of the wind to the north west. It was as if the seas sloped upwards on this line. I also observed that here they were full of a vegetation like pine branches loaded with a fruit similar to that of the mastic. . . . I noticed that when we had passed it the sea was calm and smooth, never becoming rough even in a strong wind. I found also that westwards of this line the temperature of the air was very mild and did not change from winter to summer. Here the Pole Star describes a circle of five degrees in diameter, and when it

is at its lowest the Guards point towards the right. It then rises continuously until they point to the left. It then stands at five degrees, and from there it sinks until they are again on the right. . . .

On this present voyage. . . . On coming to this line I immediately found very mild temperatures which became even milder as I sailed on. . . . At nightfall the Pole Star stood at five degrees, with the Guards pointing straight overhead, and later, at midnight, it had risen to ten degrees, and at daybreak stood at fifteen degrees, with the Guards pointing downwards. . . . I was greatly surprised by this behaviour of the Pole Star and spent many nights making careful observations with the quadrant, but found that the plumb line always fell to the same point. I regard this as a new discovery, and it may be established that here the heavens undergo a great change in a brief space. . . . I have found such irregularities that I have come to the following conclusions concerning the shape of the world: that it is not round as they describe it, but the shape of a pear, which is round everywhere except at the stalk, where it juts out a long way; or that it is like a round ball, on part of which is something like a woman's nipple. This point on which the protuberance stands is the highest and nearest to the sky. It lies below the Equator, and in this ocean, at the farthest point of the east, I mean by the farthest point of the east the place where all land and islands end. . . .

Ptolemy and other geographers believed that the world was spherical and that the other hemisphere was as round as the one in which they lived. . . . I do not in the least question the roundness of that hemisphere, but I affirm that the other hemisphere resembles the half of a round pear with a raised stalk, as I have said, like a woman's nipple on a round ball. . . .

In the latitude in which I was, which is that of Sierra Leone, where the Pole Star stood at five degrees at nightfall, the people are completely black, and when I sailed westwards from there the heats remained excessive. On passing the line of which I have spoken, I found the

temperatures growing milder, so that when I came to the
island of Trinidad, where the Pole Star also stands at five
degrees at nightfall, both there and on the mainland
opposite the temperatures were extremely mild. . . . All this
is attributable to the very mild climate in those regions,
and this in its turn to the fact that this land stands highest
on the world's surface, being nearest to the sky, as I have
said. . . . This argument is greatly supported by the
fact that the sun, when Our Lord made it, was at the first
point of the east; in other words the first light was here in
the east where the world stands at its highest. . . .

Holy Scripture testifies that Our Lord made the earthly
Paradise in which he placed the Tree of Life. From it there
flowed four main rivers: the Ganges in India, the Tigris and
the Euphrates in Asia, which cut through a mountain range
and form Mesopotamia and flow into Persia, and the Nile,
which rises in Ethiopia and flows into the sea at Alexandria.

I do not find and have never found any Greek or Latin
writings which definitely state the worldly situation of the
earthly Paradise, nor have I seen any world map which
establishes its position except by deduction. Some place it
at the source of the Nile in Ethiopia. But many people have
travelled in these lands and found nothing in the climate
or altitude to confirm this theory, or to prove that the waters
of the Flood which covered, etc., etc . . . reached there.
Some heathens tried to show by argument that it was in
the Fortunate islands (which are in the Canaries); and St.
Isidore, Bede, Strabo, the Master of Scholastic History
[Petrus Comestor], St. Ambrose and Scotus and all
learned theologians agree that the earthly paradise is in the
East, etc.[5]

I have already told what I have learnt about this
hemisphere and its shape, and I believe that, if I pass

---

5. The relevant passages in the works of the authors cited have been identified
by C. Jane, *Select Documents Illustrating the Four Voyages of Christopher Columbus* ii
(London, 1933), 36–37, although the attribution to Strabo should be to Anselm
of Laon.

below the Equator, on reaching these higher regions I shall find a much cooler climate and a greater difference in the stars and waters. Not that I believe it possible to sail to the extreme summit or that it is covered by water, or that it is even possible to go there. For I believe that the earthly Paradise lies here, which no one can enter except by God's leave. . . . I do not hold that the earthly Paradise has the form of a rugged mountain, as it is shown in pictures, but that it lies at the summit of what I have described as the stalk of a pear, and that by gradually approaching it one begins, while still at a great distance, to climb towards it. As I have said, I do not believe that anyone can ascend to the top. I do believe, however, that, distant though it is, these waters may flow from there to this place which I have reached and form this lake. All this provides great evidence of the earthly Paradise, because the situation agrees with the beliefs of those holy and wise theologians and all the signs strongly accord with this idea. For I have never read or heard of such a quantity of fresh water flowing so close to the salt and flowing into it, and the very temperate climate provides a further confirmation. If this river does not flow out of the earthly Paradise, the marvel is still greater. For I do not believe that there is as great and deep a river anywhere in the world. . . . I would say that if this river does not spring from Paradise it comes from a vast land lying to the south, of which we have hitherto had no reports. But I am firmly convinced that the earthly Paradise truly lies here, and I rely on the authorities and arguments I have cited.[6]

These propositions seem all of them most extraordinary, especially so to post-renaissance persons, and they have excited an enormous variety of responses, from the sheerly ribald to the sincerely reverent. Cohen ascribes them to physical or

---

6. Cohen, *The Four Voyages*, 216–224.

neurotic illness, a view with which many persons who have spent more than a few days at sea might sympathize.[7] The journal of the third voyage (in a section close to that which recounts the admiral's mental wrestlings over the unknown continent and Paradise) tells us that Columbus suffered far more severely from lack of sleep on this voyage than he had done on the previous two, and that agonizing eye afflictions were added to his miseries. When Columbus began this letter he was, in addition, being carried back to Spain unwillingly and in chains. Any one of these privations might explain, and excuse, in its victim, a touch of irrationality, and particularly so if the victim was, in any case, constitutionally inclined towards the self-delusory. Morison, in an article devoted largely to navigational observations (with a special section devoted to those made in this same letter), sets before us a Columbus who, at crucial moments:

> did not draw the proper conclusion from his own observations. It [that is the observation made about the Pole Star in this letter] was another instance of the curious dualism in his nature; a scientific capacity to observe, fighting against a scholastic habit of mind which squeezed all observed phenomena into pre-conceived ideas.[8]

The admiral expressed his views on Paradise, according to Morison, at one such crucial moment.

Each of these soothing draughts of reason reinforced by pity, and, in the last case, still involving no small measure of admiration, has something to recommend it. Yet none is entirely convincing. I shall attempt to argue here against

7. Ibid., 18–19.

8. S. E. Morison, "Columbus and Polaris," *American Neptune* 1 (1941), 133.

them all; and for a wholly different explanation. Columbus's account of his discovery of the Terrestrial Paradise, and of the previously unknown continent, sprang ultimately neither from navigational mistakes nor from illness, nor from an excess of scholasticism or mysticism. He simply found them where many of his medieval sources, and, in all probability, the knowledge and expectations of those to whom he was writing, had led him logically to expect them to be.

We might first recall the salient features of this third voyage, so far as we are able to establish them, beginning with those touched upon in this central letter. In his magnificent article upon Columbus's navigational skills, whose concluding words about the admiral's personality I have briefly mentioned, Morison shows that Columbus's erroneous deductions from bearings on the Pole Star, which the letter reports, may be explained in two main ways. Sometimes the cloudy or hazy weather obscured the star, especially at dawn. Sometimes the admiral's skill in middle latitude sailing, and his conviction that he was westing on latitude 5 degrees N, determined him to adjust both subsequent bearings and distances to suit. This, as we have just observed, led Morison to attribute to Columbus a curious (but not wholly unfamiliar) mixture of practicality and mysticism, infused on occasion with "foolish theories," among which he clearly numbered Columbus's conviction that he would reach, and had indeed reached, the Terrestrial Paradise.[9] It is worth pointing out immediately, however, that this last conviction is the only sign of foolishness that Morison is prepared truly to stigmatize. Given the weather conditions and the state of Columbus's instrumentation, Morison actually stresses how easy it was to mistake readings from the Pole Star, and he points out that the admiral's erroneous assessment of his latitude was based upon one widely respected at the

9. Ibid., 124–137.

time.[10] If Columbus's idea that he had reached the Terrestrial Paradise can be shown too to be a wholly rational one, then the main supports for this divided view of his personality and achievements will all fall away.

The third voyage as a whole was meant to take a more southerly direction than the previous two. The realms north of Mangi, after all, were unlikely to be as rewarding as those south of it, and there was the additional possibility that there might be an even greater continent to be discovered, and that on the Spanish side of the line drawn by the Treaty of Tordesillas.[11] Instead of heading west or southwest from the Canaries, therefore, Columbus's three ships of discovery plunged down the ocean to the Cape Verde Islands, before eventually turning westwards along the supposed parallel of 5 degrees N. At the

---

10. Columbus had taken this estimate from a bearing taken from the sun in 1485 by one Master Josephus, and which placed Sierra Leone on latitude 5 degrees N. Columbus knew by dead reckoning that, after the Cape Verde Islands, he was traveling along the same parallel as Sierra Leone, and so made the logical deduction. The fact that Master Josephus's original estimate was erroneous was not, therefore, the fault of Columbus; ibid., 128. Morison also points out that the observations Columbus made upon compass variation, reported in the beginning sections of the letter to the sovereigns quoted above, were accurate, and a real discovery (for which the admiral allowed carefully in his passage from Margarita to Hispaniola on the third voyage). Columbus was able to distinguish between this and his (equally novel) observation of the diurnal rotation of the Pole Star; ibid., 11–14. For an excellent description, and explanation for the beginner, of the use of Columbus's quadrant with its plumb-line, see E. G. R. Taylor, *The Haven-Finding Art* (London, 1956), 159. My attention was drawn to this book by Dr. Marjorie Chibnall.

11. The treaty of Tordesillas was agreed between John II of Portugal and Ferdinand and Isabella on 7 June 1494. It ruled that all discoveries made west of a line drawn 370 leagues west of the Cape Verde Islands should belong to Spain, and all east of it to Portugal. Columbus tells us, in his journal of the third voyage, that John II of Portugal had already begun to suspect that a great mainland to the west might exist, his side of the demarcation line; Morison, *Journals*, 262. There was some urgency therefore that the Spanish establish their claims to such a continent, should it be found. The text of the Treaty of Tordesillas, together with a translation into English, may be found in F. G. Davenport. *European Treaties Bearing on the History of the United States and its Dependencies to 1648* i (Washington, 1917), 86–100.

very outset, too, the Holy Trinity was very much on Columbus's mind. At the division of his fleet in the Canaries, the three colonizing ships were sent off to Hispaniola in its name,[12] he invoked it regularly,[13] and the first new island he sighted was called Trinidad. We might at this point note in passing that in the *Navigatio Sancti Brendani Abbatis* the abbot of the community of Ailbe, together with Brendan, gave honor to the Holy Trinity,[14] and that the Island of Ailbe was the last port of call on the seven-year cycle of voyages and liturgical festivities on islands, before Brendan and his company were to be released from it to find the Island of Paradise.

Trinidad was sighted on 31 July 1498, and from that moment of exultation (marked, according to Las Casas, by much praying of prayers and singing of canticles "according to the custom of mariners, at least of our mariners of Spain"),[15] Columbus's course was set all the more firmly for the hoped-for southern discoveries. Las Casas tells of the voyage along the southern shores of Trinidad, past the "island" Columbus named Isla Sancta (probably Punta Bombeador, Venezuela—Columbus's first sight of the southern continent, did he but know it) and past land which "was well populated and cultivated and contained many waters—the loveliest thing in the world—and trees right down to the sea," for which he again gave thanks to the Holy Trinity.[16] Las Casas then takes us through the treacherous tideway Columbus named Boca de la Sierpe and

---

12. See Las Casas's abstract of the journal, "the Admiral . . . dismissed the other three vessels in the name of the Holy Trinity; and he says that he implored the Holy Trinity to watch over him and all of them"; Morison, *Journals*, 261.

13. Ibid., 262 and 263.

14. J. J. O'Meara, *The Voyage of St. Brendan* (Dublin, 1976), 30.

15. Morison, *Journals*, 265.

16. Ibid., 266.

into the stormy seas of the Gulf of Paria, which Columbus called Golfo de la Ballena — the Gulf of the Whale.[17] At this point in his narrative abstract from the journal, Las Casas reports the beginnings of those reflections upon the change of climate and sea 100 leagues west of the Azores Columbus was to mention in his letter.

The experience of what he took to be a tidal bore in the Boca de la Sierpe led Columbus to expect something rather special of what we now know of as the Gulf of Paria. He was not disappointed. Sailing westwards along the southern coast of the "Island of Gracia" (Paria Peninsula), he found that fruit (he names grapes and apples and myrobolans and a type of fig-like orange, probably the guava) abounded on the surrounding lands, which he was still convinced were islands.[18] Some of the shores were so lovely he called them "jardines." Las Casas tells us of a series of other so-called islands to which the admiral gave names: Sabeta, Punta Seca, Tramontana, Punta Llana, Punta Sara; but becomes a little annoyed both at the strangeness of the names and at the fact that the admiral says no more about them.[19] Columbus remarked upon the sweetness of the sea water in the Gulf of Paria, and he sent out the caravel Correo to reconnoitre; with momentous results. For the Correo found and reported those great rivers which Columbus ultimately identified with the great rivers of Paradise.[20] He named the western corner of the gulf the "Gulf of Pearls," then, desperate to get his supplies to Hispaniola before they perished, turned back. The rivers of sweet water helped to sweep the little fleet,

---

17. "for no apparent reason"; S. E. Morison, *Admiral of the Ocean Sea* ii (Boston, 1942), 255. It in fact brings to mind the St. Brendan story.

18. Ibid., 270, 274.

19. Ibid., 274–275.

20. The Correo discovered the mouths of the Rio Grande, the northernmost outlet of the great Orinoco; ibid., 275.

seemingly by a miracle, through the straits Columbus named the Bocas del Dragon and outwards on the journey to Hispaniola.[21]

After the nerve-wracking encounter with the Bocas del Dragon between the Paria Peninsula ("Gracia") and Trinidad, and still convinced that the former, like the latter, was an island, Columbus proceeded westwards along the northern coasts of Gracia to try to assess its extent. It is at this point in his narrative that Las Casas reported a letter to his sovereigns which Columbus was clearly composing in his journal, and which expresses the wish that they will both continue their support and find Paradise through it.[22] Only a little further on Las Casas introduces those reflections of Columbus upon the Ganges, Euphrates and Nile which were quoted towards the beginning of this chapter.[23]

---

21. Of the fleet's rescue from the treacherous waters of the Bocas de la Dragon Las Casas reports: "When the wind fell, they feared lest the fresh water or the salt cast them on the rocks by their currents, and there they would have no hope. It pleased the goodness of God that from that very danger sprang safety and liberation, for the same fresh water, overcoming the salt, swept the vessels out, without a scratch; and thus they were saved; for when God wishes that one or many should live, water becomes their medicine [instead of their poison]"; ibid., 277.

22. "For it hath been seen that boundless are the treasures, and although what I say not be admitted now, the day will come when it [the enterprise] shall be reckoned for its great excellence, and to the great infamy of the people who opposed it before Your Highnesses. For though they have expended somewhat in this venture, it hath been a thing nobler and of higher estate than that which any other prince hath done hitherto, nor was it an affair to be abandoned coldly; rather it is necessary to go on with it and to grant me aid and favour. . . . Your Highnesses will leave no greater memorial; and may they ponder this, that no prince of Castile is to be found, nor have I found one in word or writing, who has ever gained any land outside of Spain; and Your Highnesses have won these vast lands, which are an Other World, in which Christendom will have so much enjoyment and our faith in time so great an increase. All this I say with very honest intent, and because I desire that Your Highnesses may be the greatest lords in the world, lords of it all I say; and that all be with much service and satisfaction to the Holy Trinity; so that in the end of your days you may have the glory of Paradise"; ibid., 276.

23. Ibid., 278.

Columbus traveled on westwards along the northern coast of
the Paria Peninsula, seeking the western side of this "island"
of Gracia and a way south round it:

> But he says that if he could not find it, he would then declare
> that it [the rush of fresh water the caravel had found] was
> a river and that both the one and the other were great
> marvels.[24]

He hands out more names on this lap of the journey: Puerto
de Gatos, Puerto de los Cabanas, Cabo de Conchas, Cabo
Luengo, Cabo de Sabor, Cabo Rico. He sights more islands
which he calls Asumpcion (Tobago), Concepcion (Grenada),
Los Testigos (The Witnesses), El Romero (The Pilgrim), Las
Guardias (the Guards), Margarita, El Martinet (the Hammer),
"which, he says, on the north side, is close to Margarita."

In order to try to show that the discoveries Columbus made
on his last two voyages (including that of the Terrestrial
Paradise) corresponded every bit as well with that inner
landscape he had built upon his medieval sources as did those
of his first two, I shall, in the first place, again make use of maps;
maps of a kind we may suppose he had. This time, however,
Behaim's globe will not be quite enough. Misgivings about its
absolute accuracy had begun to be felt, as we saw, during the
first two voyages; but, more seriously, Behaim's globe lacked
all depiction of a southern continent. Though still evidently
useful as a starting point it had, therefore, to be supplemented
by other maps of the world, and especially by ones which could
suggest the position and the outline of this continent. Such maps
and their derivatives, we should remark immediately, were liable
to suggest not merely the outline and the placing of the great
southern continent, but those of the Terrestrial Paradise too.
Thus, on the basis of many such maps, an explorer on the track

---

24. Ibid., 278.

of the unknown continent might expect to be on the track also of this Paradise, and again with the best of reasons.

Columbus was assured, as he said in his letter to his Sovereigns, that as he headed towards Trinidad, he was westing along latitude 5 degrees N; along the latitude, that is, of Sierra Leone. And he was assured of this, as we have seen, on authority he took to be expert.[25] Now, on Behaim's globe, a great island is marked southwest of the Cape Verdes and stretching almost from the equator to the parallel of 10 degrees N. This is the island Behaim marks as the Island of St. Brendan, and to which he appends the brief outline of the *Navigatio Sancti Brendani*, quoted in Chapter 3. In other words, a map or globe constructed along the lines of that of Behaim (a map, in short, of a kind we have good reason to think Columbus had) would have led the admiral naturally to suppose that the Paradise Island of St. Brendan might be found along these very latitudes, and this from the very first. So, too, would many of those supplements to Behaim which included in outline the great southern continent.

The question of whether Paradise was an island, or was to be found on the mainland of the known world, was unresolved in those medieval mappae mundi which included the great undiscovered southern continent. I mentioned, in Chapter 1, maps of the four landmass tradition, such as the map in B. L. Cotton Tiberius B. V., and also those of the Beatus tradition which delineated the antipodean landmass. These might mark the Terrestrial Paradise north of the great southern continent, and next to Cathay, but they tended to place it on the mainland. Related world maps, however, saw Paradise as an island. Also in Chapter 1, we mentioned certain maps which balanced a supposed great southern continent *against* this Paradise Island; the latter just north, the former perhaps just south, of the equator, and on the

25. Morison, "Columbus," 128–130.

supposed watery back of the globe.[26] The Lambert of St. Omer maps are instances of world maps of this kind; and so are the Corpus and Hereford world maps. Though far more schematic than Behaim, the Corpus and Hereford maps too place the island of the Terrestrial Paradise off the coast of the mainland of Cathay, though in their cases only just off this coast. Whether island or mainland, however, the Terrestrial Paradise was clearly marked on such maps, and was often marked as being close to a great unexplored southern continent. The idea therefore that "Gracia," island or mainland, might indeed be this Paradise, and might be close to the southern continent Columbus in part sought, was, then, one which logically emerged from the scrutiny of world maps of the type to which the admiral had access. We might suggest, indeed, on this evidence, that it would have been far more foolish for him *not* to have thought of the possible proximity of this Earthly Paradise at this point in his voyage, than for him to have drawn the deductions he did draw.

In the *Navigato Sancti Brendani*, the Terrestrial Paradise is depicted as an island (and close to the island upon which the Ailbe community honored the Trinity, as Trinidad was to Gracia) but some mapmakers could both show themselves aware of the Brendan story, yet place this Paradise on the mainland. Such a one is Andreas Bianco. In his world map of 1436, one which I suggested might be especially close to Columbus's exemplars, Bianco includes a curious figure, hung upon a gallows, far out in the Atlantic ocean off the coast of Africa. The figure upon the gallows has been identified with the hapless Judas of the Brendan legend, placed out in the Atlantic for his "refreshment" where Brendan found him.[27] The same map may have an echo of the story of the Hesperides and the guardian

---

26. Good reproductions of the more notable of those medieval mappae mundi which depicted the Terrestrial Paradise are to be found in E. Coli, *Il Paradiso Terrestre Dantesco* (Florence, 1897), 96–115.

27. See above, Chapter 3.

dragon.[28] Bianco kept such stories engagingly alive. It is of great interest also in this context to see that when Bianco depicts the Terrestrial Paradise, he depicts it as seemingly up on a high mountain; on a high mountain, that is, of the kind Columbus considers in his letters, and rejects as a possible site for this Paradise. Bianco also includes certain other features in his map, all of which might help towards our understanding of the deductions Columbus made on this third voyage. Among the islands Bianco places in the gulf separating Africa from the Indies, and close to this earthly paradise, are two named ones: the "ixola perlina," or island of pearls, and the "ixola colombi," island of doves, or perhaps the island of birds reminiscent, again of St. Brendan.

The least that can be said at this point is that the whole matter of the placing of the Terrestrial Paradise, and its relationship to the great southern continent, was, in the maps available for Columbus to follow, both extremely confused and deserving of the utmost attention on the part of would-be discoverers. One of the most remarkable of all the world maps available to be pressed into service for the present study is that numbered Res.Ge. AA 562 in the collection of the Bibliothèque Nationale, Paris; the so-called "Columbus Map and Chart" (see Plate 4). This is a single sheet of vellum, measuring 1,110 mm by 700 mm, and containing on its right hand side a portolan chart (which occupies some two-thirds of the space available), and on its left, separated from the chart by a band of gold, a mappa mundi, surrounded by the circles of the seven celestial spheres, and dense with inscriptions. The chart delineates the coasts of Europe, from southern Norway to the Black Sea, those of Asia along the southern shores of the Black Sea and the Mediterranean, and those of Africa to the Congo. Off the Atlantic coasts of Europe and Africa it has the islands of the

---

28. See Visconde de Santarem, *Essai sur l'Histoire de la Cosmographie et de la Cartographie* ii (Paris, 1852), 392–396 for these identifications.

British Isles, "Brasil," Iceland, "Frixlanda" (the Faroes), the
Azores, the Canaries, the Cape Verde Islands and the islands
of the Gulf of Guinea. Far west, off the coast of Ireland and
on the same latitude, a faint inscription marks the "Septem
civitatum insula," that is, Antillia.[29]

The combined map and chart have been the object of
intense discussion, the more so since Charles de la Roncière
advanced the theory that they may both have been drawn
up by Bartholomew Columbus for the great admiral himself.[30]
It is generally agreed now that the work is that of a single
mapmaker, is of Genoese origin (as evidenced by the writing,
and by the fact that Genoa is conspicuously represented
on the chart), and is of a period roughly contemporary with
the great admiral's enterprise. The Cape of Good Hope
is drawn on the world map. The discoveries of Columbus
do not appear, however, on either the map or the chart.
These circumstances suggest a late fifteenth century date
for the whole. The date of its initial composition must certainly
have been later than that at which the discoveries of Diaz
were made known, but seemingly before those of Columbus
were—perhaps, then, 1488–1493.[31] La Roncière would advance the later date to the first approach Columbus made to
the Sovereigns in 1491, or, at the latest, to the fall of

---

29. A summary description may be found in M. Foncin, M. Destombes, M.
de la Roncière, *Catalogue des Cartes Nautiques sur Vélin* (Paris, 1963), 30–31.

30. This argument is set out in C. de la Roncière, *La Carte de Christophe
Colomb* (Paris, 1924), in French, with an accompanying translation into
English. The volume contains a large facsimile, in black and white, of the
whole sheet.

31. So E. D. Fite and A. Freeman, *A Book of Old Maps* (Cambridge, Mass. 1926),
7. They (pp. 7–8) offer a summary of the arguments of la Roncière. A fuller
summary and discussion, together with an excellent enlarged reproduction of
the world map, may be found in A. Kammerer, *La Mer Rouge l'Abyssinie et l'Arabie
depuis l'Antiquité* ii (2) (Cairo, 1935), 356 and plate CXXXIII (facing
pp. 328–329).

Granada on 2 January 1492.[32] Much of la Roncière's wider argument is intriguing, but all of it is speculative. It is impossible to associate the map directly or securely with either Bartholomew or Christopher Columbus on the evidence he gives.[33] It remains true to say, however, that both map and chart were of a type Columbus could easily have seen; and the world map holds for us a particular interest, for it marks the Terrestrial Paradise, and marks it clearly.

As in the Hereford Map, the Terrestrial Paradise is depicted on the world map as an island, centrally placed off the coast of Cathay and, and especially interestingly, at about the latitude of that part of the coast of Africa which is opposite the Cape Verde Islands. It is additionally surrounded by an unbroken ring, composed of diamond-shapes (see Plate 13). The so-called Columbus Map, moreover, does not mark the Terrestrial Paradise alone off this coast, but adds another series of islands; most notably, the islands of St. Brendan's *Navigatio*. All of these islands are carefully labeled, leaving absolutely no room for mistakes. Thus, at the very top of the map (in the far north, that is) there floats the island of smoke and devils (where, it will be remembered, one of Brendan's monks was swallowed up), and below it, in the west Atlantic (en route downwards towards the Terrestrial Paradise), there follow successively the

---

32. La Roncière, *La Carte*, 20. The chart depicts, he points out, the little town of Santa Fé, constructed for the siege, as seen by an eyewitness; and Columbus was at the seige. It also shows the flag of Castile flying from the battlements of Granada, which suggests a date later than 1492. He is anxious to see in this composition the document actually presented to the Sovereigns in pursuit of their consent to the project.

33. La Roncière proves beyond doubt that the mapmaker drew upon d'Ailly's *Imago Mundi* much as Columbus did, and sometimes seemingly upon the admiral's own *postille*. He shows also that the inscription attached to the Island of the Seven Cities, or Antillia, gives an account of the rediscovery of Antillia much like that of Ferdinand Columbus, save for the fact that it says that silver was found there, not gold; *La Carte*, 10–14, 25–27. Such resemblances could spring, however, from the quite separate use of similar well-known sources.

Plate 13. *The so-called "Columbus World Map," Ms. Paris, Bibliothèque Nationale, Res.Ge. AA 562. Reproduced by permission of the Bibliothèque Nationale, Paris.*

Islands of Birds, the Island of Ailbe and the Island of Delights. Just eastwards, off the shores of the Island of Delights, is a somewhat puzzling "insula purificatorum," the Island of the Purified. This might have reference to the multifarious medieval stories of journeys of purification to the other world, undertaken by chosen persons before their entry into Paradise.

West of, and behind, the Island of Paradise, there stretches southwards the "patalis regio"; the peninsula, that is, of the

the Golden Chersonese, labeled as it is in d'Ailly and in some Ptolemaic maps. An inscription among the islands off its coast points out that the area there is full of gold,[34] a description well in accord, of course, with Columbus's own perceptions. It was in part to seek such gold that Columbus, as he says, attempted to circumnavigate that ''Gracia'' he had begun to think might be the Terrestrial Paradise. When set against such a map as this, such a maneuver and such thoughts make perfect sense.

Further into the Indian Ocean there appear on this map other items dear to the preoccupations of Columbus; an island solely for men, for instance, islands of ''monoculi,'' or one-eyed persons, and islands of people who live on raw fish alone.

Columbus's medieval mappae mundi both promoted and supported his claim that he had discovered the Terrestrial Paradise. Parts of the admiral's reading, and some few storytelling materials additional to the *Navigatio Sancti Brendani*, also provided him with evidence to fortify him in his published views. The collection which goes under the name of the *Imago Mundi* of Pierre d'Ailly is rich in information about the region around Paradise. D'Ailly speaks of the Terrestrial Paradise at several points in the *Imago Mundi* itself, and Columbus draws out these comments both in his notes to this work and, perhaps more importantly, in those to d'Ailly's abridgments of Ptolemy's *Geography*. In Chapters VII and XII of the *Imago Mundi*, for instance, d'Ailly describes Paradise as a mountain, and suggests that it might be the same place as that associated in antiquity with the Fortunate Islands. Columbus notes both these views in the margins of his copy of d'Ailly and in his letter, although, of course, to reject them in the latter, as we have seen.[35] D'Ailly

---

34. ''hic dicitur multum auri efficere''; Kammerer, *La Mer Rouge*, 356.

35. VII, ''Certain people say that on a mountain near the [torrid zone] is to be found the Terrestrial Paradise,'' and Columbus notes ''The Terrestrial Paradise is here''; XII, ''When conditions especially favourable to human life concord with other good things—fertile land and the correct amounts of

makes the point too, as Columbus does in his letter, that no author has ever committed himself as to the exact position of this land.[36] In his first abridgment of the *Geography* of Ptolemy, d'Ailly lays stress upon the temperate climate of the Terrestrial Paradise, as he does too in Chapters VII and XI of the *Imago Mundi*. Columbus makes special note of all these points upon his copy of the treatises, and again we seem to see this thought about the gentle climate of the Paradise region echoed in his letter to his sovereigns.[37]

All of these observations were clearly in the great admiral's mind as he made his southern explorations and as he wrote home to his sovereigns. Most interesting of all, however, is the passage in Chapter LV of the *Imago Mundi* in which d'Ailly, drawing grandly upon a whole parade of authors, actually tries to describe this Terrestrial Paradise. It has a fountain (Columbus makes a note of this) which divides into four rivers. It is a most agreeable place, but far away by land and sea from that in which we (Europeans, that is) live; Columbus notes this too. Further, it is so raised up as to touch the sphere of the moon, so high that the waters of the flood were unable to reach it. Not, d'Ailly goes on, that we must suppose it *literally* to touch the moon; we are merely to understand by this hyperbole that the Terrestrial Paradise is raised up in comparison with the normal level of the earth. Thus it attains to that serene air which is above this

---

sun—the region will be wholly temperate. It is probable that the Earthly Paradise is a place of this kind, and perhaps also the region authors call the Fortunate Islands.'' Columbus notes "The Earthly Paradise is perhaps the place that authors call the Fortunate Isles.'' In Chapter XLI d'Ailly comments, like Columbus, that the so-called Fortunate Isles are now called the the Canaries. This allowed the true Islands of the Blest to be placed elsewhere. *Edit.* E. Buron, *Ymago Mundi de Pierre d'Ailly* i (Paris, 1930), 198–199, 240–241, 388–391. I here correct Buron's translation of the Latin. For the passages in the letter, see above.

36. XI; ibid., 232–233.

37. Ibid., 198–199, 232–233, 646–647.

turbulent lower region which humans normally inhabit. The rivers flow down from a high mountain into a great lake, and the waterfalls fall from the lake with such a crashing and a roaring that children conceived within the region are born deaf, for their hearing is destroyed in the womb. Columbus makes a special note of all this.[38] The notion that the region of paradise was perhaps, as a whole raised up could allow Columbus both to dismiss the thought that Paradise was on a mountain and to advance those views he expressed in his letter upon the protruberance at this point on the earth.

A further source of reinforcement was to be found in the famous *Book* of Sir John Mandeville; indeed, it may be possible to find echoes of Mandeville, or at least of his own sources, in the *Imago Mundi* itself. Mandeville certainly believed both in the existence of the Terrestrial Paradise, and in its inaccessibility to man; as, it seems here, Columbus did too. In Chapter XXXIII of his *Book* Mandeville too described this Paradise:

> Beyond those isles that I have told you of and the deserts of the lordship of Prester John, to go even east, is no land inhabited . . . but wastes and wildernesses and great rocks and mountains and a murk land, where no man may

---

38. LV; ibid., 458–461. I give here the Latin of the section on pp. 458 and 460 I have rendered into English, complete with Columbus's own underlinings (I have also expanded the contractions Buron prints); "Fons est in paradiso ortum deliciarum irrigans et in quattuor flumina divisus. *Est autem paradisus* sanctorum Ysidorum, Iohannes Damascenum, Bedam, Strabum et Magistrum Historiarum (Petrus Comestor), locus amoenissimus in partibus orientis, longo terre et maris tractu a nostro habitabili segregatus, adeo altus ut usque ad lunarem globum attingat, ubi aque diluvii non pervenerunt. Non tamen est intelligendum quod secundum veritatem attingat circulum lune, sed loquendo hyperbolice eius altitudo respectu terre inferioris incomparabilis insinuat. Et quod attingit usque ad aerem quietum, supra istum aerem turbulentum ubi finis est et terminus exalacionum et vaporum humidorum. Quorum fluxus et progressus lunari corpori aproprinqua(n)ti sicut exponit Alexander. Ab illo itaque monte altissimo, cadentes aque maximum faciunt lacum, et in suo casu tamen faciunt strepitum, *quod omnes ibi incole surdi nascuntur*, quia ex immoderato fragore sensus auditus in parvulis corrumpitur, sicut Basilius et Ambrosius testant."

see, night ne day, as men of those countries told us. And that murk land and those deserts last right to Paradise terrestrial, wherein Adam and Eve were put; but they were there but a little while. And that place is toward the east at the beginning of the earth. . . . Paradise terrestrial, as men say, is the highest land of the world; and it is so high that it touches near to the circle of the moon. For it is so high that Noah's flood might not come thereto, which flood covered all the earth but it. Paradise is closed all about with a wall; but whereof the wall is made no man can tell. . . . In the midst of Paradise is a well out of which there come four floods, that run through divers lands. These floods sink down into the earth within Paradise and run so under the earth many a mile, and afterwards come they up again out of the earth in far countries. The first of these floods [which] is called Phison or Ganges, springs up in India under the hills or Orcobares, and runs eastward through India into the great sea Ocean. In that river are many precious stones and great plenty of that tree that is called *lignum aloes*, and mickle gravel of gold. . . . And ye shall understand that no man living may go to Paradise. For by land may no man go thither because of wild beasts that are in the wilderness and for hills and rocks which no man may pass, and also for murk places, of which there are many there. By water also may no man pass thither, for those rivers come with so great a course and so great a birr and waves that no ship may go ne sail against them. There is also so great noise of waters that a man may not hear another, cry he never so high. Many great lords have assayed divers times to pass by those rivers of Paradise, but they might not speed of their journey; for some of them died for weariness of rowing and over travailing, some waxed blind and some deaf for the noise of the waters, and some were drowned by the violence of the waves of the waters. And so there may no man, as I said before, win thither, but through the special grace of God.[39]

---

39. M. Letts, *Mandeville's Travels, Texts and Translations* (London, 1953), 214–217.

I have quoted from Mandeville at some length here, in the first place to show how close this passage is to d'Ailly. Mandeville's *Book*, in this respect, clearly ranked among the most respectable of geographical sources. Interestingly, the passage about the deafness induced by the sound of the rivers of Paradise goes back ultimately to Pliny. In Book VI, Chapter xxxv (181) of his *Historia Naturalis* Pliny attributes this effect to a cataract of the Nile—in the Middle Ages, one of the four rivers of Paradise. There is, however, a more important (and exciting) reason for quoting Mandeville extensively. The *Libro Copiador* contains an addition to the crucial letter in which Columbus reports to his sovereigns his discovery of the Terrestrial Paradise. It follows the sections in which the admiral comments learnedly upon his sources; and it is close, it is true, to the passage in d'Ailly's *Imago Mundi* LV referred to above. Its closest answering echo, however, especially in its account, for instance, of the plunging of the rivers underground, is to this chapter of Mandeville's *Book*. To be sure, Columbus does not here draw upon Mandeville alone. He seems still to have d'Ailly in mind, and at least one further interesting source, which will be referred to shortly. We have, however, in this variant to his letter, one more proof, if any more were needed, that Columbus both knew Mandeville, and took at least some of his stories seriously.[40]

---

40. I take the relevant passage from Rumeu de Armas's edition of this text of the letter, italicizing as he does the additional section. "San Isidro y Beda y Damasceno y Estrabon y el maestro de la Ystoria Escolastica y San Ambrosio y Escoto i todos los sacros teologos todos conciertan quel Parayso terrenal es en fin de oriente, *el qual oriente llaman el fin de la tierra; yendo al oriente, en una montana altisima que sale fuera deste ayre torbolento, adonde no llegaron las aguas del dilubio; que alli estan Elias y Enoque, y de alli sale una fuente y cae el agua en el mar, y alli haze un gran lago del qual proceden los quatro rrios sobredichos; que bien queste lago sea en oriente y las fuentes destos rrios sean divisas en este mundo, por ende que proceden y vienen alli deste lago por catar antes debajo de tierra, y espiran alli donde se been estas sus fuentes; la qual agua que sale del Paraiso terrenal para este lago, trahe un tronida y rrogir mui grande, de manera que la gente que naze en aquella comarca son sordos*"; A. Rumeu de Armas, *Libro Copiador de Cristóbal Colón* i (Madrid, 1989), 360.

Columbus's notions about the shape of the earth around Paradise have been regarded by many as the most curious of all. Morison, as we saw, explained them away as mistaken readings from the Pole Star; but Mandeville, we might note, supplies material support for them, support additional to that in d'Ailly. Mandeville avers (XX) in fact that Jerusalem occupies a high point of this kind upon the earth:

> And ye shall understand that, as I conjecture, the land of Prester John, emperor of India, is even under us. For if a man shall go from Scotland or England unto Jerusalem, he shall go alway upward. For our land is the lowest part of the west and the land of Prester John is the lowest part of the east.''[41]

Mandeville's observations were made as a result of looking down upon a globe from a height, and were based upon the assumption that Jerusalem was the center of the earth.[42] Writers who saw the equator instead as earth's center, however, and placed Paradise upon the equator at the very end of the supposed east (as d'Ailly, for example, was inclined to do), provided a splendid opportunity for the transference to this equator of the idea of upwards travel towards Paradise, or downwards travel from it. Once more we may attribute the ideas expressed by Columbus in his letter rather to the range and scope of his authorities, than to the ravings of a deranged imagination.[43]

---

41. Letts, *Mandeville's*, 129–130.

42. E. G. R. Taylor makes this point; "The Cosmographical Ideas of Mandeville's Day," in Letts, *Mandeville's*, lvii.

43. In their treatments both of the idea of upwards travel to Paradise and of the notion that the position "east" is a relative one, d'Ailly and Mandeville once more grow close together; Buron, *Ymago*, i, 248–249; Letts, *Mandeville's*, 214.

I mentioned one further interesting source. This is the *Chronicle* of John of Marignolli. John of Marignolli's account of the Terrestrial Paradise, with its four rivers flowing into the lake and crashing down in deafening cataracts, has a great deal in common with that of Mandeville.[44] Marignolli adds to Mandeville, however, in certain significant respects. John of Marignolli's description of one of the four rivers of Paradise, for instance, the "Phison," or Ganges, is fuller than that in John Mandeville. It may well have supported Columbus's later thoughts about the Orinoco, with its great rush of sweet water, as a possible river of Paradise. The Phison, Marignolli tells us, is enormous, probably the biggest river in the world. Also, it comes down through Cathay, and is full of sweet water and jewels. He has seen it.[45] A second variant to the letter on the third voyage found in the *Libro Copiador* shows us that Columbus took especial care to measure the depths of the sweet water sea off the coasts of the Orinoco, and to impress his monarchs with the size of it.[46]

From the passages in Pierre d'Ailly's *Imago Mundi* and Sir John Mandeville's *Book* to which we have referred, from the *Chronicle* of John of Marignolli, and from those writings of the Fathers and Doctors of the Church which d'Ailly, especially,

---

44. *Edit.* J. Emler, *Kronika Marignolova*, in *Fontes Rerum Bohemicarum* iii (Prague, 1878), 497.

45. "Secundus fluvius vocatur Phison, qui circuit omnem terram Evilach per Indiam et descendere dicitur per Cathay, et ibi mutato nomine dicitur Caramora, id est nigra aqua, quia ibi nascitur bedellium et lapis onichinus, et puto, quod sit maior fluvius de mundo aquae dulcis, quem ego transivi"; ibid.

46. "Y si de alli del Parayso no sale, paresce aun muy amior maravilla, porque no creo que sepan en el mundo de rrio tan grande y tan fondo, *al qual no pude llegar; en algunos lugares es en el pie largo con ochenta brazas de cordel e colgado del doze libras de plumo";* Rumeu de Armas, *Libro*, 360–361. I have set out in full the evidence for supposing that Columbus had read John of Marignolli's *Chronicle* in V. I. J. Flint, "Christopher Columbus and the Friars," in L. Smith and B. M. Ward, eds., *Intellectual Life in the Middle Ages* (London, 1992, forthcoming).

so carefully cites (thus obviating the need actually to read them),[47] we can see that the Terrestrial Paradise was a matter deserving of the most serious attention on the part of medieval exegetes, theologians, scientists, story tellers and eye witnesses. Once again, the geographical notions with which Columbus went out equipped from certain of his medieval sources make sense even of the most seemingly outrageous of his deductions and descriptions.

They may, finally, even throw some light upon some of the names he chose for his discoveries on this third voyage. Many of these names, such as Sabeta or Margarita, may be explained by the admiral's wish to compliment his sovereigns, and some of their relations.[48] Tramontana was another name for the Pole Star or the North Wind. It was used for the Pole Star by, for instance, Marco Polo. Las Guardias meant simply the Guards. Cabo de Conchas or Cabo Luengo were purely descriptive. The "Gulf of Pearls" might have reference to Bianco's "ixole perlinas," but it may have been descriptive too. Many of the names Columbus handed out on his other journeys seem to have sprung from a simple piety, especially from the seaman's piety towards the Virgin. We may explain many such names on this voyage, then, to this same urge. And yet—Trinidad, Isla Sancta (Holy Island), Gracia (Island of Grace), Asumcion (Tobago), Concepcion (Grenada)? I have already suggested that the name Trinidad may reflect in part that reverence for the Trinity reported of the community of Ailbe, and Isla Sancta and Gracia are certainly easy to connect with that same story. Then again, in the same area, we have the Golfo de la Ballena (Gulf of Paria—the Gulf of the Whale), Boca de la Sierpe

47. Buron demonstrates that many such learned references were drawn, without acknowledgment, from Bartolomeus Anglicus or Roger Bacon.

48. Sabeta may have been named for Isabella. Margarita seems to have been called after Princess Margarita of Austria, bride of the Infante Don Juan; Morison, *Journals*, 279.

(serpent's mouth), Bocas del Dragon (dragons mouths), Punta Llana (woolly or sheep point); all of these have echoes in the *Navigatio*.[49] Two of the feasts allowed to Judas for his refeshment, out in the great encircling ocean, were feasts of the Virgin.[50]

These associations are merely suggestive. It is impossible to prove from them alone that Columbus was thinking either of St. Brendan's voyage, or, come to that, of any other such Paradise story, as he attempted to circle his own suspected Terrestrial Paradise.[51] The case is different, however, when we come to two more of the names he assigned as he sailed north of the coast of "Gracia." The two are; Los Testigos (the witnesses), and El Romero (the pilgrim).[52] Here, if we look a little further into Columbus's medieval readings and stories, we do find firmer ground. The first of them, the witnesses, must surely have reference to the two prophetic witnesses of Apocalypse 11:3-12 who awaited the coming of Antichrist. Antichrist would kill them, this passage tells us, but after three days they would be resurrected, after the manner of Christ.

These two witnesses were early identified in commentaries upon the Apocalypse[53] with the prophet Elijah of 4 Kings

---

49. The whale would be, presumably, Jasconius, and the serpent and dragon bring to mind the sea beast chopped up by the second fire-breathing sea monster of Chapter 16; O'Meara, *The Voyage*, 18-19, 39-41. The dragon, of course, is echoed in the Hercules and Jason cycles.

50. The Purification and the Assumption; ibid., 58. The feast of the Immaculate Conception had not gained acceptance at the time of the writing down of the *Navigatio*.

51. Though it is worth noting that John of Marignolli speaks of the "dracones ignivomos volantes" to be encountered among the islands around Paradise; *Edit.* Emler, *Kronika*, 500.

52. Morison, *Journals*, 278-279. Morison is clearly puzzled by Columbus's name-giving here, and I have found no further discussion of them.

53. The identification may go back as far as the third century A. D.; see G. Orlandi, *Navigatio Sancti Brendani i Intoduzione* (Milan, 1968), 122.

2:11–12 (who was taken up to heaven in his fiery chariot) and with Enoch, who "walked with God" and whom God took to himself (Genesis 5:24, Hebrews 11:5). Eli and Enoch were seemingly chosen by God, then, for a special sort of removal from the world of ordinary men, just as the two witnesses were. In the Vulgate version of Ecclesiasticus 44:16, moreover, we are told specifically that Enoch, for pleasing God, "translatus est in paradisum." No orthodox commentator, however, could allow that this was the true Paradise promised by Christ, for Enoch had not died as men die.[54] That Paradise in which he and his fellow witness were placed must be, therefore—the Terrestrial Paradise. Accordingly, the city of Enoch (Genesis 4:17) can be found at the gates of this Paradise on medieval *mappae mundi*.[55] The influence of the story of Eli and Enoch, witnesses at the gates of Paradise, is also readily detectable in Irish sea-pilgrimage stories; stories, that is, of the kind we have tried to show Columbus knew, and which were also imprinted upon his maps. Eli and Enoch are specifically included in certain German and Italian versions of the *Navigatio Sancti Brendani*.[56] The idea that death-in-life might bring one to the Terrestrial Paradise was an idea, of course, central to the justification of the monastic life (was at the heart of much monastic propaganda, that is, should one wish to put the matter in this way). Thus, a monastic treatise about the two, the *Book of Enoch and Elias*, seems to have been in early circulation, and to have held a position a little similar to that of the Apocryphal Acts of the Apostles.[57]

---

54. On this, see the late seventh/early eighth century *De Mirabilibus Sacrae Scripturae* I,3; PL 35, 2154–2155.

55. The "Enos civitas antiquissima" is to be found beside Paradise, for instance, on the Hereford Map.

56. M. Esposito, "An apocryphal 'Book of Enoch and Elias' as a possible source of the *Navigatio Sancti Brendani*," *Celtica* 5 (1960), 204.

57. Ibid., 192–206. The contents of this book are discussed on pp. 197–203.

All of this suggests, then, that when Columbus named Los Testigos as he left his Terrestrial Paradise, he had the medieval apocalyptic witnesses in mind. One final piece of evidence both adds substance to this suggestion and reassures us that Columbus was no more deluded as he sailed from Paradise than he was when he first thought he had found it. This last piece of evidence lies once again in those intensely valuable and interesting additions to the central letter so recently found in the *Libro Copiador*. One such addition has just been quoted in the context of Mandeville's description of Paradise. In this second variant passage (quoted above, n. 40), Columbus adds the names of Eli and Enoch to both Mandeville's and d'Ailly's descriptions. In the original version of this letter, and in this one, Columbus adduces, too, a source additional to those given by d'Ailly for his assertions; this source is "Escoto," or John Scotus Eriugena. Each of these references takes us back to that last, enigmatic, possible source; John of Marignolli. John of Marignolli speaks of Eli and Enoch in his own extraordinary account of his journey to the edges of Paradise.[58] He also pays tribute to the authority of John the Scot. John of Marignolli, Franciscan Friar and Papal legate, no less, provided, then, substantial reinforcement for Columbus's thoughts about Paradise.

If Columbus named Los Testigos after Eli and Enoch, persons waiting on the outskirts of Paradise, then we may so explain El Romero, The Pilgrim, too. Two strong candidates present themselves immediately. One is St. Ailbe, founder of the community St. Brendan and his company found next to the Island of Paradise. The *Vita* of St. Brendan (which is more solemn than, and anterior to, the *Navigatio*) speaks of St. Ailbe, (Helveus), "peregrinus." Ailbe the pilgrim is well remembered in legend (and in those litanies which did so much to keep such legends dramatically alive) as the pilgrim-leader of a group of twenty-four who "went to revisit the Land of Promise and are

---

58. *Edit.* Emler, *Kronika*, 583.

alive there till doom.''[59] He is, then, very well qualified for the position. The second candidate is the pilgrim Macarius. The *Vita Sancti Macarii* (ultimately a Greek legend, of unknown but early date) was, in popularity and to some degree in content, the medieval land-pilgrimage story complement to the *Navigatio Sancti Brendani*.[60] The story relates how three monks set out eastwards to find the Terrestrial Paradise, and, towards the end of their journey, encounter a hermit.[61] This hermit gives the monks directions (like the hermit Paul in the *Navigatio*, and Eli and Enoch in the *Book of Enoch and Elias*). Perhaps significantly in our immediate context, however, he advises the monks not to go on but to return, and, in doing so, tells them of his own fate. He too had undertaken an earlier pilgrimage to the Terrestrial Paradise; but, when twenty miles away, he had been stopped by an angel. Vouchsafed a vision of Christ, however, he had stayed close to Paradise ever since.

The distance of "El Romero" from "Gracia" is wholly appropriate to this story; and two more aspects of it add to the probability that it was Macarius whom Columbus had here in mind. Firstly, both the pilgrim monks and Macarius describe the position and aspect of the Terrestrial Paradise in words similar to those used by Columbus in his letter. The monks sought the place where heaven joined the earth, at the ends of the earth and the stars.[62] Secondly, Bianco's map actually shows this very Macarius, sitting in his shelter beneath the mountain of Paradise.

---

59. Quoted by K. Hughes from the Irish Pilgrim-Litany she examines in "An Irish litany of Pilgrim Saints, Compiled c.800," *Analecta Bollandiana* 77 (1959), 323.

60. This was pointed out by Orlandi, *Navigatio*, 115–118.

61. The *Vita Sancti Macarii* is printed in PL 73, 415–426. I know of no translation.

62. "ubi coelum terrae se jungit," "ut finem terrae ac poli cernere quivissem"; *Vita Sancti Macarii* xvi, PL 73, 421.

It was no real wonder that Columbus poured thoughts of the Terrestrial Paradise into the ears of his sovereigns after the tribulations of his third voyage. He was in more desperate need of optimism then, perhaps, than at any other point in his career. Not all of his reading, we might remark, supported this optimism equally. Pius II, for instance, had expressed in Chapter V of his *Historia* grave doubts about the existence of that Terrestrial Paradise of which he had heard so much. The Pope reviews faithfully some of the evidence in favor of it; but then begs leave to question whether such beliefs do in truth accord with scripture.[63] Columbus simply notes that some believe the Terrestrial Paradise truly to be there. He does not mark the doubts. Perhaps he had none, or was determined to show none.[64] Certainly their acknowledgment would have undermined that passionate plea for support upon which, in this letter, he was so intent. As it was, he had much evidence with which to uphold his insistence upon his discovery of this Paradise. The thought that it might be accessible had early inspired sacrifices of the most severe, and the highest degree of expenditure and devotion. Perhaps it would inspire them again.

The decision that the unknown continent had also been discovered followed as inexorably upon the discovery of the Terrestrial Paradise as day, given time and energy, follows upon night. Many of the medieval mappae mundi we have cited gave grounds, as we have seen, for the conviction that an unknown

---

63. ''Nonnulli paradisum terrestrem sub ea coeli parte sitam crediderunt quibus sacrarum reluctatur auctoritas literarum,.quae Tigrim et Euphratem fama notissimos amnis ex Paradiso defluere commemorat, quos a septemtrionali plaga in Persicum devolvi sinum non ignoramus.'' It is tempting to think he may have had Mandeville or even Marignolli in mind here.

64. He was aware that the doubts were there. It is tempting, and perhaps not wholly fanciful, to see in his naming of El Martinet, ''the hammer,'' a reference to Henricus Martellus Germanicus, whose world map did not mark the Terrestrial Paradise.

continent might be found to the south of Paradise. Ptolemy, too, although known to be in error in the matter of the enclosed Indian Ocean, might still be allowed to provide evidence of the existence of this continent. If "Gracia" was indeed the Paradise Island—even if it were that mainland Paradise some situated near Cathay—then it must be clear to the meanest of geographers that the land Columbus found lying to the south of it must be this unknown continent. It was found to be clear accordingly, and, upon the admiral's fourth and final voyage, the fact was seemingly established beyond all possibilty of doubt.[65]

Columbus may accurately have predicted this falling out of ideas; it may have been this prediction, indeed, which led him so to stress Paradise in his letter to his sovereigns at the end of his third voyage. Today it can be hard to accept that a belief in the existence of the Terrestrial Paradise could be in any way important to the appreciation of Columbus's discoveries; let alone that it should be an essential precondition for the acceptance of the greatest one of all. At the time when these discoveries were made, however, and in the seeking of support for more of them, such an association of ideas and, above all, such an emphasis, made absolute sense.

---

65. Though he does not mark Paradise, Bartholomew Columbus is still seeking, in his own famous map, for that strait between the southern continent and Cathay which the medieval mappae mundi had led him to expect. Bartholomew's map was possibly drawn up after the fourth voyage. It was found among the contributions the Venetian Geographer Alexander Strozzi collected for the Biblioteca Nazionale in Florence. A reproduction of, and commentary upon, all of Bartholomew's sketches may be found in E. D. Fite and A. Freeman, *A Book of Old Maps* (Cambridge, Mass., 1926), 15.

—◦◉◦—— *Chapter 6* ——◦◉◦—

Columbus and His Christian World

It is beyond all doubt that Columbus thought of himself as a
Christian. References to the Christian religion pervade his
chosen readings, as we have already seen, and they inform both
his recognition of, and many of the names he gave to, the lands
he found. The supposed discovery of the Terrestrial Paradise
was, as I have just tried to show, the predictable outcome of
a Christian view of the world which, if it seemed a little fevered
at the time, was firmly declared from the very beginning of the
great enterprise.

The prologue to the journal of the first voyage (whether
written at the same time as the journal or tacked on a little later)
may perhaps be taken as setting the tone for the admiral's
Christianity:

> and I saw the Moorish king come out of the gates of the
> city and kiss the royal hands of Your Highnesses and of
> the Prince, My Lord, and afterwards in that same month,
> on the ground of information which I had given to Your
> Highnesses concerning the lands of India, and concerning
> the lands of India, and concerning a prince who is called
> Grand Khan, which is to say in our Romance tongue "King
> of Kings," how many times he and his ancestors had sent
> to Rome to beg for men learned in our holy faith in order
> that they might instruct them therein, and how the Holy
> Father had never made provision in this matter, and how
> so many nations had been lost, falling into idolatries and

taking to themselves doctrines of perdition, and Your Highnesses, as Catholic Christians and as princes devoted to the holy Christian faith and propagators thereof, and enemies of the sect of Mahomet and of all idolatries and heresies, took thought to send me, Christopher Columbus, to the said parts of India, to see those princes and peoples and lands and the character of them and of all else, and the manner which should be used to bring about their conversion to our holy faith, and ordained that I should not go by land to the eastward, by which way it was the custom to go, but by way of the west, by which down to this day we do not know certainly that anyone has passed; therefore, having driven out all the Jews from your realms and lordships, in the same month of January, Your Highnesses commanded me that, with a sufficient fleet, I should go to the said parts of India, and for this accorded me great rewards and ennobled me so that from that time henceforward I might style myself "Don" and be high admiral of the Ocean Sea and viceroy and perpetual Governor of the islands and continent which I should discover and gain and which from now henceforward might be discovered and gained in the Ocean Sea, and that my eldest son should succeed to the same position, and so on from generation to generation.[1]

The reference to the gates of the city is to the surrender of Granada by the Moors on 2 January 1492; that to the Jews, to the royal decree for their expulsion, issued at the end of March in the same year. The allusions both to the repeated requests of the Great Khan for Christian instruction, and to the difficulties of reconciling the Jewish and Christian religions, echo John of Marignolli's account of the Khan's Christian enthusiasms.[2]

---

1. C. Jane, *The Journal of Christopher Columbus* (London, 1960), 3–4.

2. *Edit.* J Emler, *Kronika Marignolova, in Fontes Rerum Bohemicarum* iii (Prague, 1878), 494–496.

They may, then, supply even more proof of Columbus's partiality for John of Marignolli's *Chronicle*, though the admiral was quite capable of supporting a faith in the Christian sympathies of the Great Khan and a suspicion of Jewish intentions, both from his attachment to court circles[3] and through his own wider reading and ambitions. This prologue is extraordinarily revealing about Columbus, from its expression of his seemingly near-fanatical zeal for the conversion of non-Christians, if necessary by force, to his clear suggestion that, should the Spanish sovereigns wish to take further to themselves the neglected powers of Rome in this respect (and perhaps in others), they would have every right to do so. We might remark too that Columbus is, from the first, in no doubt that he and his family will deserve rewards for providing the sovereigns with such Christian opportunities.

This exalted air of Christian missionary endeavor in pursuit of Christendom triumphant, these hints about the inadequacies of the contemporary papacy and its immediate entourage (especially in the making of necessary contact with the Great Khan), and this anxiety about the constant threat of Islam breathe through the rest of Columbus's letters and reports to his sovereigns. He tended to decorate his letters with an invocation to Christ and Mary, calling upon them to be with him on the way,[4] and he inclined to use a highly puzzling, but again clearly Christian, signature.[5] Dr. Rumeu de Armas

---

3. The letter of credence which Columbus carried from the Sovereigns to the Khan and other eastern potentates is printed in translation in S. E. Morison, *Journals and Other Documents on the Life and Voyages of Christopher Columbus* (New York, 1963), 30–31. Andreas Bernaldez was prominent among those who, at court, suspected both Muslims and Jews; C. Jane, *Select Documents Illustrating the Four Voyages of Columbus* i (London, 1930), cxlvii.

4. "Jesus et Maria sit nobis in via."

5. "Christoferens" or "Christum ferens"—bearing Christ. The signature is surmounted by the letters S.S.A.S.X.M.Y. Morison decides that the initials stand for both Greek and Latin words and translates them as "Servant am I

points to the intimate, even confessional, tone of the ''cartas-relaciones'' in the *Libro Copiador*,[6] and the ''Lettera Rarissima,'' written to Ferdinand and Isabella during the fourth voyage, gives especially trenchant expression to Columbus's desire for the recapture of the Holy Places of Christendom from the Moors, the rebuilding of the temple at Jerusalem and the cementing with the Great Khan of those good eastern relations he was convinced were necessary to these achievements;

> David in his will left Solomon 3,000 quintals of gold from the Indies to aid in building the temple; and, according to Josephus, it was from these same lands.[7] Jerusalem and the Mount of Zion are now to be rebuilt by Christian hands, and God through the mouth of the prophet in the fourteenth Psalm said so. The abbot Joachim said that this man was to come from Spain. Saint Jerome showed the way thither to the Holy Lady. The Emperor of Cathay some time since sent for wise men to teach him the religion of Christ. Who shall offer himself for this mission? If Our Lord takes me back to Spain, I vow in God's name to take them thither.[8]

---

of the most High Saviour, Christ the Son of Mary''; *Journals*, 202. The meaning and context of this signature is discussed at length in an outstanding book upon Columbus's spiritual affiliations and convictions; A. Milhou, *Colón y su Mentalidad Mesianica en el Ambiente Franciscanista Español* (Valladolid, 1983), 54–90. Milhou argues that Columbus invokes the Trinity, the Virgin Mary, St. Christopher, and St. John Baptist in his signature (the argument is summarized on pp. 79–80). Both St. Christopher and St. John Baptist prepared the way for Christ he points out, and Columbus's devotion to Mary and the Trinity is well established. Milhou's interpretation is a most convincing one.

6. A. Rumeu de Armas, *Libro Copiador de Cristóbal Colón* i (Madrid, 1989), 16–17. It is particularly evident in the two previously unknown private letters to the sovereigns; ibid., ii, documents VII and VIII.

7. Columbus means here the ''Aurea Chersonese,'' or modern Malay Peninsula, to which he had referred earlier in the letter.

8. Morison, *Journals*, 383. The biblical references are given in Jane, *Select Documents* ii, 104–105. He also traces some of the sources, and remarks that the allusion to the prophecy in the *Oraculum Turcicum* of Abbot Joachim of Fiora

Columbus's belief in, and constant references to, Hiram's
treasure fleet (a portion of whose rich cargoes Solomon used for
the embellishment of the temple in 1 Kings 10:12), are a part of
this same story. Such concerns seem to stand again behind the
extraordinary collection of texts the admiral and his Carthusian
friend Gaspar Gorricio put together, later known as the *Book
of Prophecies*, and they may also, at least in part, guide Columbus's
choice of, and annotations to, his books. Two books, as we saw
in Chapter 2, lead the field in the number of annotations they
contain. One, the *Imago Mundi*, was written by an exemplary
cardinal, and the second, the *Historia Rerum Ubique Gestarum*,
by a pope, no less. Pope Pius II was vehement to the point of
hysteria in his insistence upon the danger of the Turks,[9] and
he was a pope, furthermore, arguably of rather greater stature
in matters of Christian principle and practice in general than
the Borgia Alexander VI, whose pontificate (1492–1503)
coincided with Columbus's voyages. The contrast may have
been consciously felt. In his annotations, the great admiral shows
a clear interest in all of the relevant passages in these books,
and the section from Josephus (*De Antiquitatibus* VIII) which he

---

(1132–1202)) reappears in Columbus's *Book of Prophecies*. The original prophecy
does not, however, refer to Spain. This insertion appears to have been made
by Arnold of Villanova (ca. 1250–1302), and it circulated widely in the Iberian
Peninsula; Milhou, *Colon*, 375–387. The "Holy Lady" to whom Jerome showed
the way to Jerusalem is almost certainly Marcella; see Jerome *Ep.* 46, *edit.* and
transl. (into French) by J. Labourt, *Saint Jerome Lettres* ii (Paris, 1951), 113–114.
I owe this suggestion to my colleague, Dr. Philip Rousseau. The Latin letter,
supposedly directed from one woman to another, is an attractive one, and it
is perhaps not wholly fanciful to see this reference to it as a tribute to the reading
of Queen Isabella. The Queen did have the letters of Jerome in her library;
F. J. Sanchez Canton, *Libros, Tapices y Cuadros que Collecionó Isabel La Católica*
(Madrid, 1950), 56.

9. Pius reserves his condemnation of the Turks until the final chapter of Part
I of his *Historia*, but it is then very fierce, particularly in the matter of the Turks'
sexual and gustatory habits: "Gens truculenta et ignominiosa, in cunctis stupris
ac lupanaribus fornicaria, comedit quae caeteri abominantur. Iumentorum,
luporum, ac vulturum carnes, et, quod magis horreas, hominum abortiva."
He repeats it in Part II, Chapter iv.

cites as an authority in the "Lettera Rarissima" is appended by him to his own copy of Pius's *Historia*.[10] Columbus apparently took the productions of the Christian past and the perils and possibilities of the Christian future very seriously indeed.

Reverence for those who defend and wish to extend Christian realms, is manifest, moreover, not merely in the admiral's readings and writings, but in much of his behavior. He seems particularly to have admired the Franciscans, the order in the forefront of all earlier missions to the east. Both Bernaldez and Las Casas tell how Columbus appeared in Spain robed in the Franciscan habit when he returned from the second voyage in June 1496.[11] He was buried in this habit, and he may even, at some point in his life, have become a Franciscan Tertiary.[12] The admiral was a stickler, too, for the observation of the canonical hours on board ship, especially those of Prime, Terce, Vespers and Compline,[13] and it is virtually certain that he carried a *Book of Hours* with him on his voyages, one perhaps based upon that used at the Franciscan friary of La Rabida, near Palos.[14] He seems to have been a great admirer of the salvific and thanksgiving practice of pilgrimage. One of Columbus's answers to the storms he encountered towards the end of the first voyage was to order a pilgrimage to the shrine of Sancta Maria de Guadalupe—a pilgrimage which, in the event, nearly led to the capture of all

10. See above, Chapter 2. Editors and translators of this letter have not, to my knowledge, so far noted this connection.

11. The passages are quoted in Milhou, *Colón*, 43.

12. Ibid., 42–45.

13. Morison, *Journals*, 48.

14. Milhou, *Colón*, 45.

those who went on it.[15] Tradition had it that the admiral could also throw himself into the role of the Christian sorcerer. On the fourth voyage, when the fleet encountered a particularly ferocious waterspout off the coast of Panama, Columbus is said to have exorcised it by reading from St. John's gospel (6:17–20), and, clasping the Bible, traced a cross with his sword upon the sky.[16]

Skeletons, however, both rattle loudly in closets and stalk abroad. Columbus's particular brand of Christianity, as spelt out in the preface to the journal of the first voyage, seems xenophobic, antisemitic, aggressive and avaricious; unacceptable, that is, to Christianity today. And aspects of his reported activities also seem, to put that matter at its mildest, to have a whiff of hypocrisy about them. Columbus did not, for instance, marry Beatrix de Harana, mother of his second son Ferdinand, nor was he exactly truthful in his dealings with his sailors, especially not when it came to revealing just how far he was taking them from their native shores.[17] The insistence on the observation of the canonical hours, the orders for pilgrimage and the exorcising of the storm may have had as much to do with shipboard discipline as with true spiritual improvement. The wearing of the Franciscan habit was a dramatic expression of poverty and humility which accords strangely with the pursuit of honors and material rewards for himself and his family which, as we know, Columbus undertook

---

15. An account of this order, of orders for other pilgrimages and of the fate of the pilgrims, is given in the journal of the first voyage, under the entry for 14 February; Jane, *The Journal*, 166, 172–178.

16. Ferdinand tells of the cutting of the water-spout with the gospel of St. John, and Herrera of the magical gestures; Morison, *Journals*, 339 and 342.

17. The journal of the first voyage is filled with references to the admiral's deceptive reporting of distances on the voyage out, for fear the sailors might rebel at the growing length of their journey back. See, for instance, the entry for 10 September; Jane, *The Journal*, 9.

with passion. The habit of seeing his Indian converts merely as good Christian servants for his sovereigns,[18] and events such as the slave-taking raid described towards the end of his account of the second voyage by Michael de Cuneo, and clearly licensed by the admiral, rightly excite horror.[19] The eventual fate of the Taino Indians is not one Christianity could, or ever should, excuse. There is much here, in short, that proponents of a more refined religion will find now wholly abhorrent, from the manipulative theatricality Columbus seemingly enjoyed, to the cruelties and the exploitation his disoveries certainly unleashed upon native Americans.

It can be argued on the other hand, and with justice, that accusations of bad faith in matters of religion run grave dangers of subscribing to the very vices they condemn, and that the dangers are all the greater when these accusations are hurled backwards across a time-span of some five hundred years.[20] In attacking an easy and vulnerable target, such as Columbus, without an adequate appreciation of the true range of anxieties and dangers which threatened him, or an exact knowledge of the circumstances within which he acted, present-day critics can render themselves liable to like accusations of simple aggression and politically charged hypocrisy. Columbus's personality was complex in its make-up, and his actions had their roots deep in late medieval Spain. His religious beliefs and behavior were subject to pressures wholly remote from those of

---

18. ''They have no arms and are all naked and without any knowledge of war, and very cowardly, so that a thousand of them would not face three. And they are also fitted to be ruled and to be set to work, to cultivate the land and to do all else that may be necessary, and you may build towns and teach them to go clothed and adopt our customs,'' Journal of the first voyage, Sunday (!), 16 December; Jane, *The Journal*, 101–102.

19. Morison, *Journals*, 226.

20. So Milhou, *Colón*, 9–10.

a more enlightened age, and many of the skeletons to which I have pointed would not have rattled nearly so loudly in the late fifteenth century as they rattle now.[21] We must place Columbus's Christianity firmly within its historical context if we are even to begin to understand it, let alone if we wish to make moral judgments about it. It is always perilous to level accusations backwards across time. Yet, all this being said, I do in fact propose to risk some of these perils here.

In this final chapter I shall join the ranks, not, assuredly, of the accusers, but certainly of those who detect some inconsistencies between the admiral's protestations of his Christianity and his actual Christian performance. I shall argue that there really was a gulf between the ideals Columbus professed and some of the activities in which he engaged with evident enthusiasm; and that the admiral's occasional theatricality of expression is an indication of how deep this gulf in truth was. The gulf was, however, a gulf strictly of the later Middle Ages. The true, fifteenth century, inconsistencies are not the familiar ones, and some of them are the reverse of those for which we would instinctively now reach. Indeed, there stands at the root of them, and of much of the explorers' undoubted cruelty, a tortured attitude towards the acquisition and right use of wealth that might cause only amazement to much of the modern developed world. But these inconsistencies between the personally moral and the financially and politically expedient were truly present, nonetheless, when Columbus undertook his voyages; and, what is more, the great admiral knew well that they were present. The fact that he knew this so well is all-important. I shall suggest in this concluding section of the book that this recognized, but unresolved, conflict between the Christian principles Columbus and his sovereigns espoused both

21. Milhou, for instance, points to the possibility that Columbus's wish to become a Franciscan tertiary may have persuaded him not to marry. Milhou, *Colón*, 44–45.

publicly and privately, and the somewhat less-than-Christian practices the achievement of his and their ends required, produced a tension which both acted as a potent force throughout the whole of the great enterprise and in part explains (though does not of course excuse) some of the violence associated with it. When we treat of Columbus's relations with the contemporary Christian world we come, in short, upon the phenomenon known as *creative tension*. This particular creative tension underlay both Columbus's actual westward voyages and his accounts of them. It may, furthermore, provide the key to our ultimate understanding of almost all of that imaginative landscape we have here surveyed. I think it does provide this key.

To expose the tension, unearth the key, polish it and fit it gleaming (one hopes) to the lock, we must now review a strain of recent writing upon the religious dimension to Columbus's ambitions. We must review it firstly to distill from it the very important information it has to offer about the admiral's expressed religious commitments; and secondly, to offer a rather different explanation of the meaning of these commitments.

In the course of heroic efforts to plant Columbus's Christian beliefs once and for all within their late medieval context, this strain of recent writing has laid a particular emphasis upon the admiral's attachment to the orders of Friars; especially his attachment to the Franciscan Order.[22] Of a whole brew of possible contenders for Columbus's Christian attention, some of which have been mentioned already,[23] Franciscan teaching

22. The most important of the books advancing this argument are J. L. Phelan, *The Millennial Kingdom of the Franciscans in the New World* (Berkeley and Los Angeles, 1970), and Milhou, *Colón.*

23. The decadence and incapacity of the papacy, that is, the need for powerful lay influence, the pressing threats of Turks and Muslims, missionary fervor, Marian devotion, the relationship between poverty, riches and salvation; Milhou, *Colón*, 8–9.

and preaching emerged for this group of investigators as the most powerful of them all. And the emergence of this source of impulsion as the fundamental one has formed the basis for tremendous conclusions—conclusions before which, it must be said, all possible inconsistencies, and every shadow of Christian hypocrisy on Columbus's part, flee away.

Franciscan teaching, it has been argued, concentrated especially heavily upon the message of one particular book of the Bible. It concentrated upon the Apocalypse, or Book of Revelations, and it bore particularly vividly, therefore, upon events preceding, and heralding, the end of the world. In an attempt to expose the hidden message of the Apocalypse, this teaching told of the procession of human history inexorably towards the world's end, of a succession of portents of it, and of the inevitable appearance of a messianic last emperor at the limits of created time. This messianic emperor was destined to hold the bounds of Christianity against the infidel hordes which threatened it, to recapture the temple of Jerusalem from them and to rebuild it, and then, at the dying moment of creation, to do battle with Antichrist and convert the whole human race. The Abbot Joachim of Fiora (1132–1202) was a striking advocate and exponent of such teaching,[24] but the history of it goes back in Spain, we might remark, a very long way indeed, and to a period well before the Franciscans were in a position to take it up.[25]

---

24. Dante was sure that Joachim was a prophet. The abbot had a Trinitarian view of the progress of human history, a view which accommodated itself well with Columbus's devotion to the doctrine of the Trinity—a devotion especially evident on the third voyage. The doctrine of the Trinity, of course, divided Christianity decisively from Judaism and Islam.

25. In addition to the commentary on the Apocalypse by Beatus of Liébana which gave rise to some of the mappae mundi we discussed in Chapter 1, and the insertion by Arnold of Villanova, mentioned above, there were the mid-ninth century outbursts against Islam of Eulogius, Bishop of Toledo, and of Paul Alvarus, a sympathetic layman, in which Islam was also seen as a herald of the coming of Antichrist. On this see R. W. Southern, *Western Views of Islam in the Middle Ages* (Cambridge, Mass., 1962), 22–26.

This message is, of course, fraught with political possibilities.
Its potency as a means of exciting both devotion and action was,
indeed, arguably one of the main reasons for the choice of this
book of the Bible as the one, at certain times, to stress. The
attractions of teachings of this kind to those who would raise
the emotional temperature of a people, in the face of a
comfortable apathy or against a perceived enemy, are especially
obvious; and there were many such in the late fifteenth century,
and especially in the Spain of Columbus's sovereigns. Messianic
teaching was made popularly accessible in Castille, furthermore,
through such vernacular works as the *Libro del Anticristo* of the
Aragoneses aristocrat Martin Martinez de Ampiés. This, a
translation into Castillian of a tenth century apocalyptic work
in Latin, was printed in Saragossa in 1496 and reprinted in
Burgos very shortly afterwards. The *Libro del Anticristo* and other
writings of this order, such as the anti-Jewish *Epistola de Rabi
Samuel*, fired both Christian paranoia and Christian courage.[26]
It could, indeed, be difficult to separate the one from the other.

   We saw that Columbus made mention of Joachim of Fiora
in his "Letter Rarissima." Joachim reappears, also, in the
admiral's *Book of Prophecies*. In an article to which I referred at
the very beginning of the book, Dr. Pauline Moffat Watts sets
out impressive evidence in support of Columbus's especially
deep involvement in these messianic and Franciscan beliefs.[27]
Signs of this involvement are to be found, moreover, from the
moment at which the admiral began to read the compilation

---

26. These works are discussed in Milhou, *Colón*, 19–24. Interestingly, the *Libro del Anticristo* associates the Amazons, in whom both Pius II and Columbus had shown such interest, with the threatening infidel hordes. Columbus reproduces three passages from the *Epistola de Rabi Samuel* in his *Book of Prophecies*. "La exaltacion de la grandeza de Espana se compagina en Ampiés con un profundo pesimismo frente al futuro de la Christianidad;" Milhou, *Colón*, 18.

27. P. M. Watts, "Prophecy and Discovery: On the Spiritual Origins of Christopher Columbus's 'Enterprise of the Indies'," *American Historical Review* 90 (1–2) (1985), 73–102.

which goes under the name of d'Ailly's *Imago Mundi*. The cardinal's *opuscula*, annotated by Columbus in the same compilation, do, in fact, lend great substance to Franciscan messianism. Indeed, in their dependence (usually unacknowledged) upon the work of Friar Roger Bacon, and their insistence upon a procession of astrologically predictable and historically describable threats to Christianity, crowned by the last great battle of the messianic last emperor with the forces of Antichrist, they show themselves an active part of this same stream.[28]

These writings, argues Dr. Watts, led Columbus to position himself and his sovereigns at that very point in historical time at which the enemies of God were finally to be confronted, Jerusalem recaptured, and the infidel hordes won back at last for the final ruler of the world. As a result of her examination of these texts, and of Columbus's annotations to them in particular, Dr. Watts decides that:

> He [Columbus] came to believe that he was predestined to fulfill a number of prophecies in preparation for the coming of Antichrist and the end of the world . . . Columbus's apocalyptic vision of the world and of the special role that he was destined to play in the unfolding of the events which would presage the end of time was a major stimulus for his voyages.[29]

Much of the rest of Columbus's reading (the greater part of which may, on this argument, perhaps also have been influenced by the preferences of the Friars) led him, she believes, inexorably to this conclusion, and his annotations to his other books provide further confirmation that he held to it. The *Book of Prophecies*

---

28. Ibid., 86–92.

29. Ibid., 74.

(which incorporates significant sections from d'Ailly's *opuscula*) is, on this reckoning, a compelling demonstration of the great admiral's complete submission to a single overwhelming idea. There is proof, according to this thesis, that the admiral was open to this brand of Franciscan teaching from the period before his actual journeys began, and proof that its influence upon him lasted until the very end of them. His subordination to this influence, furthermore, was total. Columbus is depicted as a swimmer (although a strong one) within an overwhelming current of medieval apocalypticism, a current which bears him irresistibly along.[30] The thought-world within which he chooses to move is, on this interpretation, but a part of this same current. Columbus surrenders himself as a vehicle for messianic ambitions already fully formed. He sees his voyages simply as a necessary part of a prophetic and predestined plan of human salvation:

> In his mind . . . the New World was identified with the end of the world—the first heaven and earth passed away, there was no more sea—and the journey of the *viator*, which had begun in the deserts of the Old Testament prophets was surely almost over.[31]

This argument has much about it which is exceedingly attractive. It is well fortified with material evidence, and, in submitting the admiral's practical capacities in this way to the unifying sweep of his apocalypticism, it provides a satisfactory answer to the problem of that supposed dualism of his nature, a dualism of practicality and mysticism, which Morison seemed

---

30. "The striving to fulfill prophecy on a cosmic or global scale was a major stimulus to travel and discovery, from the early Franciscan missions into Asia to Columbus's Enterprise of the Indies, which led to his discovery of 'a new heaven and a new earth' in the Americas"; ibid., 79.

31. Ibid., 102.

to find so troubling.[32] We saw, in addition, in the preceding chapter how readily Columbus's thoughts inclined to the last days, and how many of the names he gave to his discoveries on the third voyage reflected this inclination. But there are still some disturbing aspects to such an account of Columbus's relationship with the contemporary Christian world. It is, for instance, one thing to prove that the admiral registered on occasion a deep, indeed impassioned, interest in messianic teaching of this kind. It is quite another to conclude that he registered this interest to *this* effect; that he swallowed the teaching, so to speak, so completely as to devote his whole life to its fulfillment. And is such an unresisting attitude, such a preparedness to act merely a part in a drama (though a grand part in a grand drama, admittedly), wholly consistent with the information we have from other sources about his personality? Was Columbus in general apt submissively to bow before overwhelming currents of teaching—or of anything else for that matter? The answer to the latter question, surely, is no. And then again, was Franciscan teaching on the subject of the *Apocalypse* the only one of the teachings of the Friars Columbus registered? Was it even the main one? The answer to these questions may be no, too. The strain of writing I have surveyed here tells, I am sure, a part of the story, and tells it very well; but it does not tell the whole.

In order to try and recover this whole, we might, firstly, look a little more closely into the above account of Columbus's

---

32. Morison saw Columbus's "paradisaical conceits," for example, as standing at an opposite pole to the latter's expertise in "practical navigation," and he had to resort to a notion of a "curious dualism" in the admiral's nature in order to explain the phenomenon. S. E. Morison, *Admiral of the Ocean Sea* ii (Boston, 1942), 558 and idem, "Columbus and Polaris," *American Neptune* 1 (1941), 133. It was impossible, for Morison, that Columbus's surpassing competence as a sailor and his Christianity, mystically expressed as it so often was, could run together. Jane, before Morison, had been even more insistent upon the puzzling phenomenon of Columbus's apparent "mysticism," Jane, *Select Documents*, i, cvii–cviii, liii.

dealings with the Franciscans. Now, one of the few Franciscan works we are at last in a position to prove Columbus actually read is the *Chronicle* of Friar John of Marignolli.[33] There is very little that is messianic about Marignolli's *Chronicle*. Marignolli was, it is true, writing for his patron, the Emperor Charles IV of Bohemia, and real Holy Roman Emperors do not always like to hear about Antichrist and the end of the world. But even when we make generous allowances for Franciscan tact and diplomacy, John of Marignolli still seems to show a quite singular interest in, and appreciation of, the present, the very much here and now. Marignolli is far more eloquent about the delights of this world than those of the next. It is to his preference for this world, indeed, that we owe the splendid descriptions of the "Indies" and Cathay which clearly held attraction for Columbus. The cities of the Great Khan's empire in Cathay shine with wealth and glow with silk and cloth of gold.[34] The lands round about the Terrestrial Paradise abound to this very day, says Marignolli excitedly, in healing aloes and fruits and gold and precious jewels, some of them swept there by the rivers of Paradise themselves.[35] All of these riches are there *now* to be found. They may certainly be gathered, and gathered legitimately, well before the Second Coming. Marignolli seems especially happy when these immediate delights touch upon the material sustenance of the Franciscan Friars. He waxes lyrical when speaking of the reception given by the Khan to his own

---

33. See above, Chapters 3 and 5.

34. "civitates maximas et optimas et maxime ditissimas in auro . . . serici et pannorum aureorum in tanta multitudine, ut vidimus oculis nostris, quod judicio meo excedunt totam Ytaliam"; *edit.* Emler, *Kronika*, 497.

35. "In eodem monte versus paradisum est fons maximus . . . quem dicunt derivari de fonte paradisi et ibi erumpere, quod probant, quia aliquando erumpunt de fundo quedam folia ignota et in magna copia et lignum aloes et lapides preciosi sicut carbunculus et saphirus et poma quedam ad sanitatem"; ibid., 501.

legation. The Khan assigned to the Friars, he tells us, a residence fit for a prince, and added two noble attendants so that they might all be supplied with every necessity, from food and drink to papyrus. The Khan gave them precious cloths as well, for themselves and their friends and relations. The Great Khan might well have expended as much as 4,000 marks upon them, all told.[36] Marignolli has nothing but praise, too, for the establishment provided for the Friars in Zayton, with its bathhouses, three churches and great bells. He himself added to their number of bells. He gave two more, called John and Anthony, and set them specially to ring across the Muslim quarter.[37] Columbus's reading of Friar John of Marignolli would not, then, have led him inescapably to contemplate the coming of the end of the world. It might have encouraged him instead to take a greater pleasure, though under certain strict conditions, in the riches this world could supply.

This is one instance of the variety of impacts Franciscan teaching was capable of making upon the great admiral. When we broaden our outlook still further, and turn from the possible effect of Franciscan teaching to that of the Dominicans upon him, the picture changes even more dramatically. Over 100 years ago now, the librarian of the Biblioteca Columbina in Seville, Dr. Simon de la Rosa y Lopez, called up the admiral's books to inspect them. He was presented with a box. In the box he found the five annotated works we discussed in Chapter 2; and two others.[38]

---

36. "Et sic missi fuimus ad imperialem aulam nobis honorabiliter preparatam, assignatis duobus principibus, qui nobis in omnibus necessitatibus habundantissime ministrabant in cibis et potibus et usque ad papirum pro laternis, deputatis servitoribus et ministris de curia et sic per annos quasi quatuor servierunt infinitis semper honoribus, vestibus preciosis pro nobis et familiis extollendo. Et si bene omnia computarem ultra valorem expendit quatuor milium marcarum pro nobis"; ibid., 496.

37. Ibid., 500.

38. The story is told in S. de la Rosa y Lopez, *Libros y Autographos de D. Cristóbal Colón* (Seville, 1891), 20–21.

One was a *Filosofia Natural* (sic),[39] and the other a *Summula Confessionis* of one "San Antonio de Florencia," printed in Venice in 1476. This second little book was the work of the Dominican Friar Antoninus Florentius (1389–1459), founder of the Dominican convent of San Marco in Florence and later archbishop of the same city. Usually known as the *Confessionale*, and first printed in Venice in 1474, it was a confessional guide, written in simple Latin and meant primarily, it seems, for lay persons. It was also quite extraordinarily popular in the late fifteenth and early sixteenth centuries.[40] Thus, though there is no more than a high probability that this particular copy of it was in fact Columbus's own,[41] we may be sure that he knew of it and that, either directly, or by means of copies owned by his patrons and friends, he was aware of its contents. The work of this Dominican Friar, was, therefore, especially well placed to exercise an influence upon the admiral; and it was a work which had, in addition, a great deal to say about Columbus's proposed enterprise.

Antoninus's *Confessionale* is a work of the first importance to those seeking to understand the confessional practices of the late medieval Christian world, and, in particular, the vital role these played in the life of the individual Christian. It will be remembered that, in addition to their roles as preachers and teachers, the Friars occupied a preeminent position in the late

---

39. This was the *Philosophia Naturalis* (usually known as the *Philosophia Pauperum*) of the Franciscan Friar Albertus Magnus (d. 1280), printed by Georgius Arrivabenus at Venice in 1496.

40. On the popularity of the *Confessionale* of Antoninus Florentius see the *Catalogue of Books Printed in the Fifteenth Century now in the British Museum* iv (London, 1916), 226–227. There are over 102 incunable editions of it, often in pocket-book form and overwhelmingly designed, it seems, for the lay market.

41. Taviani accepts it as a certainty, though, on Rosa y Lopez's evidence; P. E. Taviani, *Christopher Columbus the Grand Design* (London, 1985), 450 (a translation of *Cristoforo Colombo — la Genesi della Grande Scoperta*, Novara, 1974).

medieval church as confessors. Antonius's *Confessionale* is divided into two parts.[42] The first part is devoted to the confessor himself. It tells of his authority, of the knowledge he needs in order to sustain this authority, and of the deep goodness the pursuit of his profession requires. The second part treats of the ways in which penitents are to be approached and questioned. This second part takes us directly to Columbus and his own world, for, in a section (Section III) devoted to methods of questioning individuals with reference to their occupations, the *Confessionale* assigns a long chapter (Chapter vii) to merchants and traders, and so to merchant-adventurers of Columbus's kind; and the message it conveys is not an encouraging one.

The life of the merchant-adventurer is, according to the *Confessionale* replete with opportunities for every kind of sin. Interestingly, the first sin with which Antoninus Florentius concerns himself, the major mercantile sin, seemingly, of the period, is the sin of exporting arms or shipping supplies to the Turkish Sultan without papal licence (of the kind Venice, for example, had); but if this is the major sin, it is so by a very short head. There follow a whole host of others; bartering (''qui vulgariter dicitur barator'') worthless objects for precious ones (examples given are the exchange of wool or cotton for silks or spices), price-rigging, short-changing, false weighing, fraudulent quality control or no quality control at all, connivance with thieves, insider-trading, excessive profit, trading on feast days, lying in the making of marriage contracts and, of course, usury. The pursuit of wealth, either alone or as a primary object is singled out for blame. A slightly larger tolerance is extended to those who take great risks in the course of their trading. Those who carry their trade-goods over great expanses of land or sea at need are, indeed, mentioned specifically as deserving careful treatment, for they submit themselves to great danger, and may

---

42. There is no modern edition of Antoninus's *Confessionale* and no translation of it into English. My references will be to a copy of the 1476 Venice edition.

be permitted a proportionately greater reward.[43] The clear impression given, however, is that all of those engaged in trade or mercantile adventure are peculiarly prone to corruption. Few conditions can render money-making of this sort respectable or give it an honest outlet, a "finem honestum." Adequate (though not excessive) provision for one's family might perform this service, and so might care for the poor; but to trade for the purpose of treasure alone is to commit the mortal sin of avarice.[44] In another section of the *Confessionale* (II,ii), Archbishop Antoninus leaves us in no doubt at all as to the meaning of the mortal sin of avarice. Usury, false-coining and selling war supplies "ad terras infidelium" feature again, along with gambling (loaded dice seem to have been a special problem here) and prostitution. It is avarice to refuse to supply the poor, and also, and again interestingly, to be too interested in wealthy display. Once more we come upon the problem of wanting too much for one's family; a problem which brings us back directly to Columbus, and to the center of the argument I wish here to advance.

The provision of a "finem honestum," an honest outlet for money-making, was the peculiar talent of the Franciscan Friars. They had striven to come to terms with the reality of wealth from their very inception; in the case of their founder, St. Francis, with that of the mercantile wealth of his very own father. Apocalypticism and messianism, the use of this wealth in support of those who, with the last emperor, would confront the infidels at the end of the world, was one of their solutions to the problem,

---

43. "nam sine fraude assecurare merces per mare, vel per terram, et in die quaere emolumentum plus et minus, secundum quantitatem periculi, non videtur illicitum, cum substet periculo magno."

44. "Si negotiantur non propter aliquem finem honestum, puta sustentationem familiae suae ex lucro moderato, vel propter sustentationem pauperum, vel provisionem eorum pro utilitate necessariorum, et negotiantur propter avaritiam, et ad thesaurizandum, est mortale preccatum si in lucro constituunt finem, vel si intendunt lucrum per fas et nefas."

and one of evident relevance to attempts to wring money from wealthy and ambitious kings. John of Marignolli's solution, the appropriation of wealth to the use of a papal missionary legation and for the purposes of conversion, was another. To a certain degree, Franciscan solutions to the problem of the "finem honestum" for wealth could be employed by other people; and both of these solutions were of service to Columbus, as the evidence we have surveyed above shows clearly. But there are insurmountable obstacles in the way of *identifying* Columbus's method of justifying the acquisition and use of wealth with those of the Franciscan Friars, and there are still greater obstacles in the way of subordinating his ambitions to theirs. For Columbus, for all his wearing of the habit, was not himself a Friar; nor was he a papal legate, nor was he a missionary out simply to gain converts, nor was he even a servant of an established Holy Roman Emperor. He was a merchant-adventurer, identified precisely with those about whose hopes of ultimate salvation Antoninus Florentius was so discouraging. Columbus was intent upon the advancement of his family to a degree easily depictable as excessive,[45] he was a dependent of ambitious sovereigns, sovereigns relatively new to the Christian stage; and he was anxious, above all, to find gold, both for his sovereigns and for himself.

This is the real message Columbus's readings and his annotations to his books deliver; the unrelenting search for gold.

---

45. Documents in which Columbus claimed titles and hereditary rights for his family, and a levy on the profits of trade with the New World which may have risen as high as thirty percent, are printed in translation and discussed in Morison, *Journals*, 26–30. Morison shows that, although Columbus modeled the *Cartas de Donacão* which he claimed from his sovereigns upon the charters granted by the Kings of Portugal to their navigators, the admiral demanded more titles and privileges than did the Portuguese. The *Book of Privileges*, put together by the admiral shortly before the fourth voyage, is the best record we have of his ambitions for his family and his own fortune, and the *Pleitos de Colón* (law suits for their defense which dragged on into the seventeenth century) a good indication of the value of his claims. The *Book of Privileges* and the surviving copies of it are fully discussed in J. B. Thacher, *Christopher Columbus, His Life, His Works, His Remains* ii (New York, 1903), 503–565.

His annotations to his books are filled with references to gold and jewels and precious stones; references that might all be counted up, but for the tedium induced by their monotonous repetition. The search for gold is evident again in the admiral's journals, and the earliest biographical notices about Columbus report this self-same aim.[46] When his contemporary, the scholar Peter Martyr, writes of Columbus's achievements, the first thing he mentions is the admiral's discovery of gold.[47] Peter Martyr goes on to talk of spices, and indeed references to spices among Columbus's annotations to his books and in his letters seem to be very nearly as numerous as those to precious metals and jewels. But then, they were very nearly as valuable. Inscribed on the globe of Martin Behaim, for instance, there is an account of the profits to be made on the spice trade by the merchants and money-men who handled the precious cargoes as they traveled the different sea and overland routes westwards from the east — an account fit to strike terror into the hearts of cooks.[48] If even half of this account is true, then the potential profits to be made by shipmen traveling directly back to Europe via the Atlantic sea routes would have promised riches far beyond even the wildest hopes.

---

46. ". . . he inquired first for gold and for things most precious in our world." This entry is from the first Genoese biographer, Antonio Gallo, Columbus's contemporary, and it is repeated in later ones; Thacher, *Christopher*, i, 195. The letters in the *Libro Copiador* concerning the conquest and settlement of Hispaniola report this self-same primary aim; Rumeu de Armas, *Libro*, i, 19.

47. He writes in September 1493 to Count Tendilla and the Archbishop of Granada: "You remember Columbus, the Ligurian, who persisted when in the camps with the sovereigns, that one could pass over by way of the Western Antipodes to a new hemisphere of the globe . . . He is returned safe and declares he has found wonderful things. He displays gold, a token of the gold mines in those regions." Thacher, *Christopher*, i, 55–56.

48. E. G. Ravenstein, *Martin Behaim, His Life and His Globe* (London, 1908), 89–90. The inscription purports to recount information given by one Bartolomeo Fiorentino to Pope Eugenius IV. It estimates that customs are levied twelve times on the journey from Java to Western Europe, not to speak of the charges levied by gatherers, merchants and retailers. It concludes that it is no wonder spices are worth as much as gold.

This is the crux of the matter, and this is the key to that creative tension of which I spoke at the beginning of this chapter. In order for the energy necessary to sustain the voyages to be released, and the financial support they must have to be forthcoming, the struggle between Columbus's real desire for the advancement of his family and for the acquisition of great wealth for himself, his sovereigns and his patrons, and his need to render this desire Christian, both by his own standards and those of others, must somehow be quietened. That in the teaching of the Friars he could take fully to himself and employ with pleasure, and that he must defy, must somehow be reconciled, and the haunting specter of avarice be laid. Columbus had, therefore, a quite desperate need of an overarching "finem honestum." Las Casas tells how the admiral fell upon his knees in his oratory whenever he found gold or anything precious, and how he vowed before all present that he would give one-tenth of it to Christ.[49] Doubtless this helped somewhat, and so, perhaps, did the admiral's periodic appearance in the Franciscan habit. There is something to be said too for the idea that the admiral sometimes saw the voyages as a whole as great pilgrimages; scaled up versions, that is, of the pilgrimages he ordered in thanksgiving for his ships' reaching safe harbor after the first journey. This, quite as well as messianism, would explain his insistence upon Jerusalem. But the deep tension could never be wholly resolved; nor could it be dismissed. The need and the desire both to acquire wealth, and to prove to himself and to others that this acquisition was right and Christian in its purposes, was a constant source of friction and conflict, a friction arguably made all the more intense by Columbus's own

---

49. "Cuando algun oro o cosas preciosas le traian, entraba en su oratorio e hincaba las rodillas, convidando a los circunstantes, y decia 'demos gracias a Nuestro Senor, que de descubrir tantos bienes nos hizo dignos';" *Historia de las Indias*, quoted Milhou, *Colón*, 32.

wish to be, as well as to be thought of as, the best of Christians.

For there can be little doubt, I think, that the admiral's wish to live as well as he could as a Christian is sincere. Bernaldez lets slip how carefully Columbus prepared himself for the Sunday Mass on his voyages and how seriously he took this devotion.[50] He was perfectly willing to undertake all lesser pilgrimages himself, too, should the lot fall on him.[51] Bernaldez tells also of acts of kindness, and of moments which have little of the actor or grasping merchant about them, and much, again, of the devout man:

> And as soon as this cacique came alongside the ship, he began to give things from his store to the masters and to each one of the crew. It was morning, and the admiral was praying, so that he did not know of the presents or the determination with which this cacique had come . . . And directly he saw the admiral, he went up to him with a very joyous expression, saying: "Friend, I have resolved to leave the land and go myself with you, and to behold the king and the queen and their son the prince, the greatest sovereigns in the world" . . . And the admiral, having compassion on him and on his daughter and his sons and his wife, seeing his innocence and good will, withstood him and told him that he received him as a vassal of the king of Spain and of the queen, and that for the present he should remain where he was.[52]

Columbus's willingness to carry off captives did have its limits, broad as these limits may have seemed. He was sensitive,

---

50. Ibid., 150–153.

51. Jane, *The Journal*, 166. In the event, the fate of the first deputation of pilgrims rendered it unwise for the admiral to head a second as he had proposed. Lots were drawn with chick-peas, one marked with a cross.

52. Jane, *Select Documents*, 162–165.

also, to that style of bartering which Antoninus had condemned. He speaks of it in his letter about the first voyage, and of his own attitude to it:

> They [the "Indians," that is] are content with whatever trifle of whatever kind that may be given to them, whether it be of value or valueless. I forbade that they should be given things so worthless as fragments of broken crockery, scraps and broken glass and lace tips . . . They took even the pieces of the broken hoops of the wine barrels and, like savages, gave what they had, so that it seemed to me wrong and I forbade it . . .[53]

His annotations to his copy of Plutarch's *Lives* are, in the context of anxieties about moral rectitude and money-making, especially revealing. They show that the admiral was impressed by those great men of the past who could control, or, even better, correct, the human lust for wealth. He marks, for instance, a passage in Plutarch on Lycurgus, in which Plutarch tells of Lycurgus's withdrawal of all the gold and silver currency at his command, and his substitution of great weights of iron for it, precisely to overcome the vice of avarice.[54] Columbus marks too how Solon despised riches, and he makes a particular note of Phocion's contempt for the gold of Alexander the Great. Phocion, says Plutarch, deemed it a far greater thing not to have the need for such wealth than

---

53. Jane, *The Journal*, 194–196.

54. C. de Lollis, *Scritti di Cristoforo Colombo. Raccolta di Documenti e Studi Pubblicati dalla R. Commissione Colombiana* 1 (ii) (Rome, 1894), 473. Plutarch explains that the amounts required for the smallest value were impossible to carry away and hide in sufficient quantities to be rewarding. Iron is also, he notes, subject to corrosion. Edit. B. Perrin, *Plutarch's Lives* ix (Loeb, London, and Harvard, Cambridge, Mass., 1967), 228–231. Columbus had clearly read these passages in his own copy with care.

to possess it.[55] Columbus also noted that the vice of greed overwhelmed all the virtues of Crassus.[56] This preoccupation persists into others of his annotations. Against Chapter xxix of the *Historia* of Pope Pius II, for example, he makes a special note that Scythians spurn silver and gold alike.[57] Such evidence suggests, in truth, that there was a struggle. Columbus was a complex man, possessed of great personal piety and considerable reflective powers. But his personal ambitions and his public enterprises as an explorer and adventurer took him into a region of tremendous moral danger.

The idea that business enterprises of a type so evidently acceptable in the late twentieth century could be a cause of shame in the late fifteenth, might, as I have said, excite some considerable astonishment today. Money-making has its rules even now, of course. Limits are at least meant to be placed upon too naked and destructive an avarice, and upon too unbridled an acquisitive instinct. But, in the late fifteenth century, these rules were harsher. And they were very harsh indeed upon one who aspired to enter the exalted and exclusive circles of noble Christian Spain, as Columbus did. He began his quest it seems, moreover, from very little. Despite Ferdinand's fierce efforts to claim a distinguished lineage for his father, Columbus's earliest biographers all agree that he and his brother Bartholomew had a humble upbringing.[58] It is surely harder to

55. Ibid., 475, 504; i, 406–407, viii, 184–187.
56. Ibid., 496; iii, 314–317.
57. "argentum et aurum pariter aspernari"; de Lollis, *Scritti.*, 320.
58. Thus Antonio Gallo: "Christopher and Bartholomew Columbus, brothers, of the Ligurian nation, sprung from plebeian parentage and who supported themselves from the wages of wool-working (for the father was a weaver and the sons were at times carders), at this time aquired great fame throughout the whole of Europe by a deed of the greatest daring and of remarkable novelty in human affairs. Even if these had small learning in their youth, when they were come of age, they gave themselves to navigation after the manner of their race." Thacher, *Christopher*, i, 192–93. Even Ferdinand does not contest the fact that the admiral's immediate family were poor.

resist the blandishments of a life of luxury when this has rarely or never been enjoyed than when it has. There were, however, few contemporary Christian excuses offered on these grounds, and the severe rules had, especially among the Friars we may remark, both numerous and powerful advocates to speak in support of them. In fifteenth century confessional terms, an inclination towards wealth, without a justifying motive for its use, was an inclination, too, towards sin. Poverty merely made the struggle against this particular sin all the harder; and the guilt commensurately greater. Conflict of this kind can come as close to tragedy as to achievement; indeed, it did come close to both. There was no justice in the plunderings and cruelties unleashed by Columbus's voyages, and these can never, on any terms, be wholly excused. But we might remember that the admiral himself was by no means the sole author of this exploitation; nor was he the most powerful among these authors, or the one least given to restraint. He too had been a victim of social deprivation, ignorance and disdain, even violence. He was subject, then, to temptations that deserve of us an increased understanding rather than whole-hearted condemnation.

The great need he had for a "finem honestum," a justifying higher motive for his pursuit of gold for his sovereigns and rewards for his family arguably superfluous to their real needs, might bring us to look now with new eyes upon the nature of Columbus's attachment to the messianic message of the Friars. There is no doubt at all that the message is there in the works he both consulted and composed, and that Columbus appealed to it, and frequently. His journals, his letters (especially his letters to his sovereigns), and, above all, his *Book of Prophecies*, are filled with references to the recapture of the Holy Places, to the rebuilding of the temple at Jerusalem, and to the special parts his sovereigns have to play in the fight against the infidel. But he was not, I would suggest, committed to this message in its every dimension; still less was he swept away or over-whelmed by it. Had he been, those abhorrent practices noted at the outset of this chapter might have been defeated, or at least delayed. But then so, perhaps, might the discovery of America.

Columbus employed apocalyptic messages, even exploited them, as and when he wished, and because he *needed* to make use of them; a need which became all the more urgent as his true enterprise became ever more vulnerable in Christian terms. His sovereigns, we might remark, could need them too. They were not themselves immune from criticism. They, like Columbus, were subject to the message of the *Confessionale*[59] (thought not perhaps to quite the same degree). In a predicament of this order, the role of messianic emperor could seem, on many levels, heaven sent. This, then, is the true explanation of the many high-flown letters Columbus wrote to his sovereigns, filled as they are with appeals to them to listen to the prophets, appeals which rose to a height in the prefatory letter to the *Book of Prophecies*, and in that compilation itself. This, too, is the main reason behind the admiral's castigation of the Moors and his insistence that the Holy Land be rescued from the infidel. Here was a cause which might readily justify, even require, a search for gold in its service; a cause beneath which many others might be subsumed—or covered-up. Columbus might very well associate himself with friars and legates and missionaries—or, even better, through this great cause, so recast all their offices that he became the equivalent in his own or his patron's eyes. But he had to do these things because he was, and they were, so very deeply affected by other aspects of the message of the Friars, especially their teaching upon those moral dangers inseparable from the mercantile life.

I do not mean to imply that the admiral was wholly deaf to the messianic message, still less that he was cynically

---

59. Interestingly, they too were concerned about the activity known as bartering; see, for example, Morison, *Journals*, 206–208, 311. They prohibited it in the instructions for the fourth voyage. Queen Isabella had *Confessionals* in her library; Sanchez Canton, *Libros*, 63.

dishonest in his use of it. He might have been delighted had the Great Khan been found, the infidel destroyed, the Holy Places recovered and his sovereigns set fair to lead Christian monarchs to the last days of the created world, with him as their especial servant.[60] The line between convincing posturing and real conviction can be a narrow one, and the second can indubitably spring from the first. But these aims were never, I think, his primary ones. The messianic message of the Franciscans was of tremendous assistance to Columbus; but it was not his master. He needed all the friars could produce in justification of the acquisition of wealth, not because he proposed to follow them in every essential, but because, in *one* essential (and arguably the central one), he did not.

We might now return at last to that larger imaginative landscape within which the admiral chose to move, and to the pictures from it he repainted so carefully for his patrons. The *Imago Mundi* of Pierre d'Ailly, the *Historia Rerum* of Pope Pius II, the *Travels* of Marco Polo, the *Chronicle* of John of Marignolli, mixed saints' lives, liturgical echoes and legends; all of these resources are, as Dr. Watts has proved, at one with the messianic and missionary messages Columbus wished to convey. The *Navigatio Sancti Brendani* and, if I am right about his knowledge of them, the stories of Sinbad, would have offered spectacular reinforcement to the sense of moral worth and Christian wonder attachable to adventures, even trading adventures, across the sea. The *Confessional* of Antoninus lends additional strength to the notion that they may have been turned to consciously with this in mind. But the *Book* of Sir John Mandeville, Plutarch's *Lives*, Pliny's *Natural History*, Ptolemy's *Geography*, Seneca's

---

60. It is worth remarking here, however, that the success the Turks had had in cutting off the land routes to the east for Christian traders constituted an important stimulus and support for westward exploration by sea; K. M. Setton, *The Papacy and the Levant* ii *The Fifteenth Century* (Philadelphia, 1978), 333–334. Columbus's attitude to the infidel may, then, have been a little ambivalent.

Tragedies and (if Milhou is right), the *Commentaries* of Julius Caesar?[61] These works fall into a different category; but we may offer an explanation for Columbus's interest in these different works which is similar, in many respects, to that which we have offered for the others. For this is the library, or a part of the library, of a well-read, well-cultivated Christian humanist. Again, the admiral is approaching through his reading (though perhaps flatteringly this time, rather than defensively), his possible patrons in Spain.[62] Few things are, after all, so comforting and pleasing as to be told that the ideas and plans for a momentous enterprise are in essence the same as one's own, and that one has long had them both in one's library and in one's capacious mind. Archbishop Alfonso de Fonseca (1475–1534) was only one among many powerful ecclesiastical leaders whose minds were already so cultivated, and who might therefore be susceptible to, and sympathetically inclined towards, such flattery.[63] The mental chords Columbus touched here were, in short, chords already attuned to please influential ears. The world Columbus reads about and offers, the appeals and enticements he adduces, in fact the whole of that imaginative landscape we have tried here to reconstruct, are admirably adjusted to accord with the ideas and expectations of such a Christian gentlemen — or lady. And it was, I would suggest in conclusion, deliberately so adjusted.

---

61. Milhou points out that Columbus referred to these in a letter to Pope Alexander VI, written in 1502; Milhou, *Colón*, 11.

62. Much work remains to be done upon the typical library of the late fifteenth century Castillian renaissance gentleman, but there are helpful and suggestive indications in J. N. Hillgarth, *The Spanish Kingdoms 1250–1516* ii (Oxford, 1978), 175–182. For wise words upon the acceptability in cultivated noble and ecclesiastical circles of Ptolemy's *Geography* see J. B. Harley, *Maps and the Columbian Encounter* (Milwaukee, 1990), 23–24.

63. Hillgarth, 181. Buron lists many of the impressively educated ecclesiastics Columbus knew; E. Buron, *Ymago Mundi de Pierre d'Ailly* i (Paris, 1930), 22–23.

Queen Isabella, so vital to the undertaking as a whole, is a particularly important figure in this context. Columbus's reading, and his enthusiasm for stories, are peculiarly well directed to that which we know of the reading and enthusiasms of Queen Isabella of Castille. The queen seems to have enjoyed learned enterprises, in addition to mercantile ones. She strove to become a Latinist, one who translated the letters of the scholar Peter Martyr for her (perhaps slightly less enthusiastic) consort, and many of the books for which Columbus expressed a fondness Isabella had in fact in her library.[64] She showed a clear interest, too, in heroic travelers' tales, an interest easy to extend, as we have seen, to Christian heroics. The letter Jaime Ferrer wrote to the admiral on Isabella's behalf in August 1495, for instance, is filled with such literary reference, and with sea stories of precisely the kind we looked at in the first section of this book:

> And what must we say of the magnanimous and unconquerable knight Hercules, who leaving the delightful and polite Greece with a great army, navigated the Western regions with innumerable dangers and encountered the tyrannical arrogance of Geryon, Antaeus and other evil knights: and in testimony of his great virtue many prosperous cities in our Spain, built by him, are shown. Of the great Alexander . . . this monarch subjugated the regions of the east . . . more to expound the doctrine of human life to his subjects, than from a greedy ambition for kingdoms. And surely, the Prince of Knighthood, the honour and glory of the Latins, Julius Caesar, must not be

---

64. Plutarch, Virgil and Aristotle, for example, as well as an account of the twelve labors of Hercules, Mandeville, the *Catholicon* of John of Genoa, and the *City of God* of St. Augustine. Many of Isabella's treasured tapestries, too, some of which certainly traveled with the court and so were available to be seen by Columbus on his visits, depicted heroic exploits and pilgrimages. One of the earliest descriptions of these that has reached us was compiled, interestingly, by Columbus's helper with his *Book of Prophecies*, the Carthusian Gaspar Gorricio, then Isabella's secretary. Sanchez Canton, *Libros*, 42–45, 50, 55, 67, 111–114.

forgotten, who, extending his imperial banners over the universal world, made known the laudable and moral doctrine of the Romans. And after these Knights worthy of remembrance, because the greater part of the world was without faith, without which our good works are not sufficient, it pleased our Redeemer to send His obedient disciples to different parts of the world, preaching the truth of our Holy Law. . . .[65]

An ability to conjure up a shared world soothing enough in its familiar outlines to inspire confidence in the possibilities of the as yet unknown, filled with great adventurers of at least sufficient probity to quieten moral alarms, and replete above all with that sense of Christian wonder we discussed in the very first chapter; all this was a very great resource indeed. It was a resource Columbus used to the full—particularly perhaps upon the queen. Columbus is not in general known as the best of psychologists; but this was excellent psychology. We might note also, in passing, how very vulnerable were all involved in this mental landscape to the vagaries of the newly invented art of printing—and to the whims of publishers not themselves wholly devoid of mercantile ambition. Here is matter for another study. There is level upon level of influence to be uncovered; and to be understood with sympathy.

Columbus could, then, navigate the turbulent waters of the contemporary Christian world in which he lived almost as well as he could the stormy waves of the Atlantic, or the perilous reaches along the coasts of his Terrestrial Paradise. There is no dualism in his personality. The impression of dualism is simply, and paradoxically, the result of the multitude of abilities he displayed in his single purposeful pursuit of westerly trade and discovery. He could please ecclesiastics and friars. He could attract sovereigns, knights, gentlemen and ladies; even, on

65. Thacher, *Christopher*, ii, 367–368.

occasion, his own sailors. By playing upon carefully chosen instruments he could charm from them ideas they hardly knew they had. The power of his siren songs was, it is true, not limitless, and the playing became a little desperate towards the end of the enterprise, when the rewards were not as evident as the admiral had hoped, rivals were many and, most importantly of all, the inconsistencies between the pursuit of these rewards and the Christianity of the great enterprise as a whole became ever more clear. But the admiral's skills in the service of his overriding intention were evident to the very end.

If, at the conclusion of this excursion through Columbus's mental and pictorial world we have come upon an element of the manipulative in it, this should by no means be allowed to diminish, still less to cloud the variety of, the great admiral's achievements. We might prefer now, it is true, to place him rather upon the slopes than the heights of Olympus, and we might have to part those veils of the Christian mystic which have been placed recently around him. We may have to range him, in short, among the ranks of the human race. For all this, however, Christopher Columbus remains one of the most talented and, perhaps above all, one of the most imaginative human beings ever to have lived; one driven, furthermore, by a courageous trust that his hopes would be realized to which exceedingly few now can aspire.

—————⟨⟩————— *Appendix* —————⟨⟩—————

The Voyages and Discoveries of Columbus

1. 3 August 1492–15 March 1493. Three ships, the Nina, the Pinta and the Santa Maria, were built and fitted at Palos, on the Rio Tinto in Southern Spain. From there they sailed via the Canaries to discover San Salvador (Guanahani, Watling Island),[1] Santa Maria de la Concepcion (Rum Kay), Fernandina (Long Island), Isabela (Samoet, Crooked Island), Chipangu (Colba, Juana, Cuba) and Hispaniola (Bohio, Cibao, Haiti, Dominican Republic). The settlement of Navidad was founded on Hispaniola. Columbus returned via the Azores to Lisbon, then Palos.

2. 13 October 1493–11 June 1496. Upwards of seventeen ships set out from Cadiz and sailed, again via the Canaries, to discover Dominica (Charis, Carib, Dominique), Santa Maria Galante (Mariegalante), Todos los Santos (Les Saintes), Santa Maria de Guadalupe (Guadeloupe), Santa Maria de Monserrate (Montserrat), Santa Maria la Redonda, Santa Maria la Antigua, San Martin (Nevis), Santa Maria de la Nieve (Saba), San Christobal (St. Kitts), Santa Anastasia (St. Eustatius), Santa Cruz (Ayay, Saint Croix), Las Once Mil Virgines (Virgin Islands), Gratiosa (Vieques, Crab Island), San Juan Battista (Boriquen, Carib, Puerto Rico) and Mona (Amona). Columbus

---

1. I cite in the first place the names Columbus himself gave to his discoveries, and then record in brackets other names by which they seem to have been, or are, known.

215

returned to Hispaniola to find Navidad deserted, and the garrison dead. Anchor was dropped off Hispaniola, near the site of the future city of Isabela, 2 January 1494. 24 April–29 September 1494, from Hispaniola, Cuba was further explored and Sant Iago (Jaime, Janahica, Jamesque, ?Babeque, Jamaica) discovered. 12 June 1494, Cuba was officially declared part of a continent. 10 March 1496 Columbus set sail with two ships from Isabela, Hispaniola, for Cadiz, arriving there 11 June.

3. May–October 1498. Columbus departed Sanlucar de Barrameda with three ships for discovery and three for colonists and provisions in late May 1498. Via Madeira, the Canaries, and the Cape Verde islands, the discovery fleet found Trinidad, Gracia (Venezuela), Paria (on the northern coast of Venezuela), Asuncion (Tobago), Concepcion (Grenada), and Margarita. From Margarita he went back to Hispaniola. He was sent back to Cadiz in chains on the La Gorda in early October, and reached there by the end of the month.

4. 3 April 1502–7 November 1504. Four ships, sailing from Seville, via Cadiz and perhaps the Canaries, made landfall, 15 June 1502, at Matinino (Martinique). They skirted Hispaniola, Jamaica and Cuba, and anchored off Honduras in late July. From Cape Honduras the fleet discovered and explored the Mosquito Coast of Nicaragua, and the coasts of Costa Rica, Veragua and Panama. Forced in to refit after the loss of a caravel, the expedition was marooned on Jamaica for a year and five days. Columbus and the few survivors of the expedition embarked from Santo Domingo on Hispaniola on 12 September 1504 and reached Sanlucar de Barrameda on 7 November.

Outline of Life
b. Genoa, Italy, August/October 1451, d. Valladolid, Spain, 20 May 1506. Columbus was related to the Genoese family of

Colombo and worked for an important merchant house in Genoa. As their agent he visited Chios. He survived sinking in a sea battle off Cape St. Vincent in 1476, and went to Lisbon. There he and his brother Bartholomew set up in business as chartmakers. In 1477 he went to Ireland and Iceland, seemingly under the flag of the Portuguese marine, and lived in Madeira for a while. In the period 1482–1484 he captained a merchant vessel for at least one voyage to equatorial West Africa. In 1485 he went to Spain to begin his attempts to find patronage there for the voyages of discovery. His plans were rejected by the Talavera Commission in 1490, and early in 1492 Ferdinand and Isabella of Aragon rejected them again. Santangel procured a new hearing and the Queen accepted the plans a little later in the same year. 28 May 1493 Columbus was given the official title of Admiral of the Ocean Sea and the Indies.

In 1479 in Lisbon, Columbus married Dona Felipa Perestrello e Moniz, sister of the Captain of Porto Santo near Madeira, and had by her one son, Diego. After her death in 1485 he had another son, Hernando (Ferdinand), b. 1489/1490, by his mistress Beatriz Enriquez de Harana.

Bibliography of Works Cited

Editions and Translations of Primary Sources

Edit. J. H. Bridges, *The Opus Maius of Roger Bacon*, 2 vols. (Oxford, 1897).

Edit. and *transl.* E. Buron, *Ymago Mundi de Pierre d'Ailly*, 3 vols. (Paris, 1930).

Transl. R. F. Burton, *The Book of the Thousand Nights and One Night*, 4 vols. (London, 1894).

Transl. J. M. Cohen, *The Four Voyages of Christopher Columbus* (Harmondsworth, 1969).

Edit. J. Emler, *Kronika Marignolova* in *Fontes Rerum Bohemicarum*, iii (Prague, 1878), 492–604.

Edit. and *transl.* L. Giovannini, *Il Milione con le Postille di Cristofero Colombo* (Rome, 1985).

Edit. Th. Graesse, *Jacobus a Voragine Legenda Aurea Vulgo Historia Lombardica Dicta* (Leipzig, 1850).

Edit. and *transl.* W. H. Green et al., *Saint Augustine City of God*, 7 vols. (Loeb, London and Cambridge, Mass., 1965–1981).

Transl. C. Jane, *The Journal of Christopher Columbus* (London, 1960).

Edit. and *transl.* C. Jane, *Select Documents Illustrating the Four Voyages of Columbus*, 2 vols. (London, 1930).

Transl. B. Keen, *The Life of Admiral Christopher Columbus by His Son Ferdinand* (London, 1960).

Edit. and *transl.* M. Letts, *Mandeville's Travels. Texts and Translations*, 2 vols. (London, 1953).

Edit. W. M. Lindsay, *Isidori Hispalensis Episcopi Etymologiarum sive Originum Libri XX* (Oxford, 1911).

Edit. C. de Lollis, *Raccolta di Documenti e Studi Pubblicati dalla R. Commissione Columbiana*, 14 vols. and supplement (Rome, 1892–1894).

Edit. and *transl.* F. J. Miller, *Ovid, Metamorphoses*, 2 vols. (Loeb, London and Cambridge, Mass., 1984).

Edit. and *transl.* F. J. Miller, *Seneca, Tragedies*, 2 vols. (Loeb, London and Cambridge, Mass., 1968).

Edit. Th. Mommsen, *C. Iulii Solini Collectanea Rerum Memorabilium* (revised edn. Berlin, 1958).

Transl. S. E. Morison, *Journals and Other Documents on the Life and Voyages of Christopher Columbus* (New York, 1963).

Transl. J. J. O'Meara, *The Voyage of St. Brendan* (Dublin, 1976).

Edit. and *transl.* B. Perrin, *Plutarch's Lives*, 11 vols. (Loeb, London, and Cambridge, Mass., first publ. 1914–1926, repr. 1967).

Edit. and *transl.* H. Rackham et al., *Pliny Natural History*, 10 vols. (Loeb, London, and Cambridge, Mass., 1942–1984).

Edit. A. Rumeu de Armas, *Libro Copiador de Cristóbal Colón. Correspondencia Inedita con los Reyes Católicos Sobre los Viajes a America*, 2 vols. (Madrid, 1989).

Transl. G. Ryan and H. Rippenberger, *The Golden Legend of Jacobus de Voragine* (London, 1941).

Edit. and *transl.* R. C. Seaton, *Apollonius Rhodius, the Argonautica* (Loeb, London, and Cambridge, Mass., 1967).

Edit. C. Selmer, *Navigatio Sanch Brendani Abbatis* (Notre Dame, Ind., 1959).

Edit. and *transl.* H. St. J. Thackeray and R. Marcus, *Josephus* (Loeb, London, and Cambridge, Mass., 1966).

Edit. and *transl.* J. J. Tierney, *Dicuili Liber De Mensura Orbis Terrae* (Dublin, 1967).

Transl. J. F. Webb, *Lives of the Saints* (Harmondsworth, 1965).

H. Yule, *Cathay and the Way Thither*, 2 vols. (London, 1866).

————, *The Book of Ser Marco Polo*, 2 vols. (London, 1903).

Secondary Works

A. R. Anderson, *Alexander's Gate, Gog and Magog, and the Inclosed Nations* (Cambridge, Mass., 1932).

A. d'Avézac, *Les Iles Fantastiques de l'Ocean Occidental* (Paris, 1845).

————, *Notice des Découvertes Faites au Moyen Age dans l'Ocean* (Paris, 1845).

L. Bagrow (revised R. A. Skelton), *History of Cartography* (London, 1964).

C. R. Beazley, *The Dawn of Modern Geography*, 3 vols. (London and Oxford, 1897–1906).

W. L. Bevan and H. W. Phillott, *Medieval Geography: An Essay in Illustration of the Hereford Mappa Mundi* (London and Hereford, 1873).

E. Coli, *Il Paradiso Terrestre Dantesco* (Florence, 1897).

G. R. Crone, ''The origin of the name Antillia,'' *The Geographical Journal* 91 (1938): 260–262.

F. G. Davenport, *European Treaties Bearing on the History of the United States and its Dependencies to 1648* i (Washington, 1917).

C. Deluz, *Le Livre de Jehan de Mandeville, une "Geographie" au XIVe Siècle* (Louvain-La-Neuve, 1988).

O. A. W. Dilke, *Greek and Roman Maps* (London, 1985).

D. B. Durand, "Tradition and innovation in fifteenth century Italy," *Journal of the History of Ideas* 4 (1943), 1–20.

————, *The Vienna–Klosterneuburg Map Corpus of the Fifteenth Century* (Leiden, 1952).

M. Esposito, "An Apocryphal 'Book of Enoch and Elias' as a Possible Source of the Navigatio Sancti Brendani," *Celtica* 5 (1960), 192–206.

E. D. Fite and A. Freeman, *A Book of Old Maps Delineating American History from the Earliest Days down to the Close of the Revolutionary War* (Cambridge, Mass., 1926).

V. I. J. Flint, *Ideas in the Medieval West: Texts and their Contexts* (London, 1988).

————, "Christopher Columbus and the Friars," in L. Smith and B. Ward, eds., *Intellectual Life in the Middle Ages* (London, forthcoming).

M. Foncin, M. Destombes, and M. de la Roncière, *Catalogue des Cartes Nautiques sur Vélin* (Paris, 1963).

H.-C. Freiesleben, *Der katalanische Weltatlas vom Jahre 1375* (Stuttgart, 1977).

J. B. Friedman, *The Monstrous Races in Medieval Art and Thought* (Cambridge, Mass., 1981).

M. I. Gerhardt, *Les Voyages de Sinbad le Marin, Studia Litteraria Rheno-Traiectina* 3 (Utrecht, 1957).

E. P. Goldschmidt, *Hieronymus Münzer und seiner Bibliothek* (London, 1938).

J. B. Harley, *Maps and the Columbian Encounter* (Milwaukee, 1990).

————— and D. Woodward, eds., *The History of Cartography* i (Chicago and London, 1987).

J. Heers, "De Marco Polo a Christophe Colomb: comment lire le *Devisement du Monde*," *Journal of Medieval History* 10 (1984), 125–143.

J. N. Hillgarth, *The Spanish Kingdoms 1250–1516*, ii *1410–1516* (Oxford, 1978).

K. Hughes, "An Irish Litany of Pilgrim Saints Compiled c. 800," *Analecta Bollandiana* 77 (1959), 305–331.

M. Jomard, *Les Monuments de la Géographie ou Recueil d'Anciennes Cartes* (Paris, 1858–1862).

A. Kammerer, *La Mer Rouge, l'Abbyssinie et l'Arabie depuis l'Antiquité* ii(2) (Societé Royale de Géographie d'Egypte, XVI, Cairo, 1935).

J. Larner, "The Certainty of Columbus: Some Recent Studies," *History* 73 (1988), 3–23.

W. Levison, "Das Werden der Ursula-Legende," *Bonner Jahrbucher* 132 (1927), 1–164.

A. Milhou, *Colón y su Mentalidad Mesianica en el Ambiente Franciscanista Español* (Valladolid, 1983).

K. Miller, *Mappae Mundi. Die altesten Weltkarten*, 6 vols. (Stuttgart, 1895–1898).

S. E. Morison, *The Second Voyage of Christopher Columbus from Cadiz to Hispaniola and the Discovery of the Lesser Antilles* (Oxford, 1939).

—————, *Admiral of the Ocean Sea: A Life of Christopher Columbus*, 2 vols. (Boston, Mass., 1942).

—————, "Columbus and Polaris," *American Neptune* I (1941), 6–25, 123–137.

—————, *Christopher Columbus Mariner* (London, 1956).

A. E. Nordenskiöld, *Facsimile Atlas to the Early History of Cartography* (Stockholm, 1889, repr. New York, 1961).

───── , *Periplus* (Stockholm, 1897).

L. Oliger, "De anno ultimo vitae Fr. Iohannis de Marignollis missionarii inter Tartaros atque episcopi Bisinianensis," *Antonianum* 18 (1943), 29–34.

G. Orlandi, *Navigatio Sancti Brendani* i *Introduzione* (Milan, 1968).

J. L. Phelan, *The Millennial Kingdom of the Franciscans in the New World* (Berkeley and Los Angeles, 1970).

J. R. S. Phillips, *The Medieval Expansion of Europe* (New York, 1988).

C. de la Roncière, *La Carte de Christophe Colomb* (Paris, 1924).

E. G. Ravenstein, *Martin Behaim, His Life and His Globe* (London, 1908).

S. de la Rosa y Lopez, *Libros y Autographos de Cristóbal Colón* (Seville, 1891).

D. A. Russell, *Plutarch* (London, 1973).

F. J. Sanchez Canton, *Libros, Tapices y Cuadros que Collecionó Isabel la Católica* (Madrid, 1950).

Visconde de Santarem, *Essai sur l'Histoire de la Cosmographie et de la Cartographie*, 3 vols. (Paris, 1849–1852).

───── , *Atlas Composé de Mappemondes et de Cartes Hydrographiques et Historiques*, 3 vols. (Paris, 1845).

K. M. Setton, *The Papacy and the Levant*, ii *The Fifteenth Century* (Philadelphia, 1978).

T. Severin, *The Brendan Voyage* (London, 1978).

R. A. Skelton, *The Vinland Map and the Tartar Relation* (New Haven, 1965).

R. W. Southern, *Western Views of Islam in the Middle Ages* (Cambridge, Mass., 1962).

P. E. Taviani, *Christopher Columbus, the Grand Design* (London, 1985), translated from *Cristoforo Colombo—La Genesi della Grande Scoperta* (Novara, 1974).

E. G. R. Taylor, *The Haven-Finding Art* (London, 1956).

J. B. Thacher, *Christopher Columbus, His Life, His Works, His Remains*, 3 vols. (New York, 1903).

R. V. Tooley, C. Bricker, and G. R. Roe, *A History of Cartography* (London, 1969).

P. W. Watts, "Prophecy and Discovery: On the Spiritual Origins of Christopher Columbus's 'Enterprise of the Indies,'" *American Historical Review*, 90 (1–2) (1985), 73–102.

Index

225